HOW TO MAKE YOUR
ELECTRIC GUITAR
Play Great!
by Dan Erlewine

HOW TO MAKE YOUR
ELECTRIC GUITAR
Play Great!
by Dan Erlewine

The electric guitar owner's manual

Backbeat
Books

San Francisco

Dedication

Dedicated to my wife Joan, and daughters Meredith and Kate—with love.

Published by
Backbeat Books
600 Harrison Street
San Francisco, CA 94107
An imprint of The Music Player Network
United Entertainment Media, Inc.
Publishers of
Guitar Player magazine
and MusicPlayer.com

Distributed to the book trade
in the U.S. and Canada by
Publishers Group West
1700 Fourth Street
Berkeley, CA 94710
Distributed to the music trade
in the U.S. and Canada by
Hal Leonard Publishing,
P.O. Box 13819,
Milwaukee, WI 53213

Library of Congress Control Number: 00-136124
ISBN 0-87930-601-7

Printed in the United States of America
02 03 04 05   5 4 3 2

Editor: Meredith Erlewine
Design: tom@erlewinedesign.com
Production: Daniel D. Erlewine
Cover photos: Tom Erlewine, Summer Blevins
Photo Credits: Many thanks to my friend Brian Blauser of Athens, Ohio, for his photos from our many "setups of the stars" road trips. Brian Blauser's photos appear on pages 63, 64, 108, 113, 117, 118, 119, 123 and 127. Thanks also to Paul Natkin of Photo Reserve for his great photo of Albert King (page 128).

Special thanks to all those who provided guitars and information: Allparts Music Corp.; Baker USA, Custom Guitars; Buzz Feiten Design; Carruthers Guitars; Dominick Ramos Guitars; Dunlop Mfg. Inc.; Epiphone/Gibson; Fender Musical Instruments Corp.; Fishman, Inc.; Fred Gretsch Enterprises, Ltd.; FRET-King Guitars, Parts, and Accessories by Trev Wilkinson; Fretware Guitars; GHS Corp.; Gordon-Smith Guitars; GraphitAll (Rene Martinez); Graph Tech; Gruhn Guitars; Ibanez Guitars; J. D'Addario & Co.; JM Rolph Pickups; Joe Barden Pickups; Lindy Fralin Pickups; Parts Is Parts (John Sprung); Paul Reed Smith Guitars; Sadowsky Guitars; Seymour Duncan Pickups; Stevens Electrical Instruments (Michael Stevens); Stewart-MacDonald's Guitar Shop Supply; Suhr Guitars; Tom Anderson Guitarworks; Tom Holmes Pickups; Tone-Pros; TV Jones Guitars; Vintique; Washburn International; WD Music Products, Inc.

Table of Contents

Evaluating a Guitar

Setup Tools

The Eight Steps to a Supreme Setup

step 1
Fretboard cleaning and installing strings

step 2
Adjusting the truss rod

step 3
Nut adjustment and maintenance

step 4
Bridge and tailpiece maintenance

step 5
Whammy bars

Putting it all Together

How They Do It: A Guide to the Great Setups

Introduction

Electric guitars that are set up correctly shorten the learning curve for beginners and set the stage for advanced players to take their music to the next level. Unfortunately, even most advanced players don't know how to perform the tried-and-true tricks of guitar setup that will make a guitar rock and roll.

Most electric guitars are factory made and roll off the assembly line in amazingly playable shape. Still, after shipping, settling and the inevitable shrinking and swelling associated with climate adjustment, it's a rare guitar that plays anywhere near its potential directly off of a music store wall. Not surprisingly, used guitars present their own setup challenges. I never expect any guitar—new or used—to satisfy me until I've set it up to suit my style.

A setup is the combination of tweaks and adjustments you can make to your guitar so that it suits your style and preferences. A good setup can eliminate typical problems like fret buzz, strings noting out on high or low frets, poor intonation, string height (action) that is either too high or too low, strings that won't stay in tune, unbalanced pickup output, and tremolos which, if used, put the guitar hopelessly out of tune. Music store repair staff can set up your new (or new to you) guitar so that it plays the way you want it to, but if you're like me you want to do the work yourself.

That's what this book will teach you how to do. You'll master adjustments that can make the difference between a guitar that sounds bad (or even good) and a guitar that sounds great. A long time ago I learned that with some simple tools and some common sense I could make my guitars sound just the way I wanted them to—and so will you. And really, the best person to set up your guitar so that it plays the way you want it is you, so have fun!

Dan Erlewine

Evaluating a Guitar

Having run a repair shop for more than 30 years, I can spot a guitar's needs for setup or maintenance in no time flat and usually can suggest ways to make a guitar sound better than its owner even thought possible. By following the guidelines below, I seldom overlook a problem and can chart the course for a supreme setup. This evaluation is an absolute must when you're guitar shopping, too. It may help you negotiate a better price—or decide that even the best repair person in the world won't help the guitar you're considering.

Put your guitar (or the one you're thinking about buying) through these paces, making a list of possible trouble spots. The 1967 Gibson Trini Lopez I use to illustrate the steps of the evaluation happened to exhibit everything we need to cover.

Play the guitar

Play the guitar from one end to the other for as long as it takes to get a feel for its "action"—the feel of

how that particular guitar plays and responds to your touch. Then check the clearance between the bottom of the strings and the top of both the 12th and 1st frets. That distance will greatly affect the action, as will the amount of straightness or "relief" you deliberately adjust into the neck and fretboard. Relief is a measurable gap, or upward bow, in the fingerboard, caused by the string's pull and/or a deliberately loosened truss rod. In some cases, relief eliminates strings buzzing against frets (caused by the long, elliptical pattern of a plucked string shown in the drawing below). I'll go into more detail about relief beginning on page 19.

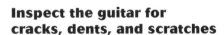

Inspect the guitar for cracks, dents, and scratches

I always inspect a guitar under good lighting, looking for cracks, dents, dings, and scratches. This may not affect a setup, but it might affect how much

I'm willing to pay for an instrument (new or used). This close inspection also protects me from customers who carefully look over their

guitars for the first time after they've spent money to set them up—they often "find" scratches that were already there! Hold the guitar at an angle so that it catches the light—any hidden marks will jump out.

Inspect and feel the back of the peghead for any sign of a crack or break (especially on used Gibsons with mahogany necks, which are notorious for cracking across the grain). A good example of a broken peghead is the ES-335 below, which I've reglued and will touch up with lacquer. You must have a broken peghead repaired before you start any setup.

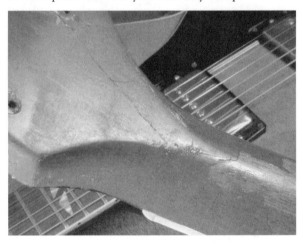

Test the neck for strength and twist

Rest the guitar body face up and on the bottom back edge of the lower bout, support the peghead, and pull down from the center of the neck. You'll know immediately if the neck is strong and stiff or weak and rubbery. Stiff necks are best because you can easily control them with a little truss rod adjustment. "Rubber" necks, caused by weak or inferior wood, may never straighten out because the pull of the strings is too much for even the truss rod to correct. Refretting usually will straighten out a weak neck, but not always.

With the guitar in this position (the neck pointing straight at you), you

can see if the neck has a twist toward either the bass or treble side. If it does, the peghead usually will dip in the direction of a twist—in this case, slightly toward the treble side, but not enough to affect playability. I avoid buying a guitar if it has a discernable twist—but a wee bit doesn't bother me.

Sight the neck for straightness or relief

With the guitar on its side (the playing position),

close one eye and sight along the fretboard edge. Sight first on the bass, then the treble side, to see if the neck (and especially the fretboard, because it is the playing sur-

face) is either straight, back-bowed (away from the strings) or up-bowed (toward the strings). A straight neck is a desirable starting point for any setup; you may be able to adjust a slight up-bow (relief), but back-bow is always bad because it will cause the strings to buzz against the fretboard.

Another way to check for relief is to use the strings as a straightedge (above), fretting a string toward each end of the fretboard while stretching one finger toward the center and pressing the string down. If it moves, you have relief; if it rests on the frets, the neck is straight (or maybe even back-bowed).

Professional guitar techs use notched straightedges (below), which skip over the potentially imperfect frets and "read" the fretboard surface itself. The frets are only as accurate as the surface they are pressed into. The notched straightedge identifies fretboard humps and valleys instantly, helping a tech decide whether a complete refret might be better than a fret leveling and crowning (a "fret dressing").

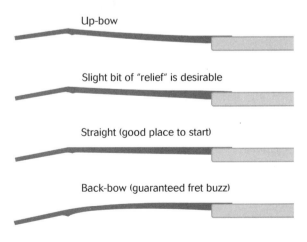

Up-bow

Slight bit of "relief" is desirable

Straight (good place to start)

Back-bow (guaranteed fret buzz)

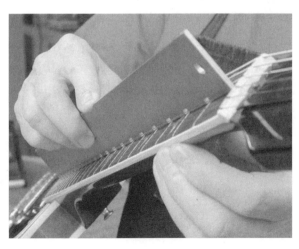

Check a bolt-on neck's alignment in the pocket

Stand the guitar upright and look at the neck straight on to see if it is aligned, with the outside E-strings running equidistantly in from the edges of the fretboard. Strings that lean toward either the bass or treble side will have a tendency to fall off the edge. It's easy to re-align such necks (see "Shifting a Bolt-On neck" on page 81).

Inspect the nut's shape, string slots, and action

Look closely at the nut—almost any nut needs a little bit of cleaning. Slots like the ones pictured above are too deep, and can catch strings when you bend or tune and cause a "chinking" sound. The strings should rise gradually from the tuner to a contact point directly at the nut's front edge.

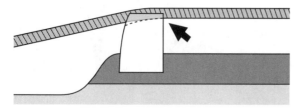

The slots above are so wide that the strings move sideways when you bend them. Ultimately, the owner of this guitar will need to have a professional replace the nut (unless he or she reads my *Guitar Player Repair Guide*, and has a bent for do-it-yourselfing).

Check the fret condition and height

Closely inspect the fretboard. Check (or measure) the fret condition and height, looking for pitted frets, rough fret ends or loose frets (look for loose inlays, too). With a thumbnail or fingernail, feel for sharp fret ends at the edge of the fretboard—these may need a professional's attention.

Not everyone agrees on the "right" height for frets, and there are many fretwire sizes. Players like me, who like to bend strings or whole chords, prefer high frets (i.e., frets that are .045" high after any fretting, fret-leveling, rounding, or crowning). I'm satisfied with .040", or even .038", but when the fret height gets into the mid-.030" range it becomes more difficult to bend strings. Some jazz and coun-

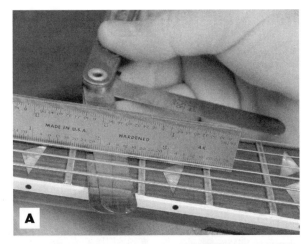

A

B

is a quick and inexpensive way to make an accurate tool. They're the most delicate tools for testing fret height, fret relief, and even the string height at the nut (see page 28).

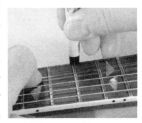

Loose frets are nothing but trouble because, if undetected, they don't level properly during fret leveling and dressing (whether at the factory or in a repair shop). They sink down as the factory or repair technician levels the fretboard with a file or sanding block, then spring back up after the tool passes, causing high frets that buzz and exposed, sharp fret ends. Even worse, loose frets sound bad! To find loose frets on any guitar, but especially on inexpensive models, pull the treble E-string out of the way and tap on every fret end, listening for either a solid "clink" that indicates a tight, well-seated fret, or a quieter, hollow "thud," indicating a loose fret. Loose frets are easily fixed by any trustworthy repair tech who's good with superglue.

Make sure the truss rod works

Remove the truss rod cover and, using the proper adjustment tool (a nut driver, Allen wrench, or screwdriver), check to see if the truss rod works and how well it adjusts the neck. Removing this truss rod

cover (below) exposed a botched repair job: lacking the proper 5/16" nut driver, someone had gouged out the wood to make room for a larger socket.

try players, however, who rarely bend strings, prefer low frets—even as low as .025".

I measured the lowest frets on this Trini Lopez with feeler gauges stacked together until they matched the fret height—the frets were .028" high. You can do the same with any inexpensive feeler gauge set from your local auto parts store (A). Or, use guitar strings to check your fret height (B)—in this case a .028" string did the job. Supergluing various gauges of guitar string to popsicle sticks (C)

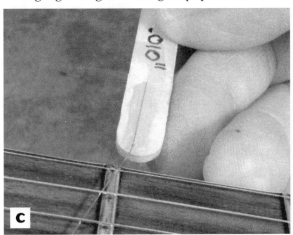

C

The person tightened the rod so much that the wood compressed under the nut and required four half-moon washers to take up the slack. I usually use only one washer as a bearing surface for the brass truss rod nut (called an acorn nut on a Gibson). See why you need to evaluate before you buy? The owner didn't even know there was a problem, having never looked under the truss rod cover!

This job was repairable, but tricky. The gouging had thinned the back of the peghead so much that tiny cracks were developing (above). I had noticed these when I inspected the rear of the peghead and thought they might simply be finish cracks, but something seemed fishy so I held off my decision. After clever woodworking, gluing, fiberglassing and painting, the guitar was fine—but it cost the owner $400! He wouldn't have bought the guitar if he had known beforehand, or certainly would have paid less.

If this truss rod had been normal (in the photo below, you're looking at a healthier nut) I would have made a mark to show where the rod was adjusted. Then I would loosen the rod before trying to

tighten it. Loosen the rod by turning it counter-clockwise (the direction of the arrow in the photo at right) You'll learn all about that on page 19.

Determine and compare the fretboard and bridge radii

In the setup section we'll make sure the radius of the bridge saddles matches the fretboard radius, so determine the fretboard radius now. The strings on the bridge below don't quite touch the 12" radius gauge because the bridge is slightly collapsed—a common problem on older Gibson Tune-O-Matic bridges (we correct a collapsed T.O.M. bridge in the

bridge maintenance section on page 48). Even without removing the strings, you can check the approximate fretboard radius by pressing all of the strings against a fret and then reading across them with a radius gauge. Most Gibson electrics will have a 10" or 12" fretboard and bridge radius.

Check the condition of the bridge and tailpiece

This bridge was in pretty good shape, but needed a good cleaning (below). The studs that the bridge rests on were bending forward, though, and we'll fix that on page 49. The tailpiece is a simple trapeze style with some nice Trini Lopez decoration on it—nothing wrong there. The other common Gibson

tailpiece is the "stop-bar" style. The most common problem with tailpieces is rusted and corroded plating caused by sweat, although sometimes stop-bar height-adjust screws rust tight.

Check the tuning keys

Detune and retune the tuning keys to make sure they work. Check for loose hex nuts and mounting screws, and be sure that the screw that holds the key onto the shaft is secure. On most tuners, this screw not only holds the tuning key, or "button," on, but it determines how stiff or loose the key will be.

Make sure screws and hardware are secure

Test all of the screws to make sure they're not stripped. Check control cavity cover plates, pickup surrounds, output jack covers (on Telecasters, Les Pauls, Stratocasters and all like models), pickguards, strap buttons, etc.

Check the electronics

Plug the guitar into an amp and play it. Turn the volume and tone controls (also called pots, short for potentiometers) from 0 to 10 a number of times. If they're stiff, cleaning and flushing with contact cleaner usually loosens them up and does away with any crackling sound caused by the dirt. Listen for electrical shorts (no conduction) or bad solder joints

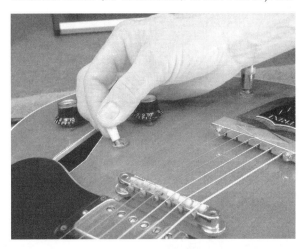

(indicated by crackling, intermittent sounds or no conduction). Move the selector switch back and forth, too, listening for the same unwanted noise. Use any steel object to tap on the pickups in each selector switch position to make sure they're working. Wiggle the guitar cord in the jack—it'll crackle if the jack is loose or there's a problem with the wiring.

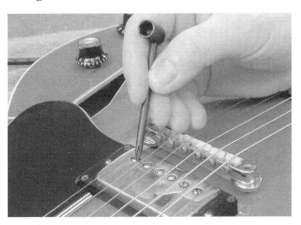

Even if you don't find any problems during the above checks, inspect the wiring. Open any accessible electronics compartments and look for tight, shiny solder joints. Dull, grainy-looking solder joints often cause intermittent crackling or make no contact at all. If you have a hollow-body guitar, or a semi-hollow like this one, inspect inside with a mirror. Here's a great trick: break the plastic back off of an inexpensive plastic, convex, "fish-eye" mirror from an auto parts store (the kind that you can stick to your car's rearview mirror). Tape a piece of string to it and lower it through the F-hole, (in this case a diamond-hole—part of the great looks of a Trini Lopez). Here I could see all of the original

You're done! Now you know what to address when you set up your guitar, using the steps beginning on page 108.

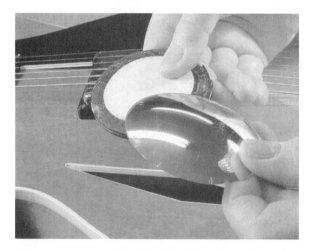

electronics, as well as loads of dust, lint, hair, dirt, food, and rust. It needed a good cleaning.

On vintage instruments, remove the pickups and make sure they're original—these were, and that's crucial when investing in a vintage instrument. Some people take parts from guitars and replace them with less valuable parts—then sell the guitars as original. Buyer beware!

Setup Tools

If you're a tool lover, you're bound to make a few trips to the hardware store before you're done reading this book. However, I tried to make the book as tool free as possible so you wouldn't need to make a major investment in specialized guitar repair tools to set up your own axe. I did pretty well, too—even including a set of punch-out vinyl radius gauges at the back of the book. Radius gauges, as you will see, are an important tool for setting up a guitar correctly. Along with your new radius gauges here are the basic tools used in this book:

1 Side cutters (any nipper that will cut strings)

2 String winder (optional)

3 Screwdriver: large flat-blade (5/16", 1/2")

4 Small adjustable wrench (Crescent wrench)

5 Tweezers or hemostats come in handy

6 Allen wrenches:
Fractional (Imperial): 3/64"; .050"; 1/16"; 5/64"; 3/32"; 1/8"; 9/64"; 3/16"
Metric: 1.5mm; 2mm; 2.5mm; 3mm; 3.5mm; 4mm; 5mm; 7mm, 8mm

7 Sockets: 1/4", 5/16", 7mm, 9/32", 8mm

8 Screwdrivers:
Small phillips (0, and 00 size)
Larger phillips (#1, and #2 size)
Small flat-blades (1/16", 5/64", 3/32",1/8")

9 Razor saw (I use the smallest X-acto brand)

10 Any type of electronic tuner

11 Six-inch ruler graduated in 64ths

■ Lighter fluid (naphtha) for cleaning

■ Lubricant (Vaseline, 3-In-1 oil, Teflube, white grease, etc.)

■ Clean rags or paper towels

■ Guitar polish or fine automotive polish

■ Fine-toothed metal file (a hardware-store lawnmower sharpening file is good, and so is a spark-plug file from the auto parts store)

■ Homemade nut files (see how to make them on page 30)

■ Homemade feeler gauges (see how to make them on page 28)

■ Low-tack drafting tape (art supply store)

■ Long straight edge (the long edge of a carpenter's L-shaped "rafter-square" from any hardware store works for checking neck straightness)

The Eight Steps to a Supreme Setup

After the pre-setup evaluation reveals a guitar's good and bad points, you should approach a setup in the following order, correcting minor problems along the way. Your guitar—especially if it's brand-new—won't require some of the maintenance work listed (it could though). If that is the case, skip that task and go on to the next step. Any number of minor problems may pop up during the evaluation or the setup that you must take care of before the setup can continue. Some situations may even call for a visit to a guitar repair shop before the setup is done.

1 Fretboard cleaning and installing strings

Many of the guitars I deal with are used, road-worn instruments that have spent too many nights in bars and clubs. It's automatic for me to clip off dirty (sometimes even rusty) strings…the fingerboard is usually even dirtier. Unless a customer requests that I not clean the fretboard, I do that right away. If the fingerboard needs cleaning, but the strings are in good shape (a rare occurence), I'll go ahead and do the setup with a dirty fretboard so as not to waste a good set of strings. Then I clean the fretboard when I re-string, just before setting the intonation. Let's assume, however, that your guitar is used, has dirty strings and needs a fretboard cleaning.

A

Remove the strings by clipping them close to (A) the tuner's string post and the bridge (B). Throw away the main part of the strings that you just removed, then 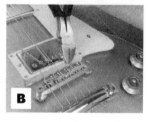 B carefully lift the tailpiece away from the body (C) to remove the old string ends. If you're not careful, the tailpiece can fall on the guitar's face and dent it (due to the lack of string tension). Finally, carefully re-

move the string wraps remaining around the string posts to avoid scratching the peghead— I prefer to use tweezers or hemostats for this (D).  C

Removing the strings from guitars with tremolos can be a little tricky. Clip the strings close to the bridge, but leave enough string length to grab onto (E). Then push the loose string ends through the tremolo block until you can grab their "ball ends" (F) and pull them out. (Ball ends, the round brass pieces that the string is twisted around during manufacturing, hold a string in place in the bridge or tailpiece). If you do happen to cut the strings too short, you'll need to poke  D  E 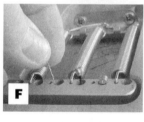 F a sharp, hooked tool up into the tremolo block and pry the strings out.

If you use a string winder, follow this advice: When removing or installing strings on Fender and Fender-style guitars with six-in-line tuners, set all the tuning keys vertically to make room for your string winder to work without knocking into the adjacent tuner as you wind. If you're installing strings, wind them until they become tight enough to hold fast, but still leave the keys vertical. Then, when all the strings are on and you don't need the winder anymore, you can tune to pitch with your fingers. (Fender six-in-line tuners are close together.)

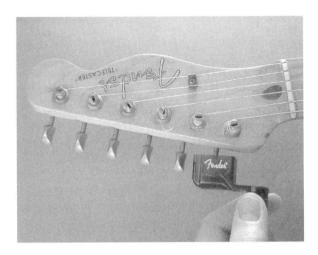

Moist breath treatment

Now the fretboard is ready for my signature moist breath treatment. My motto for cleaning any fretboard is "less is best," so I start with the most non-invasive approach: I loosen mild dirt or a sticky film with moist breath, then remove the dirt with a clean rag or paper towel. Moisten the fretboard surface, several frets at a time, by breathing on it—up close, hot, and moist. Follow immediately with a clean, dry rag or paper towel, drying the moisture and polishing the surface simultaneously. It will lift off any mild dirt. This is how I approach any fretboard that isn't particularly dirty, but especially vintage Fender "maple necks." Most fretboards are made from ebony or rosewood, which are hardy woods that stand up to cleaning with solvents. Vintage maple necks, however, have no fretboard. The lacquered surface of the maple neck is the fretboard, so you must be careful cleaning the finish—it may be brittle or cracked. Here, after the moist breath treatment, I'm using my fingernail to press a paper towel right along the

edge of a fret to remove the dirt. The old lacquer finishes on these maple necks will stand up to cleaning with solvents, but you must be careful—don't saturate the rags.

If the moist breath treatment isn't doing the trick, I start with a rag barely dampened with hot water and follow with a dry paper towel. The dampness lifts the dirt and the towel wipes it away.

Solvents

Sometimes fretboard dirt is really caked on, almost as though it's been baked on. You can soften it with any number of wetting agents before trying to remove it with the scraping

and steel wool methods described next. Try saliva first—it may sound crude, but saliva will soften anything (I use it first on any dirt, and even on finishes). These photos show dirt along a fret being cleaned with saliva—with good results! Dip a cotton swab, or a clean paper towel or rag, into a small amount of any of the following (one at a time, not mixed together): saliva, mineral spirits, naphtha (lighter fluid), or a guitar polish or cleaner. You may need to let a wetting agent rest on the dirt for a minute or two before the dirt is soft enough to remove—but keep an eye on it.

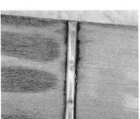

Scraping

You can scrape away heavy buildup with any number of tools—used credit cards are good. I also like the sharp edge of a Stewart-MacDonald plastic radius gauge because it follows the fretboard surface, and if you use it sideways you can scrape right up to the hard-to-reach corner of the fret. Even though credit cards and radius

gauges are made of plastic, they can mar the wood if you press too hard, so pay attention to the amount of pressure you apply.

For really tough jobs, however, scrape with single-edge razor blades. After marking one side of the blade as a reference, draw the blade's sharp edge against another hard steel object to "turn," or "burr," the razor blade's edge. The burr does a great job of scraping. Push the blade with the marked edge facing the direction of the push for the for the burr to do its work.

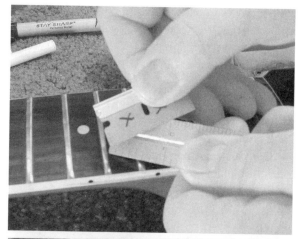

Steel wool

Fine steel wool (0000 grit) removes dirt fast and you can press it into the corner of the fret against the fingerboard with your thumbnail or a fingernail. Make only as many sideways strokes (across the fretboard's width) as are needed to remove heavy dirt along the fret edge; follow those with lengthwise strokes going with the direction of the wood grain

in between the frets. This keeps cross-grain scratching (even with 0000-steel wool, which is very fine) to a minimum.

Important: *Never use steel wool on maple neck finishes! It will remove the shine instantly!*

Lubricating dry fretboards

Occasionally, once or twice a year perhaps, consider adding a little lubrication to ebony or rosewood fretboards. I do it automatically on customer's instruments when I see that they need it—especially if the fretboard was exceptionally dirty and I used solvents to remove the dirt (solvents draw the natural oil from the wood and leave the wood parched and dry looking).

My preferred fretboard treatment is pure raw linseed oil (not the "boiled" variety). You can find this at art supply stores and paint stores. Nothing gives the deep rich look to rosewood or ebony—or makes light, bland-looking fretboards look dark and beautiful— as linseed oil does. Most of all, it forms a thin finish on the wood that feels good to play on and makes the fretboard easy to clean throughout the year. Use it only when you think you need it.

Many say that linseed oil stays on the fretboard and frets, remains sticky, and never dries. I don't understand that—they're doing something wrong. I have used the same can of linseed oil for 30 years—

it is still good, and still works its magic. This oil penetrates well into the wood, and if removed quickly and thoroughly, feels dry to the touch. I swab linseed oil on quickly and sparingly, let it rest one minute, then remove it thoroughly with paper towels or soft rags. I avoid slopping it along the fret edge, working carefully and stopping at the fret edge. I don't want to run any oil under the fret and down into the fretslot for fear of loosening the fret or making the fretslot oily and less likely to hold a fret.

Sure, if you leave a thick pool of linseed oil along the edge of the fret, or if you are sloppy with it and get it on areas other than the fretboard, the fretboard will get sticky because linseed oil takes a long time to cure. (It cures on contact with oxygen.)

A number of fretboard preparations have come and gone over the years, and they all work. Some, called "lemon oil," are  simply mineral oil with a lemon scent. Lemon oils disappear quickly from the surface, as if they evaporate rather than soak into the wood. After using lemon oil, I don't feel as if I've added much to the wood or gained much protection. They are a nice softener and cleaner, however, for caked dirt. Other preparations use linseed oil mixed with other additives, or are petroleum based.

Whatever oil you wipe on, let it rest only briefly on the wood, then wipe it off carefully—removing as much as you can. Finish by dry-polishing or "burnishing" the fretboard with a clean, dry rag. What you can't remove is in the wood and will rejuvenate it and help keep the fretboard clean.

Note: *All oils—especially linseed oil—create heat when left on crumpled paper towels or rags. They can spontaneously combust in as little as two hours. Dampen used rags with water, put them outdoors to evaporate, then dispose of them.*

String installation

You'll be installing a fresh set of strings just before setting the intonation in the final setup step, but it's a good idea to install a set now if the existing set is old, dirty, or rusty. If they're OK, and the gui-

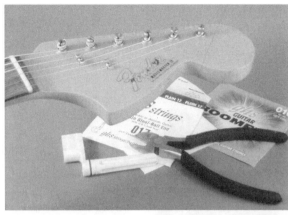

tar's fretboard is clean, leave them alone until one breaks—then replace just that one. While the strings are off, check that all adjustable parts of the tuning keys are snug, including the mounting screws that fasten them to the peghead. Now you're ready to install a fresh set of strings, using one of the following methods.

There are two main electric guitar styles that you're likely to string, and Gibson and Fender guitars best represent those styles. There are hundreds of other guitars built in the same basic styles used by Gibson and Fender. Fender necks are made from a 1" thick maple slab; therefore, the peghead has no angle. Gibson necks do have angled pegheads, because they're cut from a much thicker piece of wood, so you need to string them a little differently. The majority of Fender (and Fender-style) necks are the bolt-on variety (the neck fastens to the body with wood screws and is removable). Most Gibsons and other similar brands have "set necks," meaning that the neck is glued permanently into the body. I'll show you several methods to string both Fender and Gibson-style guitars. I'll also show you how to string using several popular locking tuners, but I'm going to leave stringing guitars with locking nuts for the tremolo section starting on page 56.

Remember: *A guitar string can have a mind of its own. Be sure to wear eye protection and watch out!*

INSTALLING STRINGS ON FENDER AND FENDER-STYLE GUITARS

Fender (and similar) electric guitars have a unique tuner with a "Safeti-Post." The Safeti-Post has a split shaft with a small hole in the center to accept the sharp string ends and save players from bloody string pokes. The Safeti-Post also puts an extra kink in the strings that standard tuners can't, an advantage because kinks help keep the string from slipping. This extra kink comes first, where the string exits the tuner shaft hole (A). A second kink (which happens on normal, non-Safeti-Post tuners also) occurs as you wrap the string tight around the edge of the slot to begin your string wraps (B). The kinks made by a Safeti-Post tuner look like this (C).

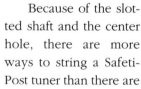

Because of the slotted shaft and the center hole, there are more ways to string a Safeti-Post tuner than there are for other types of tuners. Here are my favorite methods, demonstrated on a single guitar—a lovely 1965 Fender MUSICMASTER. For each method, start with all of the tuner's Safeti-Post slots in line with the length of the peghead and the strings.

STRING TREES

On Fender instruments (and all similar bolt-on neck styles), because the peghead does not tilt, hold-downs called string trees pull certain strings close to the peghead (always the high E- and B-strings, often the G- and D-strings). String trees create an angle from the tuner post to the string nut, and the angle keeps the strings from popping out as you're playing. Without string trees, even if you wound the entire E- and B-strings onto their posts until the strings hit the grommet on the peghead face, you still wouldn't have enough string angle at the nut. Thanks to string trees, you don't need excess string winds on the treble strings, which is nice because excess string winds stretch and slip, making it hard for the string to hold tune.

The Fender MUSICMASTER shown here has two factory-installed string trees. One is screwed directly to the peghead face, the other is raised on a string-tree spacer (someone removed the factory spacer from under the E- and B-string tree, most likely to further increase the angle to the nut). Quite a variety of string trees exists in the replacement parts market, and some even have rollers (to ease friction when a string is bent or the tremolo is used). The bass A- and E-strings don't have string trees because they get a natural angle from being close to the nut, but you still must wind enough string on the post to create a good angle—without overdoing it and getting too steep of an angle. For more about string trees, see page 37.

For any stringing method on a Fender-type guitar, cut each string length two-and-a-half string posts past the tuner you're stringing—photo top left opposite page, the E-string has been "measured" and clipped. This amount of extra string length (it's about 2-1/4") winds far enough down the post to create a good angle for the E- and A-strings, the D- and G-strings if they don't have a string tree, and the E- and B-strings. This is subject to string gauge and

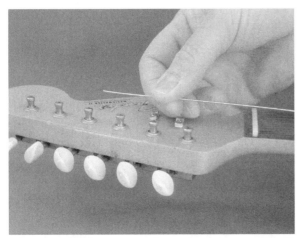

other personal tastes. Unless otherwise noted, all of the installation methods below use the two-and-a-half-post cut.

FENDER STYLE, METHOD ONE

I'm installing this low E-string in the simple manner that the Safeti-Post was intended to be used. For many players, strings installed this way stay in tune adequately, especially for those using heavier jazz-gauge and flatwound strings. Other players use one or more techniques of "locking" each string in place, particularly for thinner, unwound strings.

Measure and cut the string using the two-and-a-half-post method described above, then poke the string end down into the hole. Bend it forward—this makes the first kink at the edge of the hole. Bend it sharply around the slotted edge—there's the second kink. After you've made the kinks, if you're right-handed, hold the string slack in the right hand as you wind all the string downward with the left. Two-and-a-half to three winds gives sufficient string angle to the nut to keep the string from popping out of the nut slot. The correct approximate angles for strings installed on Fender pegheads are: 11 degrees for the low E, 9 degrees for the A, and 4 to 5 degrees for the D and G. The B-

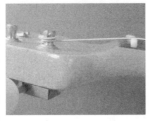

and E-strings have their string tree to produce the 4 to 5 degree angle that keeps the string from popping out of the nut slot.

FENDER STYLE, METHOD TWO

I gave this A-string a different, but popular, locking wrap that doesn't use the Safeti-Post center hole (the Safeti-hole). Cut the string two-and-a-half posts longer than the tuner post, just like the E-string above, but don't poke it down into the hole. Instead, holding the string slack in one hand, use your other hand to sharply bend the last 1/2" of the string end toward the center of the peghead (A). Then, as the first wind comes around the post (B), cross the string up and over the bent string end (C). The next time around, the string goes under the string

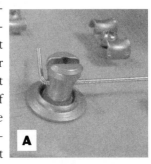

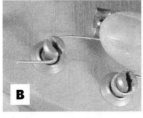

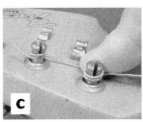

end, locking the string between the over-and-under winds. The resulting tie looks like the bottom photo (D). It has two kinks and a locking wrap, and the remaining wraps go downward to achieve the angle to the nut. (The A-string, since it is farther from the nut, has a lower angle.)

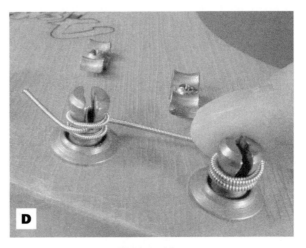

FENDER STYLE, METHOD THREE

Let's do the D-string with another wrap. This method uses only two kinks and does not use the Safeti-hole, but allows you to control the angle of the string and number of winds because you start winding at the bottom—right where you want the string winds to end up!

Without cutting the string to length, tightly pull all the slack around the post (A). Wrap the string around the post from the bottom to the top (B). After three full wraps, hold the string

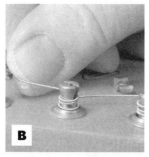

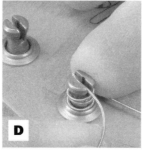

against the post with your finger. With your other hand, pull the string tightly back through the slot toward the nut (C). Next, make a sharp bend with the loose end, or tail, in the opposite direction (D) and press the tail firmly against the post. Keep holding the wraps tight as you start the winds. Once the coil of winds tightens, clip the tail close (E) and tune to pitch.

FENDER STYLE, METHOD FOUR

I learned this wrap from my great friend and guitar advisor Dave Hussong of Fretware Guitars in Franklin, Ohio. Hussong's a fine player and one of the world's leading vintage guitar experts and dealers. This non-Safeti-hole wrap uses two kinks and a string against the post to keep it from slipping.

Instead of cutting to length, pull the string tight through the slot (F), wrap the loose end toward the center and kink it well. Continue wrapping the string

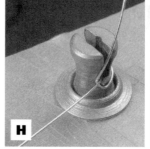

back around the post, under itself (G), and up against the post (H) just as you start to make your turns—catching the end against the post with the wrap, and wrapping downward (I).

FENDER STYLE, METHOD FIVE

Here's another good tie for the unwound strings. It uses the Safeti-Post, and comes from my friend Lindy Fralin, who not only makes great pickups, but plays a mean blues guitar. Fralin doesn't like it when his guitar is out of tune.

Poke the string end down the Safeti-hole, wrap the string halfway around the post, then go back through the slot (J) with a second loop. This second wrap should cross over the first kink (K) and go downward for the remaining wraps. If you count the kink coming out of the post hole, you have four kinks here plus a locking wrap! Tighten these wraps, and the lock is exceptional (L).

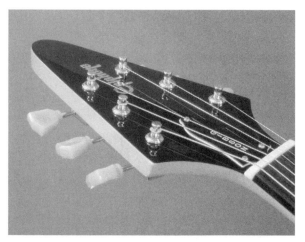

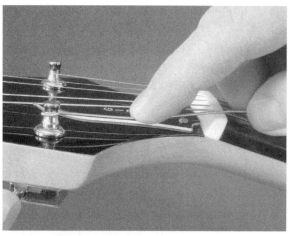

INSTALLING STRINGS ON GIBSON AND GIBSON-STYLE GUITARS

Gibsons and similar models have angled pegheads, which is the most traditional neck construction (compared to Fender's "slab" neck construction). In traditional neck construction, the neck is band-sawed from a good-sized billet of wood (usually mahogany or maple). This creates a beautiful, one-piece neck, which does, however, have have a natural weakness—the "short" grain where the peghead angles back from the nut. This is why one-piece mahogany necks have a tendency to crack at the rear of the peghead, just down from the nut, if you drop or mistreat them.

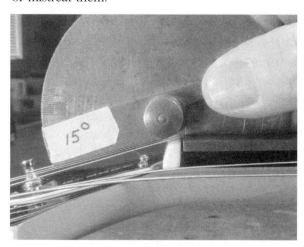

Gibson's peghead angle ranges from 14 degrees to 17 degrees, which creates a good string angle at the nut. String trees are unnecessary on such angled pegheads, and generally only one to three wraps are needed.

This is how I string Gibsons and many similar makes (in this case a Gibson Epiphone Flying-V). *Don't forget your eye protection!*

GIBSON STYLE, METHOD ONE

This is how the factory installs strings—it's a non-locking installation that allows for quick installation and easy removal without undue kinking and breaking. I use this method at the beginning of a setup or when making a new nut so I can take the strings on and off a number of times.

Holding enough slack in your hand to make a wind or two, poke the string end through the post hole, kink it sharply toward the center of the peghead and slightly upward, then start to wind. Keep tension on the string as you wind the wraps downward and as you guide the string into its nut slot. Slowly release the slack as you tune the string to pitch

GIBSON STYLE, METHOD TWO

I use this locking wrap to install strings after a set-up is done—right before I set the intonation. It is much like Fender Method Two, but without a split-shaft Safeti-Post.

Pull the string through the tuner post hole tight, then pull back about 1-1/2" of slack. Create a kink toward the center of the peghead and start winding. Wind over the loose end on the first turn, and under the second turn, locking the string end in

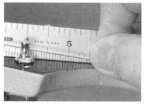

between wraps. Bend the loose end sharply upward and clip it close.

Note: *String manufacturers recommend making a sharp bend in wound strings before cutting them to keep the winds from unraveling.*

GIBSON STYLE, METHOD THREE

This wrap is much like Fender Method Three, but again, without a Safeti-Post tuner. It allows you to control the angle of the string and number of winds because you start winding at the bottom—right where you want the string winds to end up.

Turn the tuner until the post hole is at a right angle to the nut and pull the string tight around the post, make one wrap, and hold the wrap tight against the post with your free hand. Still holding the wrap, poke the loose end through the hole, continue wrapping until the coil tightens, then kink the tail sharply back and up before clipping it close.

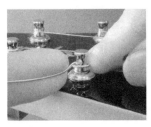
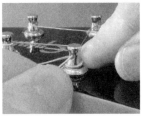

GIBSON STYLE, METHOD FOUR

Here's an excellent locking wrap for the unwound (treble) strings that has a unique kink of its own.

Holding the slack string, poke the string through the hole and make a sharp kink toward the center of the peghead. Wrap the loose end back toward the nut, under itself, and bend it up against the post as you make the first turn to lock it against the post. Continue wrapping the string downward.

Next, bend the end sharply over a thin screw-

driver to kink it before trimming it short. Although harder to remove later (you must clip off the kink before you remove the string), the kink prevents painful string pokes.

STRINGING UP LOCKING TUNERS

Locking tuners clamp on the string, which is pulled taut through the post hole (no slack is left behind). Clamped tight in this position, a string tunes to pitch with a half-turn or less and no string winds are wrapped around the tuner post. The idea is that without string wraps, the string has no potential for stretching and slipping. There are a number of locking tuners on the market. Shown below are the Gotoh top-locking vintage Kluson replacement, which comes in several models to retrofit both Fenders and Gibsons, (A Sperzel locking tuner is pictured on page 40); and the PRS locking tuner.

GOTOH LOCKING TUNERS

Gotoh's locking tuners, shown here on a Strat-style guitar, are simple to use. They create a good angle to the nut because the stringpost hole is low—keeping the string

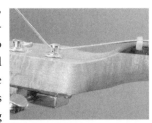

close to the face of the peghead. The tuner post, removed for demonstration in the photo, threads over the string lock pin and into the tuner body.

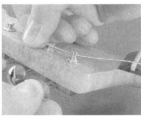

Run the string straight through the hole and pull it tight. As you turn the tuner's key, the stringpost draws down onto the locking pin and captures the string, at which point you can let go of the string end and tune to pitch. Although it's really not necessary, you can place a coin in the shallow slot in

the top of the string post to hold the post as you turn the key to get an extra-tight lock.

PRS LOCKING TUNER

One of the most unique and cleverly designed tuners is the one used on Paul Reed Smith (PRS) guitars. As with other locking tuners, the strings reach pitch before the string ever makes it around one whole post turn. That's how fast PRS tuners grab the string and get it to pitch. Here's what I tell my customers who own PRS guitars:

To remove an old string, push the lever in (A) the direction shown to release the cam-lock that holds the string. In photo (B), I removed the top and the wing lever so you can see the cam slot and better understand how it works; as the cam turns, more and more metal comes to bear against the string until it finally grabs it tight and turns it around the post.

Reassembled, (C) the tuner is in the stringing position. The outer housing, or string clamp, is

turned with the lever pointing toward the tuning key in the 10 o'clock position. This leaves a wide-open slot for the string to thread into (D), if the cam is turned to its most open position. Pull the string through the slot and hold it tight as you turn the knob. When the cam comes around it will grab the string and you'll be at pitch instantly (E).

2 Adjusting the truss rod

Truss rod adjustment is the first setup step that deals with adjusting something—and adjustments are what setups are all about. For guitars with adjustable truss rods (most modern guitars), few setups would be complete without at least tweaking the truss rod. Some guitar necks are perfect and don't require adjustment—if you have one of those, don't mess with a good thing. Of course, if you're just learning to set up guitars, you won't know if your neck is adjusted correctly until you've read this chapter.

You need to know how to adjust a truss rod in order to straighten an up-bowed neck, loosen a back-bowed neck, and to adjust controlled straightness or relief into the fretboard when setting the action.

Up-bow and back-bow are illustrated on page 3. Up-bow refers to a fretboard that curves in the direction of the string pull, creating a valley that makes for high, stiff action. Back-bow refers to a fretboard with a hump in the center, which occurs when a truss rod is so tight that it causes the neck to bow away from the string pull. Back-bow makes a guitar completely unplayable because the strings buzz against the humped frets. Relief is a controlled up-bow deliberately adjusted into a straight neck to give string-to-fret clearance for the vibrating strings (not every guitar needs, or benefits from, relief—it is up to a player and his or her style).

Although I'm separating truss rod adjustment into its own step, truss rod adjustment (controlling the fretboard's straightness) goes hand-in-hand with setting the string height at the bridge and at the nut to produce the overall action desired. I felt it would be easier for readers to understand these adjustments if I separated them into steps. A professional, however, will adjust a truss rod while raising and lowering the bridge; watching, measuring, and adjusting neck straightness or relief; and measuring and adjusting string height at the nut—all simultaneously, almost like a dance.

Truss rod adjustment tools

You need only a few simple tools to adjust truss rods. Depending on the guitar brand, these tools may include a 5/16" flat-blade screwdriver; a No. 2 Phillips-head screwdriver; socket-head nut drivers in 1/4", 5/16", 7mm (9/32" will substitute for 7mm), and 8mm sizes; and Allen wrenches in these fractional and metric sizes: 1/8", 9/64", 3/16", 1.5mm, 2mm, 2.5mm, 3mm, 3.5mm, 4mm, 5mm, 7mm, and 8mm.

Truss rod types and how they work

If you cut a variety of electric guitar necks down the center lengthwise and exposed their truss rods, you'd find many variations: some are installed on a curve while others are installed straight; some are U-shaped metal channels; and some are simple, round steel rods with threaded ends. All adjustable truss rods exert pressure on the neck in the opposite direction of the pull of the strings to straighten up-bow. Some truss rods, called two-way adjustable rods, also exert pressure toward the pull of the strings, and can straighten back-bowed and up-bowed necks (see drawing above right). Some necks are not adjustable at all, and inexpensive guitars such as old Kays, Harmonys, and early imports have necks that adjust poorly even though they have adjustable truss rods. Most other guitars' necks adjust satisfactorily.

You always adjust a truss rod by tightening or loosening a nut. Some nuts screw on to the threaded end of the truss rod (vintage Gibson, Guild, Gretsch and Fender models), other nuts are part of the rod (PRS). While you can remove some nuts for cleaning and lubrication (photo above), others aren't removable due to the truss rod's construction.

Many guitars adjust at the peghead end with either a socket driver or an Allen wrench. Others—

On a typical truss rod, the adjusting nut is threaded onto the rod. Turning it clockwise tightens the rod, pulling the anchor end closer and pulling the neck back. Loosening (turning counter-clockwise) allows the neck to bow back. Remember: "lefty-loosey, righty-tighty."

A dual-action rod works differently:

The adjusting nut is welded to the "active rod." The active rod is threaded through anchors fastened to each end of a "fixed rod." Turning the adjusting nut pushes or pulls against the fixed rod, bowing the neck either way.

vintage Fender guitars and their many clones, in particular—adjust at the body end with either a flat-blade or a Phillips-head screwdriver (or an Allen wrench, as is the case on some imports), Usually, imported guitars require metric tool sizes and American-made guitars require fractional and decimal tool sizes.

Easy adjustments

We'll start with easy truss rod adjustments first. I selected a good range of guitars, some with standard one-way adjustable rods and some with two-way systems.

STANDARD ONE-WAY TRUSS RODS

Vintage Fender, Gibson, Gretsch, Guild, Harmony, Kay, and most imports.

1 To tighten the truss rod and straighten the neck (away from the pull of the strings, removing relief and lowering the strings), turn the adjusting tool clockwise.

2 To loosen the truss rod and give relief to the fretboard (toward the pull of the strings), turn the tool counterclockwise.

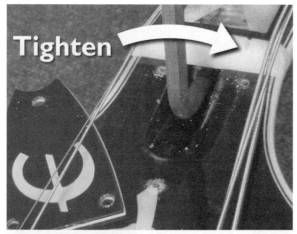

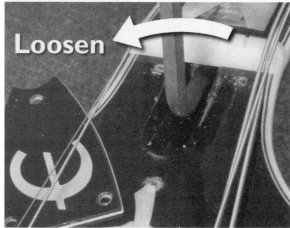

Note: *Loosening a truss rod nut can't harm anything. If you overtighten the nut, however, you can cause damage by stripping the threads of the truss rod nut or the rod itself or twisting the threaded portion off of the rod. Either way, the truss rod is useless and in need of replacement—an expensive job.*

Always loosen the adjusting nut before you tighten it so you know that you're starting at the beginning of the nut's travel. This also is a good time to clean and lubricate the nut's interior threads, and the exposed threads of the truss rod. An ideal neck adjusts perfectly with a quarter or half turn. Do NOT start turning a truss rod nut like you would a wing nut. Once snug, the adjusting nut will do its work immediately. It's not like winding a clock! In extreme situations a nut may require a full turn—but be careful.

TWO-WAY TRUSS RODS

Fender's Bi-Flex truss rod, used on many recent models, and the PRS double-action truss rod (used since 1992) are examples of two-way truss rods. Each adjusts the neck in either direction. A num-

ber of smaller companies and individual luthiers also build with one of several two-way adjustable truss rods that are man-ufactured by several guitar shop suppliers. Two-way rods save the day when a neck decides to backbow in a reverse-warp away from the strings.

Fender supplies a 1/8" long-reach Allen wrench to adjust its Bi-Flex truss rod, which is accessible through a hole in the peghead under the string nut. Above, my shop-mate Elliot John-Conry uses the string as a straightedge before using the 1/8" Allen wrench to adjust the neck of his Fender Lone-Star Strat—a version of Fender's American Standard Strat that uses the Bi-Flex rod.

Paul Reed Smith guitars use a truss rod nut that resembles Gibson's traditional acorn-nut, but the PRS nut (A) is welded to the rod and is not removable. Like Gibson's nut, the PRS adjusts with a 5/16" socket driver (B). Unlike Gibson's long-shafted T-handled wrench (C), the PRS wrench has a short socket with a right-angle handle that allows it to drop into the truss rod cavity to do its work.

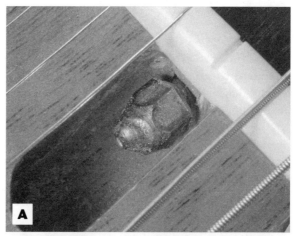

1 To tighten the truss rod and straighten the neck (away from the pull of the strings, removing relief and lowering the strings), turn the adjusting tool clockwise, as with the standard rods above.

2 To loosen the truss rod and give relief to the fretboard (toward the pull of the strings), turn the tool counterclockwise.

3 To straighten back-bow that is causing the neck to curve away from the strings, loosen the truss rod counterclockwise until you feel the slack "zero" point (you will feel no tension), then continue turning counterclockwise until you feel resistance—you are forcing the neck upward and straight.

Many imported guitars have adjustable truss rods that you can access at the peghead and adjust with an Allen wrench. The shorter portion of the L-shaped Allen wrench needs to be pretty long for some models. If you don't have a factory-supplied wrench for your guitar, find a shop that can heat and bend a T-handled Allen wrench as shown.

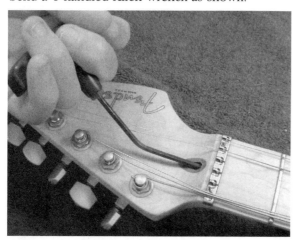

Making difficult truss rods work

Easily adjustable truss rods are no problem, but more difficult necks can be downright frustrating. Therefore, I'll highlight two problematic ones: A 1977 Gibson Les Paul Standard, and a 1995 Fender Bajo Sexto baritone guitar. These two guitars cover all troublespots, and you'll see that hard-to-adjust necks require some help. (If your truss rod adjusts easily, consider yourself lucky.)

USED 1977 GIBSON LES PAUL STANDARD

After close evaluation, I chose this 1977 black Les Paul Standard for a number of the book's setup steps because it had many of the problems that you must address during a complete setup. One of

those problems was a heavily up-bowed fretboard despite a very tight truss rod.

1 A layer of white paper towel with a desk lamp pointed at it makes a bright backlight for comparing a straightedge to the fret top. This guitar had a ton of relief and a truss rod that felt really stiff as I loosened it to clean and lubricate the nut.

2 I always mark the truss rod nut to remind me where it was when I started. Then, using the correct tool (a 5/16" socket in this case), I remove the truss rod nut before  even trying to tighten it any farther. I use a dental probe or hobby knife to clean any dirt, rust, and lacquer from the truss rod threads and the metal half-moon washer that the brass acorn nut tightens against. It's amazing how much junk you find on the threads.

3 I lubricate the truss rod threads, the interior threads of the acorn nut, and the face of the half-moon washer with Vaseline, Teflon lubricant, or

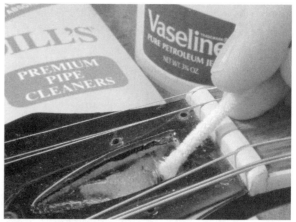

sewing machine oil before replacing the acorn nut and tightening it until it is just snug. Then I back off the acorn nut until it is loose.

4 With this neck, knowing how stiff the acorn nut felt, I knew that I should "help" the neck reach adjustment. I loosened the strings and placed a small block of soft wood (pine from a 2x4) at each end

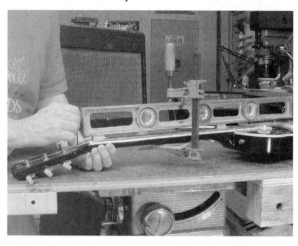

of the fretboard and spanned them with my carpenter's level. Protecting the back of the neck with a rubber-padded block, I used a small bar clamp to back-bow the neck into quite a curve before tightening the acorn nut.

5 I ended up with a back-bow (reverse curve away from the strings, the opposite of what I started with)—note the first fret falling away from my straightedge… I

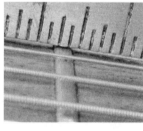

needed to loosen the truss rod (counterclockwise).
6 I gave the neck .002" of relief—almost perfectly straight—and continued with setting the action.

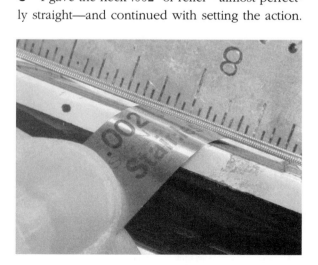

If you don't have the tools mentioned above, have a friend hold the guitar body firmly on a table, with the neck hanging out off the edge, while you pull back on

the neck as you adjust the truss rod. Another method (when working alone) is to clamp the body to the table while you make the adjustment as my friend Luke Berchowitz demonstrates here on his Fender Strat Plus. The wrench Berchowitz is using is an inexpensive T-handle Allen wrench.

1980S SUNBURST LES PAUL

While I was working on the '77 Les Paul, a 1980s sunburst Les Paul came in for a refret. It needed help just like the black one, but it had a more severe problem. The truss rod was as tight as it should go, yet there was still a whopping .027" of relief at the 9th fret. Also, an unusual amount of exposed truss rod thread was showing. This was

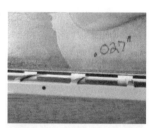

caused by the acorn nut bearing against the steel half-moon washer—the overtightened truss rod compressed the neck wood and forced the half-moon washer into the neck (similar to the problem the Trini Lopez had in Pre-Setup Evaluation, and also to one coming up next with a Fender guitar).

I marked the existing nut position, removed the acorn nut, added a second washer, cleaned the truss rod threads, and lubed them with Vaseline. I also lubed the face of the half-moon washer to cut down on friction, and replaced the worn acorn nut with a fresh one. Then the acorn nut grabbed on fresh threads (notice how little threaded rod is showing). With

23

the same type of help I gave the Les Paul above, the neck adjusted perfectly straight without taking the truss rod nearly to its limit. This was a relief because the owner had purchased it used—without ever looking under the truss rod cover or determining that the rod worked. If the owner, or the wrong person, tried to further adjust this neck I believe the threaded end of the rod would have snapped off—not a good thing!

1995 FENDER BAJO SEXTO BARITONE GUITAR

Here I'm demonstrating, in detail, two ways of adjusting the vintage-style Fender truss rod at the body end. This neck was hard to adjust because it is long (it has a 30" scale length) and has heavy-gauge strings. It was well worth the effort, however. It's my Bajo Sexto, a baritone Telecaster made by the Fender Custom Shop that I bought used. I later "antiqued" the body. When tuned *E* to *E* and an octave lower than standard, baritone guitars also are known as six-string basses. Fender made a version in the 1960s. Common tunings and string gauges for the baritone range are *E* to *E, B* to *B,* and *A* to *A.* I use the A- tuning, and all three tunings are listed on page 26.

Having played other Bajo Sextos that had necks adjusted perfectly straight and good action—even low action considering the string gauge—I was confident that I could adjust mine. When I purchased the five-year-old guitar, the neck was up-bowed and had .050" of relief at the 9th fret. The gap is mea-

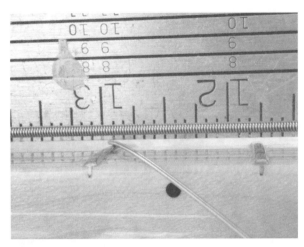

sured here with a .050" guitar string. This neck had a problem common among some Fender necks (even shorter, standard-size necks): they are over-tightened by owners who don't realize that they need to help the neck into proper adjustment. This is especially true with longer necks, but we see the same problem with standard guitar necks, too.

When a truss rod nut is adjusted too tight, sometimes the nut moves forward and compresses the wood in front of it instead of straightening the neck (the strength of the particular piece of wood is a factor). To avoid this, as we did with the Les Paul, help the neck reach the desired adjustment with the truss rod nut loose. Then, hold the neck in that position while tightening the rod. Below I demonstrate two ways of adjusting Fender necks and deal with the wood-crushing problem at the same time.

METHOD ONE

This is the way many people adjust Fender necks, and it is effective, but I don't like it because too often the screwdriver mars either the neck pickup, the pickguard, or both. In this case the neck is not removed entirely from the body (I prefer to remove the neck).

1 Loosen the strings. I like to tie the strings with a rubber band or use a capo so they don't spring out of the tuners and flop all over the place.

2 Loosen the four neck mounting screws with either a Phillips- or flat-head screwdriver (vintage Fenders use straight-

slot screws, later models use Phillips head). Don't remove the screws, just loosen them.

3 If the pickup is springy, push it down and tape it to hold it as low as pos-
sible. Tip the neck until the truss rod adjustment nut (a barrel-shaped nut slotted on the end) will show enough that you can get a thin-bladed, long-handled screwdriv-er into the slot. You'll on-ly be able to get the blade into half of the slot—not a good idea if you need to apply much pressure because the nut

can break without the full slot taking the load. This is a "quickie" truss-rod adjustment, and is OK for necks that adjust easily—but not for me.

METHOD TWO

The best way to adjust Fender and Fender-style necks is to remove the neck entirely so that you can adjust it properly—with a screwdriver tip in the full slot (you can use either a Phillips- or flat-blade screwdriver). The downside of this method is that often you'll have to take a neck on and off four or five times before the rod is adjusted to your satis-faction. Experience is a big help, and professionals often know when they have it right and get the ad-justment the first time around—like me right here.

1 Remove the strings carefully from the tuners so they'll go back on easily and won't break. Lay the treble strings to one side and the bass strings to the other to keep them from tangling.

2 Remove the four neck mounting screws—hold your fingers around the screwdriver tip to keep the screwdriver from slipping onto the finish (although it would-n't matter here because I "aged" the finish to make it look old).

3 Lay the guitar on a soft towel and either remove the neck from the body or lift the body away from the neck. Now, set the body and the strings care-fully aside.

4 Now you can really see the nut and how much it has moved. Re-move the nut, lubricate it with Vaseline or other lu-bricant, then replace it in the neck.

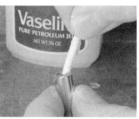

5 (Optional.) This is a good solution that I use of-ten for the crushed-wood problem. Place a brass spacer down the hole first to make up for the space lost by the compressed wood. This moves the truss rod nut back where it should be and allows it to get a fresh grip on the truss rod threads. I make these spacers on a small lathe, but I have used hardware store flatwashers that I ground and filed until they were small enough to fit in the hole. I have always thought this would be a great product for a suppli-er to offer. If you want to try this trick, stop by any machine shop, show them the problem, and they can make a spacer in minutes.

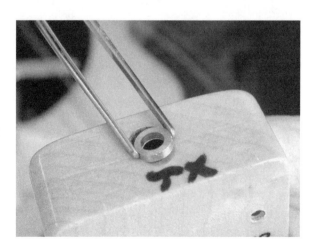

6 With or without the spacer, have the truss rod totally slack as you lay the neck face down on padded blocks of wood and sight it. Clamp some  back-bow into it, taking care to pad the center of the neck (here I'm using a Stewart-MacDonald cork-padded neck support).

7 When you have clamped a comfortable, but not scary (don't break it!) back-bow into the neck, tight-  en the truss rod nut. The truss rod is just a thin piece of metal—and now it doesn't have to do the job by itself.

8 This neck now has a great deal of back-bow, but it will straighten with string tension. It's a  guessing game, and I won't know if I've suc- ceeded in straightening the neck until it is back on and strung to pitch.

9 The neck is still just a little too backbowed. I give it a little "chiropractic" bend in the middle to lessen the rod's grip, and then double-check that I am really at pitch—the string tension will pull that back-bow out.

10 If there's no hurry, I leave the neck strung overnight to settle in be- fore making a judge-  ment. The truss rod will continue to exert pres-

sure (or give way to the string pressure), and the neck may look different the next day. In this case I didn't wait, and with a capo on to free one hand I checked the neck's straightness. It was perfect— a good guess!

Common baritone tunings and appropriate string gauges

Listed from low (bass string) to high (treble string), these tunings are the same intervals as standard gui- tar tunings but start and end on different notes. The string gauges also are listed. D'Addario makes a set of six-string bass strings for the *E* to *E* tuning, and Fender offers a set that works for either the A-tun- ing or the B-tuning.

A Tuning: (*A, D, G, C, E, A*), using .066", .056", .046", .036", .026" (unwound), and .016 gauge strings, respectively.

B Tuning: (*B, E, A, D, F#, B*). B-tuning uses the same string gauges as the A-tuning above. A good medium-to-heavy guitar set (.013 to .056") will work.

E Tuning: (*E, A, D, G, B, E*—one octave lower than standard), using .072", .062", .052", .042", .032", .022" gauge strings (all wound), respectively.

My four-piece band has drums, bass, and two guitars, so when I play baritone I am in between the range of the bass and the guitar—sort of in the cel- lo range. The resultant voice of the baritone is sim- ply wonderful—plus, since I have absolutely no idea where I am on the fretboard, I play music from the heart (not just lick after memorized lick).

That's it for truss rods—plenty of help for get- ting your guitar's neck where you want it to be. Let's move on to the ends of the neck—the nut and bridge. We'll start at the nut.

3 Nut adjustment and maintenance

A guitar's nut, or string nut, has slots for the strings to rest in. The exact front edge of the slots (where the nut face meets the blunt end of the fingerboard) is one of two string contact points, or witness points, that determine if a vibrating string's speaking-length is well intonated. The other witness point is where the string, coming from its fastening point in the bridge base, last touches the saddle and becomes part of the speaking length. These contact points also are called take-off points—from them the string is free to take off and produce sound.

The nut slots space the strings comfortably across the fretboard and hold them in place. Traditional (nonmechanical) nuts are made of bone, ivory, plastic, brass, aluminum, steel, graphite, Graph Tech, Delrin, Corian, Tusq, and other materials. Of these materials, bone is my favorite for a standard nut on a non-tremolo guitar. However, the self-lubricating qualities of some of the synthetics (such as Graph Tech and Delrin) make them a better choice for guitars with tremolos, string-benders, D-tuners, and other pitch-altering devices.

Traditional nuts are found on Gibson, Gretsch, Fender, Epiphone, Guild, PRS, and other guitars. Mechanical nuts usually are cast or machined from metal (some have plastic parts) and include locking nuts, roller nuts, and adjustable nuts. Mechanical nuts are a product of the modern guitar age and are generally associated with locking tremolo guitars.

The placement, shape, height, and string slots of the nut—as well as the angle of the string from the tuning key post to the rear edges of the nut slots— is a critical factor in determining good string support and alignment in the nut and accurate intonation. Equally critical are the shape, height, and location of the bridge saddles and string angles from the bridge saddles to the tailpiece. Unlike most mechanical bridge saddles and nuts (easily adjustable), traditional nut adjustments require hand filing, sanding, and shaping skills. All nuts are replaceable and adjustable to some degree. Although replacing a traditional nut usually should be left to a professional, there are many minor nut adjustments you can make to insure that any nut is doing its job. All of these adjustments relate to the string height at the nut.

Measuring string height at the nut

Factories normally send out new guitars with the strings on the high side (they're low enough to play, but high enough to guarantee no buzzing at the first fret). Most players aren't satisfied with factory set-ups, which is understandable because the factory setups are pretty generic. Even guitar stores with a policy of setting up showroom guitars err on the high side—future buyers' preferences are not yet known. Also, after a guitar leaves the factory, the humidity level of its new environment can greatly affect the wood and therefore the guitar's setup— why set the nut (or make any critical adjustment) within thousandths until it's necessary?

The specifications given throughout the action setups beginning on page 108 cover a variety of guitar models and player preferences. Those measurements are only guidelines, however, and in the case of factory specs are often on the high side for new guitars (a used guitar, of course, may well have strings that have worn too low in the nut slots). You can compare your string height at the nut to the any of the specs, but playing the guitar and looking at the string height are the most valid tests.

MEASURE STRING HEIGHT IN THE PLAYING POSITION

You should take your measurements with the guitar on its side in the playing position because the neck's flexibility, combined with the weight of the neck and tuners plus the forces of gravity, causes it to fall forward while you're playing. Any close measurements made while the guitar is lying on its back will be far from accurate. Even worse is propping the peghead on something, which adds unnatural neck relief. You may return the guitar to your bench, vise, or neck rest to make slight adjustments, but check it often in the playing position.

And remember, although separated for instructional purposes, the neck, bridge, and nut adjustments go hand-in-hand as part of the overall action adjustments that are the components of a setup. Any measurements taken at the nut wouldn't mean much if the neck was not adjusted correctly, or if the bridge saddle height and string height over the frets were far too low or high. Here you are just learning what to do at the nut during a setup.

THIRD-FRET PRESS TEST

A quick test for determining if your nut is too low is to press the strings down at the 3rd fret and tap each string at the 1st fret to see if it moves. There must be at least some clearance between the bottom of the strings and the top of the 1st fret—if the strings rest directly on the 1st fret during this test, they probably will buzz open. You can measure this clearance by clamping a capo at the 3rd fret so both hands are free to measure the gap with guitar-string feeler gauges.

MY FAVORITE FEELER GAUGES

I have boxes of feeler gauges that I often use, but they're clumsy for some jobs. I prefer to measure string clearance at the 1st fret, and relief, with pieces of guitar string fastened to a wooden stick with superglue. With the singular, small diameter of a string it's easier to see whether or not it touches as you drag it between a string and the top of the a fret. Guitar strings only go as low as .008", so for a .004"

measurement I cut a thin strip from a .004" feeler gauge. Capoed, these strings measured .004" under the treble E-string and .008" under the bass E-string—plenty of clearance.

Checklist for a perfect nut

In my opinion, the perfect nut would pass this checklist:

1 It would rest clean and tight in its slot, and all adjacent surfaces would contact precisely. The nut would be held in place with a small amount of water-soluble glue (hide glue, Elmer's, or Titebond), thinned with water (3 parts water to 1 part glue) so there is just enough strength to hold the nut in place.

2 It would look good. None of the exposed edges would be sharp, and the outer surface would be polished and would have as few file marks or sanding scratches as possible.

3 The outer E-strings would be neither too far from, nor too close to, the edge of the fretboard (according to the particular player's preference).

4 Each guitar string would rest cleanly in its respective nut slot. Most nuts that I make have string slots that support approximately 1/2 of a string's diameter. This is plenty of slot to keep a string from popping out of the nut during playing and bending,

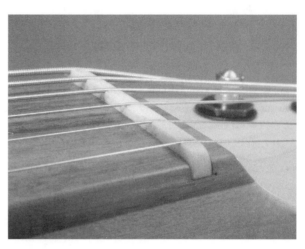

yet it leaves enough string free to produce a clean sound. The nut slot side walls and the rounded bottom of the slots would match the string width and diameter, but would be smoothed and polished until they were slightly larger than the actual string size, allowing the strings to move during tuning or tremolo work.

For tremolo guitars fitted with a traditional nut, some repair technicians file flat-bottomed nut slots because the strings catch less and move more freely on a flat surface. Others (myself included) shape the nut like the Sadowsky nut shown here to illustrate steps 4, 5, and 6, and 7. Sadowsky uses a lubricated nut material, and adds a small amount of powdered graphite to his shaped slots at the final setup.

5 Each string would angle gradually from the tuner toward the back of the nut at an appropriate angle: one that provides enough downward pressure to keep the string in the slot, but not so much as to cause the string to bind in the slot.

6 Viewed from the side, the point at which the string contacts the nut would be a gradual, rounded ramp, leaving enough nut material to support the string and give the slot years of wear. (See illustration, page 4.) The string would rise gradually to the nut's front edge (the string's take-off point), insuring good intonation. An angle that is too steep and sharp will leave a brittle, weak front edge that will wear out fast—dropping the string in the slot and likely causing it to buzz on the first fret.

Loosen a string and lift it from the slot and you'll see where the string has burnished (made smooth and glossy) the contact area. You don't want to see a contact area *behind* the take-off point—that indicates a poorly filed "uphill" nut slot that increases the string length and causes the string to note flat. This is a problem that must be fixed. If the strings are high enough in the nut you may be able to correct this problem by properly back-filing and lowering the string in the slot. Otherwise, you must resort to the nut-shimming, slot-filling and reshaping, or nut-replacement options mentioned below (or head to your local repair shop).

7 The string slots would widen slightly (filed in the shape of a slightly rounded "V", away from the string) as they approach the back edge of the nut. This allows the string freedom 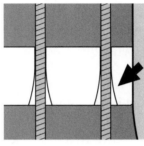 to move and angles it toward its respective tuner post.

8 String spacing would please the player. For me, looks and feel are most important. I don't cut slots that are an exact division of the space between the outer E-strings because it places the thicker-wound strings too close together.

I prefer a comfortable blend of all the string diameters so the strings look and feel right. I do this by eye because calculating it is too time consuming. Some players prefer different string spacing at the nut, such as:

■ Squeezing the treble strings closer together then the bass strings.

■ Strings spaced closer to the bass edge than the treble edge to keep the treble strings from falling off the fingerboard. This is handy for many 1970s Fenders with a heavy "roll-off," or rounding, at the edge of the fingerboard.

■ Strings that are spaced exactly within the space available between the outer E-strings. This makes the bass strings closer together than treble strings.

COMMON NUT PROBLEMS

Now that you know whether your strings need to go higher, lower, or remain the same at the nut, here are a number of common scenarios you may face:

1 You're satisfied with the string slot depth (string height), and the nut slots are clean, well shaped, and not too deep. You need only make sure the slots are correctly back-filed to ensure that the string is leading off the front edge for good intonation.

2 You're satisfied with the slot depth, but the guitar is used and the slots have collected sweat and dirt. You should clean them and they may benefit from a little back-filing and polishing.

3 The slots are too high and simply need to be filed lower. Depending on how much you lower the slots, you may or may not need to remove excess material from the top of the nut to keep the nut slot sidewalls from pinching and muting the strings.

4 The slots are too low. There are several solutions: 1) Replace the nut entirely (most often a job for a pro); 2) loosen the nut and raise it with a shim (you can do that if you can get the nut loose without wrecking anything—often a nut loosens easily); 3) fill in the slots, then recut them to the desired depth. Solutions 2 and 3 are temporary, because shimmed nuts lose tone from resting on a shim, and filled nut slots not only lose tone but eventually will break down because the fill material is not as solid as the original nut material.

5 The slots are too shallow to keep the strings from popping out of their slots. On Fender-style guitars, simply adding a second string tree or lowering the existing one(s) may help keep the string down. In most cases, however, you must replace the nut or, if the strings are high enough, lower the slots.

6 The string-to-string spacing is irregular, or the outer strings are too close to the edge of the fretboard. It is best to have the nut replaced, but for a temporary fix, shim the nut and reposition the slots with the filing techniques shown here.

7 The nut is fine, but made of plastic (common on inexpensive guitars). Consider having a professional replace the nut with one made from bone or some other nut material that is appropriate for your guitar (guitars equipped with tremolos may benefit from a slippery nut material such as Graph Tech or Slip-Stone).

NUT WORKING TOOLS

If you're looking to get deep into setup and work on more than a few guitars, consider investing in a starter set. With the few tools shown here—a razor saw and three nut files—I can make any nut or re-

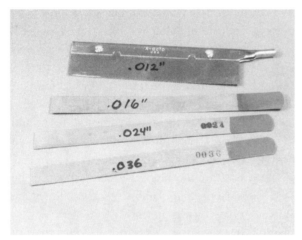

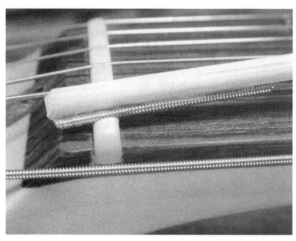

work any existing nut. You'll find that in Step 4, "Bridge and tailpiece maintenance," these same tools serve double duty by fitting and reshaping bridge saddle slots. You also can make your own nut files that will slowly lower nut slots and clean and polish quite well.

The specialty files mentioned above cut round-bottomed slots in guitar or electric bass nuts. Pictured below are two types of nut files offered by Stewart-MacDonald: The six plastic-handled, V-shaped files have teeth on the sides as well as the bottoms, and each edge is a different size, ranging from .016" to .120".

The sixteen other round files have smooth sides. Each of their two cutting edges is the same size, ranging from .010" to .109". I use both styles—"Vs" to cut the  slot in a hurry because they widen as they deepen; and "rounds" to accurately shape and smooth the slot bottoms. *"V" on left, "round" on right.*

MAKE YOUR OWN NUT FILES

Do-it-yourselfers can make nut files by supergluing several gauges of round-wound guitar strings to wood dowels. Making a nut from scratch with these would be tedious, but they're fine for slightly modifying and lowering slots, or for burnishing (polishing) the nut slot bottoms. You also can shave

wood away to better expose the string and wrap the "file" with sandpaper. Coarse grits (220-400) lower the larger slots quite well, and fine grits, as in the photo (1200 and up), will polish any snags in the nut slot bottoms.

CLEANING NUT SLOTS

Keep in mind that nut adjustments are the most difficult to make because the strings are at their lowest point on the fretboard. Even a single stroke of a nut file or sandpaper, meant only to clean away dirt, can lower a string too much and cause a buzz—so work carefully and check your work often. Additionally, measurements are only a guideline. It's more important to use your eyes first—look at the string height—then use your sense of touch. Compress the strings (in the playing position) and see how they feel, that's what really counts.

For cleaning and light-duty back-filing of nut slots, you need only to loosen the strings, lift them from their slots, and rest them on the peghead face. Place three strings on each side of the nut and protect the finish with low-tack drafting tape. For more heavy-duty nut work you'll have to remove the strings entirely, either at the peghead end or the bridge end, to keep them out of your way.

■ Remove dirt and grease with a paper towel or thin rag dipped in lighter fluid. Work the towel or rag through each slot with any thin objects that can guide it without scratching the slot.

■ Wrap whatever appropriately sized tools you have with 1000-grit or finer wet-or-dry sandpaper (available at auto parts stores) and polish the nut slot bottoms until they shine.

■ Place a tiny dot of lubricant into the bottom of each nut slot. Use Teflon spray (sprayed into a container and applied with a toothpick), Vaseline, powdered graphite, pencil lead, or any of several products made especially for nut lubrication such as Guitar Grease or the special lubricant developed and marketed by Rene Martinez as "GraphitAll." (Martinez was Stevie Ray Vaughan's famed guitar tech and is an awesome player in his own right.)

BACK-FILING NUT SLOTS

■ Inspect the nut slot. If a back-angle is needed (items 5 and 6 on page 28), use any of the tools and sandpapers mentioned to gently file a slightly rounded back-angle. All the slots in the nut pictured needed at least some cleaning, and most needed back-filing. After starting to back-file the low E-string with a sandpaper-wrapped file, I put some pencil lead in the slot to show where the sandpaper was hitting.

Then I switched to just a wound guitar string to finish the round slope to the front edge. As you can see in the photo, I did the same to the A-string. If the slot is close to being where you want it, a guitar-string file alone will remove small amounts of material, but not too much, too fast.

■ I cleaned the high E-string slot with a razor saw—gently, and only pushing out the dirt from the slot. I shaped the B-string with a real nut file—the saw would do the job, too.

QUIZ: What's wrong with these pictures?

ANSWER: I'm not being careful enough. Even though I have lots of experience, I should have applied tape around the nut to protect the surrounding area from slips and scratches (see the '59 Tele nut job below for a proper tape-off job).

FILLING IN NUT SLOTS THAT ARE TOO LOW

This well-worn 1959 Fender Telecaster had the coolest input jack cup I've seen. Made from a 1950s Fender amp logo, it's a piece of folk art that no future owner should change. When it arrived in my

shop, the guitar almost played—but the strings snapped and buzzed because the nut slots were too low, especially the D-, B- and A-strings, which were so close to the 1st fret that I didn't bother measuring the gap. Pits in the fret didn't help the buzzing problem either. The guitar's owner was about to sell it, and he hoped I could eliminate the buzz without removing the original nut (and realized it was a temporary fix).

Before working on the nut, I checked the other end of the guitar to make sure that the height and radius of the bridge saddles were set correctly to produce an accept-

able overall string height (action). If a saddle is too low, or if its bridge saddle radius does not match the fretboard radius, it could cause a string to be too low at the nut. I'll show you a little bit about bridge setup before continuing.

The radius wasn't correct: the D-string was too high at the bridge (which meant it would buzz even

worse if I lowered it at the bridge to match the radius), and the G-string was too low. The rest seemed fine, so I adjusted the D- and G-strings correctly before continuing with the nut. However, while adjusting the saddles, I decided to give them a good derusting and cleaning. They were in pretty bad shape. The G-string height screw had a broken slot—no wonder it was out of adjustment! I stopped right there and cleaned all the parts (see "Cleaning rusted bridge parts" in Step 4)—just as I would in an actual setup, going back and forth between setup steps to keep the ball rolling.

With the bridge saddles clean, working, and adjusted properly, I did a quick neck check (looking for straightness or relief) with a capo installed at the 1st fret (as on page 26). I found almost no fretboard relief—my preference. With the capo still on (to eliminate the nut height as a factor in the overall action), I used a ruler to measure the string height at the 17th fret and found it perfectly acceptable, ranging from 5/64" (bass side) to 4/64" (treble side). Fender measures action height at the 17th fret because the neck is most stable where it's bolted to the body. I knew if I could raise the nut slots just a little, the guitar would play—with the original vintage nut intact.

I used low-tack drafting tape, a less-sticky masking tape that won't pull the finish off, to protect the brittle finish around the nut. I made it even less tacky by sticking it on and off my apron a couple of times. On top of the drafting tape I put some thicker, more durable tape for extra protection. Next I used a clean, smooth-cut, flat file to remove bone from the top of the nut (there was way too much anyway, since the string slots were so deep). I saved the bone dust on a piece of paper taped behind the nut—we'll use it later.

I cleaned out the slots that needed to be raised by scraping away dirt with an X-acto blade (bottom left), then I used my homemade nut file to expose fresh bone. After degreasing the slots with lighter fluid, I packed bone dust into the slots with the X-acto blade and carefully brushed away all the excess. Using a plastic toothpick as an applicator, I placed a drop of water-thin superglue on the dust. It soaks into the bone dust and, when dry (several hours later), the bone dust is part of the nut.

After the glue was dry I used my string file to reshape the slot, then wrapped the file with 500-grit sandpaper to polish the slot. An X-acto saw is good for cutting the thin slots. Follow the saw with the folded edge of 500-grit sandpaper. I ended up "bone-dusting" the low E-string, too. After sanding the file marks off the nut top, I removed the tape on

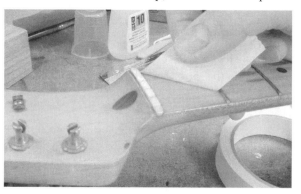

the bias—you're less likely to pull up finish when you pull at an angle. With a set of new strings, this guitar was ready for market.

REMOVING EXCESS NUT MATERIAL THAT IS MUTING STRINGS

The nut shown on the next page is a good example of nut slots that are filed too deep. The nut is on a Fender Lone-Star Strat (a version of the American Standard) that belongs to my apprentice and shop mate, Elliot John-Conry. I helped Elliot take care of this job.

The string height at the nut was fine—we determined that by looking at the nut, playing the guitar, consulting the setup specs, and by using guitar string feeler gauges. The nut slots were simply too deep and a bit tight. The deepness causes the tightness, which in turn mutes the strings' brilliance when played open. The deep slots also can pinch strings during tuning or bending, producing a "chinking" sound or holding the string out of tune (especially

with a tremolo). Finally, the nut's sharp factory edges made playing uncomfortable. Elliot lowered the top of the nut to expose some of the string and give it a cleaner, brighter, sound, and carefully rounded and dulled the sharp edges at the same time.

First Elliot taped off the area with several layers of low-tack drafting tape. Next, he removed the excess nut material with a smooth-cut file, the kind sold in hardware  stores for sharpening lawn mower blades. Before Elliot used the file, he dulled and rounded its sharp edges on a block with coarse emory cloth. Then he used a fingernail file to smooth off the remaining file marks, gently round the hard corners, and remove the hard edges of both the front and back of the nut. Since the string touches only the contacting surfaces of the nut slot it rests in, there is no reason not to remove the hard, sharp edges above the string slots.

Elliot finished up with a quick run-through of sandpapers ranging from 400 grit to 1000 grit. Then he buffed the nut with a dry paper towel and some of Stewart-MacDonald's #1202 buffing compound, which is a paste, not a liquid. I prefer not to use liquid polishing compounds because I believe they soak into the nut material and soften it.

When Elliot removed the tape, he pulled it on an angle and from each side in toward the center to avoid pulling up lacquer from the fingerboard edge. This is very important, especially on new guitars, because the finish is still curing! Now the nut felt good to the touch, looked good, and the slots were one-

half the diameter of the strings—plenty of slot to hold them in place, but not causing muting or pinching.

GLUING A LOOSE NUT

As Elliot was stringing up he felt a little of the nut overhanging the edge of the nut slot. Then, to his surprise, the nut moved in the slot! Perhaps it was glued in too lightly or not  at all, or maybe the shaping and sanding loosened the glue that had been there. Elliot loosened the strings and propped them up off the fretboard on a 1/2" wood dowel inside a length of 3/4" plastic tubing (the tubing won't harm the strings). It's a good way to keep strings out of the way without removing or harming them while doing quick work on a nut. He pried the nut out with his fingernail.

Neatly, he applied a small amount of white (PVC, or Elmer's) glue in the bottom of the nut slot, using a toothpick as an applicator, and set the nut in place. Quickly but gently, and before the glue set, he replaced all the  strings in the slots (trying not to mar a nice polish job). After tuning the two outside E-strings up enough to press the nut down, he centered it, then firmly pressed it into its final position. Elliot tuned to pitch quickly, taking care that the nut didn't shift under the unbalanced string pressure, and let the string pressure clamp the nut while it dried.

Note: *We thinned the glue so the nut would remove easily—3 parts water to 1 part glue. Finally, Elliot and his Lone-Star were ready to ride again!*

SHIMMING A TRADITIONAL NUT

It's often obvious that someone has removed a nut on a used guitar and shimmed it with bad materials such as matchbook covers. The previous owner may not even have succeeded in raising the nut to a good playing height. You may want to re-shim the nut with a better material so that it is high enough that you can rework the nut slots (and remove any excess material afterward, as we did above). In most cases, a nut like this will remove easily because it no longer is tight in the factory slot—a light tap should free it. However, if the nut doesn't want to budge with a gentle tap, have a repair technician remove the nut and then follow the steps below. Don't risk harming your guitar by manhandling your nut!

Following is an easy, cautious way to shim a nut. Remember, however, that nut shimming is a temporary solution because anything sitting between the nut and the wood of the neck is a tone robber. But I have shimmed (and still do) hundreds of nuts when necessary.

Clean the surfaces of the nut by rubbing it on some 220- to 320-grit sandpaper taped to a flat surface. Don't overdo it— just clean off the dry, crusty glue. Carefully clean the nut slot in the neck that the nut rests in, too. If there is glue on the end of the fingerboard, "chop" vertically with a sharp, single-edge razor blade or chisel. Clean the

nut slot bottom with a file if you have one that fits (file from the treble and bass sides toward the center to avoid chipping finish off the edge), or scrape with the razor blade. Clean the sharp corners of the slot bottom with any scrap of steel (a nail works, if sharpened like a chisel with a smooth-cut metal file).

If the strings are resting directly on the fret, you have a pretty good idea of how thick your shim must be. A good, thin shim material is a guitar string envelope—it's almost transluscent, like rice paper. After

soaking in superglue, the color of the paper looks good on traditional nuts made of bone or light- or off-white material. For a graphite nut shim, first color the paper black with permanent marker, let it dry, and then do the gluing. The paper measures .003", so knowing that you can determine how many layers you'll need.

Cut several strips of the string package larger than the actual nut dimension and set them aside. Tape a good-sized square of waxed paper on a hard, flat, disposable surface. Place your shims on one end of the waxed paper; on the other, squeeze out a thin, 2-1/2" long bead of medium-viscosity superglue and spread it out with a cotton swab. Set the nut bottom in the superglue, then quickly press it down on a shim and hold it tight and flat for a couple of minutes. Superglue accelerator will hasten the drying if you spray some on the bottom of the nut before jamming it onto the glue and paper—I prefer not to use it though, because I think accelerator weakens the joint.

When the shim is dry, continue to rest it on the hard, disposable surface, and use a very sharp X-acto knife to trim the shim close to the nut bottom. Repeat the

process until you have the height you need, then use a smooth file and sandpapers to shape the shim to meet the nut. The superglue soaks into the paper and makes it hard, and it almost looks like bone or another light nut material. Now install the nut into the slot and make whatever adjustments are needed. Nut shimming is easy! (If you're lucky enough to have an easily removable nut.)

SHIMMING A MECHANICAL NUT

Mechanical nuts, like Fender's LSR Roller Nut, are easy to raise or lower using thin (.005" and .010") stainless steel shims 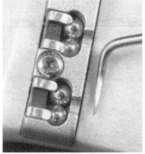 (Fender dealers can provide these). Be extremely careful removing the two tiny screws that hold the nut in place! The one shown here was bungled by someone who used the wrong size, or a dull-bladed, Phillips screwdriver—all the clean edges of the screws were destroyed, and since the plating was scraped away, the Phillips slots began to rust.

Always clean any grease, dirt, and rust from screw slots before trying  to loosen a screw—especially tiny screws like these because they're difficult to find. I cleaned these with the sharp point of a dental probe. I could barely get these screws out or back in again. Drop the nut and its mounting screws into a solution of lighter fluid and light oil, such as sewing machine oil, to clean and lubricate the parts. Use 3 parts lighter fluid to 1 part oil.

The shims are loose in the slot so be sure to keep them in their correct order while you clean any parts. The treble side had two .010" shims superglued together to make .020"; on the bass side, there was one .010" shim. Neck slotting tolerances and wood hardnesses vary, so you may need a shim as low as .005" or as high as .020" to get the correct nut height. It's doubtful that you would go higher than .020", but possible you would need to go lower than a factory-supplied .005" steel shim. If you do need to go lower, use aluminum foil in combination with Fender's shims, if necessary. In the case of this guitar, the factory nut shims were the correct thickness for good string height over the 1st fret.

After the nut is back in place, lubricate the roller ball bearings very lightly with Dupont Teflon "dry" lubricant. Spray the lubricant into a small plastic cup—the carrier/solvent evaporates quickly, leaving

behind the Teflon, which makes a good lube for nuts, bridges, truss rods, and other parts.

Note: *Wear protective gloves when handling these chemicals.*

Using lubricated nut material with traditional tremolos

Traditional tremolos can work smoothly and return to pitch well when used in combination with a traditional nut made from a self-lubricating nut blank such as Graph Tech or Slip-Stone and a set of locking tuners.

Tom Jones, of TV Jones Guitars (see page 120), honed his tremolo nut-making skills working on Brian Setzer's Bigsby-powered Gretsch 6120s. Jones also builds his own Gretsch-inspired guitars. On his own tremolo guitars, and on Brian Setzer's Gretsch, Jones uses a special, chemically lubricated Delrin that makes a wonderful nut for tremolo guitars. Jones happened upon it by chance, and sent me some to try. It doesn't sound quite as bright as Graph Tech but it has more lubrication. Tom was kind enough to share his source, and now Stewart-MacDonald sells it as Slip-Stone. Consider having a professional replace your nut with one of these materials.

Any nut must be shaped very carefully, but especially a nut used with a tremolo. After experimenting with both V-shaped, flat-bottomed, and round-bottomed slots, I prefer round bottoms because they're easier to shape and control since I have round files. Besides, I burnish the slots well enough that they don't bind.

I burnish the slots with a guitar string, dipped in paste buffing compound, of the gauge and type that will be used in the slot. Sometimes I even polish the slot bottoms with a wide, waxed dental floss.

Notice that the strings in this Graph Tech nut are well exposed in the slots, but that the B- and E-strings rest a little deeper—they are the ones most likely to pop out during a string bend.

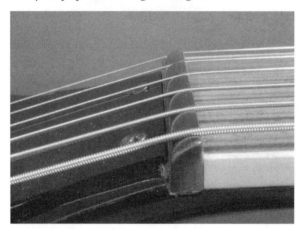

Working with locking nuts

When I first saw the Floyd Rose locking tremolo system, followed by Kahler's version, I was intimidated by locking string nuts—how inescapable! With a shop full of tools and years of experience, I still approached these strange birds with caution—I didn't know the "right" way to adjust them. Years have gone by now, many locking tremolo systems have come and gone, and a variety of locking nuts with them. Unlike the earliest versions, today's locking tremolo systems are easy to adjust and set up. We'll deal with the peghead end of these systems, the locking nut, right now, and cover the other half—the locking tremolo—in Step 5 (page 77), which covers bridges, tailpieces, and tremolos.

Locking nuts are used only with locking tremolos that have fine-tuning capabilities, and they are never used on guitars with standard tremolos such as Strats and Bigsbys because, of course, you wouldn't be able to tune the guitar! Locking nuts are difficult to install from scratch, but they are easy to adjust and maintain.

Today's most popular locking nuts and locking tremolo systems are the Floyd Rose-licensed versions. Ibanez, which manufactures almost all of the hardware and pickups for its guitars, equips its guitars with Floyd Rose-licensed systems. I had several Ibanez models with locking tremolo systems in the shop for this book, including a seven-stringer. These models have different EDGE tremolos, but their locking nuts are the same.

In a locking nut, strings are locked against the

bottom of the hardened-steel nut body by three string clamps called pressure pads (also hardened steel), which are fastened tight with 3mm Allen-head machine screws. These string clamps mount with their back ridges running lengthwise, along the neck. The entire nut body rests on a flat surface machined into the neck at the fingerboard end, and is held fast by two 2.5mm Allen-head machine screws and washers installed from the rear of the neck.

Viewed from the side or end, you can see that the nut body has a gradual, rounded slope toward the string take-off points at the nut's front edge (where the scale-length begins) to insure good intonation. A retainer bar is mounted at the backside of the nut to hold the strings down against the nut body at a steeper angle than occurs naturally. Without the retainer (below), the strings would sit high at the rear of the nut, and go sharp as the string clamp was tightened. Even with the Ibanez peghead angle, the retainer bar is necessary. Imagine how important the retainer bar is when a locking-nut is installed on "slab-construction" necks built in the Fender-style, with zero back angle on the peghead.

Note: *Even when perfectly adjusted, the pressure pads will sharpen the string an almost imperceptible amount that can be corrected by a tweak of the locking tremolo's fine tuners.*

One of the great things about a Floyd Rose locking nut is that it is machined to the same radius as

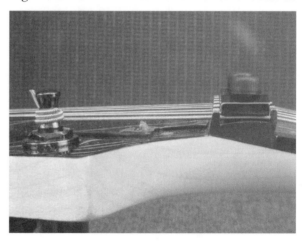

the fretboard of the model on which it's installed. Floyd Rose nuts are available in several different radii and widths, and some companies—Ibanez for example—have their own proprietary custom sizes. When you have a perfect radius across the fretboard, you need simply adjust the overall nut height, or the height of the treble or bass sides individually, to suit your style. After all of the nut work just covered, what could be easier?

To remove the nut for height adjustment, remove the two rear screws at the back of the neck. Hold the nut tight against the neck until the screws are free, then lift the nut away with the instrument laying on its back and the nut facing upward. If any shims are under there, you'll want to know how they were placed—it'll be too late if the shims fall

out before you get a chance to see their order. The two steel washers are used with the nut mounting screws to keep them from over-compressing the wood.

This shim is a "medium" Ibanez factory shim—one piece of .3mm (.012") brass shim stock punched on a press to match the nut base. (Ibanez has shims that are available in thicknesses of.1 mm, .3 mm, and .5 mm [.004", .012", and .020", respectively]), which the company refers to as thin, medium,

and thick. These sizes cover most shimming situations. Notice that I marked the treble side with a pen for later reference.

You can increase or decrease on either the bass or treble side by adding an additional shim, removing one, or cutting off a piece of shim to use on only one side or the other. Any shim material will increase the nut height if you place it between the factory shim and the bottom of the nut. Ibanez dealers stock shim packs of all three sizes (the thinnest is most often used). Also, any good machine shop will have many sizes of thin brass shim stock if you

want to make your own. Aluminum foil makes good shim stock because it's thin (.001"/.02mm) and allows you to make subtle adjustments. Try not to use soft shim materials, such as wood or plastic, that might rob your guitar of tone.

This guitar had not been readjusted since leaving the factory. With a straight neck (no relief), and comfortable action at the 12th fret, I tried the "capo

test." Capoed at the 3rd fret, I measured a 1st fret clearance of .004" on the treble E-string, and .008" on the bass E-string. With the capo removed, the (actual) clearance measured .013" and .022", respectively—a comfortable factory action that could go lower by replacing the .012" shim with two .004" shims stacked together (lowering the overall nut by .004"). I tried it, and it was perfect.

String trees, tuning keys, and string angle to the nut

I put string trees (hold-downs) and tuning keys (also called tuning pegs or tuners) in the nut section because they have a big effect on whether or not a guitar nut will do its job—especially on guitars with bolt-on slab necks that have no peghead angle. Mounted between the tuning keys and the rear of the nut, string trees provide downward pressure (for the treble E- and B-strings in particular) to keep the strings in their respective slots. Guitars with traditional angled pegheads don't need string trees, but they do benefit from a good set of tuners.

As for the tuners' contribution to the string angle at the nut on non-angled pegheads, today several versions of shortened-post tuners provide the desired angle and downward pressure without the need for a string tree at all (in some people's opinions—not necessarily mine). These shortened-post tuners have string post holes that are closer to the peghead face than normal tuners. Both shortened-post tuners mentioned below also are locking tuners, which add tuning stability to any guitar.

STRING TREES

On a Fender peghead, the natural string angle (without a string tree) from the treble E-string tuner to the nut is about 2-1/2 degrees, depending on how many downward string winds are used. That's barely enough rise to keep the treble E- and B- strings in their slots, let alone allow you to play them with any gusto. The G- and D-strings have sufficient angles, especially if you wind some extra string down the post. String trees are unnecessary for those strings and can create too much of an angle—many players remove the second tree. The A- and low E-strings naturally have good string angles. If you use too many string winds, the angle will become too great. To avoid that, some players wind the low E-string upward to decrease the string angle.

A good string angle for non-angled pegheads is between 6 degrees and 12 degrees. Less is better, as long as the strings have enough downward pressure to remain in the nut slots and produce good tone. This is why many makers like Jackson, Ibanez, and others use a slightly back-angled peghead on an otherwise slab-style neck. This FRET-King Elan 60 (above), built by Trev Wilkinson, has an 8 degree peghead angle—optimum, in Wilkinson's opinion, for good downward pressure, with good pitch return. The peghead requires no string tree, and with a lubricated nut, the floating tremolo returns to pitch.

Fender's first two string trees were the round, steel type used in the early 1950s and the stamped

metal "butterfly" that came along in 1956. Both trees have convex string slots on their undersides, and were screwed flat to the peghead face. To increase the downward pressure behind the nut, Fender moved the tree closer to the nut. In the new location, the string tree was in line with the A-string tuner rather than the G-string tuner. It has remained in that approximate position ever since.

In 1959, Fender added a 1/8" high to 5/32" high hollow-tube spacer to reduce friction at the string tree and decrease downward pressure at the nut (so strings would return to pitch better). In 1971, the company added a second string tree for the G- and D-strings. Fender may have added the second tree because it had switched from Kluson tuners to its own F-stamped tuners with higher string posts (the Safeti-post string slot was more than 1/16" higher than the slots on the vintage posts, decreasing the angle to the nut).

In 1983, Fender fitted many Stratocaster models with Ezy-Glider string trees. The one-piece Ezy-Glider's new L-shape eliminated the need for a spacer, and its smooth, round string grooves produced little friction. It was the predecessor of today's Graph Tech and roller string trees, which also are one piece and stand  off the peghead without a separate spacer. In the photo, from left to right are: (Front row) Fender's vintage round and butterfly trees; (Back row) Fender Ezy-Glider, Graph Tech, and the roller string tree. On today's Fender Vintage reproductions, both vintage string tree styles still are in use, and you'll find the butterfly on a number of nonvintage models. Not all string trees have nice smooth rounds on the bottoms.

Of the vintage Fender-style string trees, I think the butterfly tree works best, mounted with a 1/8" to 5/32" spacer that provides enough, but not too much, of the necessary downward pressure, while also allowing the string to move through the spacer with less friction. However, roller string trees and Graph Tech trees work better than the vintage trees, but don't have the vintage look.

String trees need special attention when used on tremolo-equipped guitars that don't have locking nuts or on nontremolo guitars—whenever you want strings to return to pitch after bending them or using the tremolo. No matter how well made or well lubed your guitar nut is, if friction at the string tree(s) causes the strings to hang up, they may not return in tune. If you can remove a string tree and still be satisfied that the treble E-string has a solid sound and stays in its nut slot, by all means do so. Or, if you have a Strat already equipped with short-shaft Sperzel tuners and no string tree, and are happy with it, fine. However, I think that all Strat-style guitars (necks with no peghead angle) need a string tree for at least the E-string. Since most string trees are made for two strings, you might as well put the B-string in there, too. It needs the added downward-pressure almost as much as the E-string.

Another consideration is the thickness of the peghead—it can limit how many string winds you can fit in before the string hits the grommet on the face of the peghead. Fender pegheads range from anywhere between 1/2" thick to almost 5/8" thick, depending on the year—one more thing to add to the mix.

TUNING KEYS

Unless you buy really cheap tuners, it's hard to find bad ones these days. Stamped-housing (non-die-cast) tuners, such as the Kluson Deluxe reproductions manufactured today, are better than the origi-nals were, thanks to nylon bushings and improved gearing. The assortment of non-die-cast tuners in the photo, clockwise, are: Kluson's diamond-shaped lined-back version (no longer available); Fender's Kluson six-in-line tuner; the same Kluson in a three-on-a-side version with a plastic "keystone" knob; Fender F-stamped trapezoid-shaped tuner; and a Grover Imperial.

The first die-cast tuner was the Grover Rotomatic, and because it tuned better than the Kluson, thousands of Gibson players replaced their Klusons with Rotomatics in the 1960s. Die-cast tuners wouldn't fit on Fender pegheads until the six-in-line "mini" versions came along years later. If the improved Kluson-style tuners of today had existed back then, players probably wouldn't have had

Grovers (and later Schallers) installed on their guitars so readily, and more vintage guitars would remain original. In the photo are some typical die-cast tuners, from bottom left to right, clockwise, they are: Grover Roto-Matic; Grover Rotomatic show-ing hex nut and washer; Schaller M6; and an Ibanez tuner.

TUNING KEY WEIGHT AFFECTS THE SOUND

I improved the tone of a Gibson Les Paul by retro-fitting it with new Kluson-style tuners. Previously, someone had replaced the guitar's original, diamond-shaped Klusons with Grover Rotomatics. This guitar is on its third set of tuners! According to the owner, the Les Paul regained a lighter, brighter, more authentic tone after the heavier Grovers were removed and the lighter Klusons were installed. The original tuner holes didn't match the new Kluson replacements, but plugging the holes with wood and drilling new ones didn't leave a trace. Luckily, the Grovers didn't leave a bad footprint in the lacquer, either. That's not always the case.

DIE-CAST TUNERS

Grover Rotomatic, Schaller M-6, and other similar tuners are die-cast with all the internal workings permanently lubricated and sealed. The key (also called a knob or button) on each die-cast tuner fastens on-to the key shaft with a machine screw and washers that space the key from the tuning key shaft. The keys are removable, so I was able to clean and

39

lubricate the two washers—a nylon washer and a "wave" washer, which provides spring tension so that by tightening or loosening the machine screw you can control the key's stiffness. The Sperzel tuners shown here were filthy—I removed them and degreased the bodies with a cotton swab dipped in the cleaning solution mentioned earlier (page 35). I soaked the hex nuts and their washers in the same solution, then cleaned the nylon spacers and wave washers separately. Reassembled, the tuners worked like new.

Routine tuner maintenance simply involves tightening or loosening the machine screw that fastens the key to the shaft. It's also a good idea to tighten a die-cast tuner's hex nut on the face of the peghead occasionally, such as during a string change. Any loose parts connected to the string will rob tone and contribute to a guitar

being out of tune. Non-die-cast tuners, such as the Kluson style, have permanently fixed keys that you cannot remove, tighten, or loosen.

Tip: *Fender six-in-line tuners are quite close together—turn all the keys in a vertical position when installing strings to make room for the stringwinder. After all the strings are on, tune to pitch.*

LOCKING TUNERS
WITH LOW TUNING POST HOLES

Locking tuners have been a Godsend for helping guitars stay in tune. The two most popular styles are those made by Gotoh and Sperzel, left and right, respectively, in the photo. These tuners have low post holes (close to the peghead face) to increase the string angle to the nut, generally without the need for string trees. In use, the string is pulled taut through the post hole and clamped—re-

sulting in almost no string winds around the post before you reach pitch. The Gotoh tuners lock by drawing the interior-threaded tuner post cap down onto a pin. Once the string is locked, the tuner winds the string. Sperzels lock via a bottom-mounted knurled thumbwheel and pin. Both Gotoh and Sperzel are excellent locking tuners, and each has its advantages and disadvantages, depending upon your needs:

■ Gotohs are lighter and less expensive. They make a great replacement for vintage Klusons, since they retain the vintage weight and sound at the peghead. Also, their string post holes, at 1/8" from the peghead face, are even lower than the shortest string post holes on the Sperzel locking tuners with shortened post-hole heights (resulting in slightly more angle at the back of the nut).

■ Sperzel tuners are die cast and permanently sealed and lubricated. Like all good die-cast tuners, and because they are a higher quality, they may last longer than the less-expensive Kluson-style reproductions. Sperzels are heavy, adding more mass and weight to the peghead, which some say creates more sustain, or a "darker" sound.

Sperzel tuners have three post heights. The total length of the posts measure 3/4", 13/16", and 27/32" from short to long. When the tuners are installed, the distance of the post holes above the peghead face (and therefore the string angle to the nut) depends upon the thickness of the peghead and which tuners are installed. Fender, for example, uses three short (on the E-, B-, and G-strings) and three medium (on the D-, A- and E-strings) post heights. Usually, on Fender guitars, the distance of the post holes from the face will be 1/4" and 5/16" respectively.

Sperzel's standard six-in-line tuner set includes two each of all three sizes, and the company's three-on-a-side set (for angled pegheads) uses all medium-height posts. Sperzel manufactures custom post-heights for some makers. For example, Roger Sadowsky uses Sperzel tuners with custom post hole heights that measure 5/32" on the E-, B-, G-, and D-strings, and 15/64" for the low E-and A-strings—slightly higher than the Gotoh, but lower than standard Sperzels. However, Sadowsky still uses a roller string tree for the E- and B-strings. I agree with him that it is necessary.

My all-time favorite tuner was the first version of Ned Steinberger's ingenious tuner, pictured here with an original Gibson RB-250 banjo tuner. The RB-250 tuners came on the Firebird and are notorious for slipping. The Steinbergers mounted at the rear of the peghead, like banjo tuners, had locking posts, and used a machine screw instead of gears to draw the string down into a hole. They tune up or down equally well. A later, silver version is still in use on some Gibson models, but it doesn't work as well as the earlier version. Speaking of banjo tuners, the Firebird uses rear-mount banjo tuners—I replaced three of them on my Fire-

bird with Keith banjo D-tuners that drop the low E-, A-, and treble E-strings a whole step into G-tuning instantly, and the other three with old Steinbergers.

The gear ratios of all of today's tuners range from 12:1, 14:1, 15:1, and 16:1. Study parts catalogs to find out what a given tuner's gear ratio is. Also, in the interest of science, I weighed a number of tuners, and the difference in weight between Klusons and the die-cast models is significant.

Without hex nuts, mounting screws, or bushings, here are the weights, in ounces, for six (a set) of the most popular tuners:

WEIGHTS OF POPULAR TUNER SETS	
GROVER ROTOMATIC	8.8 OZ.
SCHALLER M-6	7.7 OZ.
GIBSON/SCHALLER M6	8.6 OZ.
KLUSON DELUXE 3-ON-A-SIDE, (PLASTIC KEYSTONE KNOB)	4.8 OZ.
NEW KLUSON 6-IN-LINE	5.9 OZ.
GOTOH KLUSON LOCKING TUNER	4.95 OZ.
OLD KLUSON 6-IN-LINE	5.0 OZ.
SPERZEL	5.4 OZ.
GROVER IMPERIAL:	10.3 OZ.

Bridge and tailpiece maintenance

There's no better way to learn how guitar hardware works than to take it apart and clean it. Bridge parts must work smoothly. It isn't possible to address every conceivable bridge maintenance and adjustment situation, but those I do address should teach you not to be afraid of working on your guitar, and, I hope, will inspire some creativity on your part (see "Squeezin' the strings," and "Crooked bridge ahead," below).

I selected the guitars and bridge styles that seemed most common (mostly old standbys that set the standards still being followed today), but threw in a few newcomers too—hardware that may be new to many readers. If you're able to clean and adjust the hardware shown below, you deserve a "guitar mechanic" degree, and those bridges or tailpieces not described will fall easily under your spell.

Good coupling = good tone

When it comes to electric guitar bridge and tailpiece hardware, the name of the game is "coupling." I learned the term from Trev Wilkinson, a veteran bridge and tremolo designer, and maker of FRET-King Guitars, in Birmingham, England. Bridge and tailpiece hardware should be solid and well coupled, or fastened, to the body—transferring the string's energy to the guitar so that it can produce the sound and tone we crave. Whenever hardware gets too complicated, or is not well coupled, loss of tone results.

Coupling occurs not only where the bridge or tailpiece hardware meets the body, but also within the hardware itself—wherever parts meet or connect. Below is a fine example of a simple, well-cou-

pled bridge made by John Smith of Gordon-Smith guitars in Manchester, England. The one shown here is the tremolo version, but he makes a non-trem version too, with a standard two-stud mount. It's cast from stainless steel, which keeps a good finish without being plated. The solid barrel bridge saddles use only one good-sized height-adjustment screw. The saddles can't tip because their ends are held tightly by the bridge casting—allowing only enough movement for setting the intonation.

Graph Tech String Saver replacement saddles

Before dismantling, cleaning, and replacing parts, consider the advantages of using Graph Tech's low-friction, lubricated polymer saddles. You can use them to replace a number of saddles, including Strat-style bridges, six-saddle Tele bridges, and Gibson's ABR-1 Tune-O-Matic and Nashville bridges.

Graph Tech saddles are especially popular with players who break strings often. You will not break strings as often on Graph Tech because it is not hard like steel. Graph Tech saddles produce a different sound than steel, which some players prefer (and some don't).

As for whether or not Graph Tech's lubricated qualities help strings return to pitch better when bent or tremoloed, I think that to some extent its softness counters its lubricating qualities—especially on wound strings. If the string winding makes an imprint in the saddle (or nut slot), the string will catch on the imprint (not slide over it). Graph Tech will help your strings return to pitch if your repair tech (or you) perfectly shapes, polishes, and burnishes the string slots. I have a Graph Tech nut and saddles on my Gibson Firebird. It's not too expensive or difficult to install a set on your guitar and see if they're for you. In addition, you are far less likely to break strings on these saddles than with many conventional steel saddles.

Cleaning rusted bridge parts

Here are two Fender Telecasters (a '59 "top-loader,"

and a '67 model), and a 1977 Gibson Les Paul Standard from Fretware Guitars in Franklin, Ohio. Their owner, Dave Hussong, wanted me to thoroughly look them over before he put them up for sale. All of the bridges needed work....

Tele bridge saddles

The original, vintage Tele bridge has had a number of different bridge saddles over the last 50 years. Four versions of saddles were used on traditional three-saddle Telecaster bridges,

and probably as many on the six-saddle variety. I prefer the early '50s smooth brass version (shown here on a '52 Tele) or the mid-'50s smooth steel saddles (shown below on a '56 Tele), because there are no string grooves cut in them—the strings wear their own grooves over time, or you easily can file slots where you want them.

Another three-saddle bridge is the all-thread rod version (used from '58 to '68), which came in two styles. The earliest ones, from the late '50s, had a finer thread than those used throughout most of the 1960s. With either of these all-thread versions, good string-to-string placement is more difficult to achieve than with smooth saddles (and the sharper threads are very tough on strings). If I owned a '59 Tele with these saddles, I

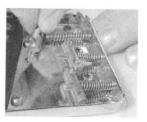

would replace them with smooth ones and save the originals.

Another style is smooth steel saddles with string grooves machined into them, used from 1968 until 1983. The grooves are well spaced, but if the outside spacing is too wide for the neck you can't do much about it and your strings may fall off the edge.

Many players complain about poor intonation with the standard three-saddle Tele bridge because strings are intonated in sets of two rather than individually—hence a number of six-saddle individually adjustable Tele bridges came along in the mid-'70s. For those who want the true Tele sound, however, the three-saddle bridge produces it best, in either brass or steel, because two strings holding something down gives you twice the coupling of one string.

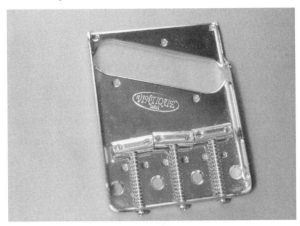

A saddle option available for three-saddle bridge lovers is the retrofit Danny Gatton Tele Saddle, drilled to sit at an angle for superior intonation. These were developed by Danny Gatton and Jay Monterose. (Monterose's company, Vintique, manufactures a number of high-end, custom Tele replacement parts.)

Vintique bridges, by the way, are ground dead-flat on the underside before plating for better coupling to the body. Except for on a vintage piece, I would flatten the bottom of any Tele bridge (after removing the pickup, of course) on a flat surface with 80-grit wet-or-dry sandpaper glued to it (or on a belt-sander) to remove the burrs, dips, and warping caused by the stamped-metal manufacturing process. The coupling to the top improves, and you'll hear the difference!

GIVING UP THOSE ROUGH AND RUSTY WAYS

Starting in late 1958, Fender used a top-loading Tele bridge for about a year. These guitars did not string through the body, nor did they have rear-drilled holes and string fer-

rules in the body (they string through six holes at the rear of the bridge plate). This '59 Telecaster's bridge saddles were rusty and appeared to be in rough shape, and the screw slot was broken off of the B-string saddle-height screw and would need to be replaced. The parts cleaned up nicely, though.

The guitar played in tune, so I jotted down each saddle's location by measuring from the front of the saddles to the rear of the bridge. Several places in this book I use the following "solution" to clean dirty metal—3 parts lighter fluid with 1 part light household oil. Here I used it to saturate

all the exposed metal surfaces of the threaded parts to help loosen them before going at them with a screwdriver. I used a long-shaft, Phillips-head screwdriver to approach the saddle's length-adjusting screw heads dead on, rather than at an angle (in which case the screwdriver doesn't get a full grip on the screw—photo next page).

I stored each saddle's parts separately to keep things in order, and filled a clean catfood can with the lighter fluid mixture for the first de-rusting. The rust began coming off immediately. After the first

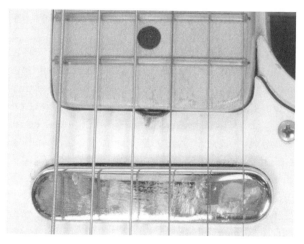

soaking, I wiped off the parts, borrowed a set screw from a mid-60s smooth-grooved saddle (it's the same size machine screw: 6-32 thread) and dropped the parts into a second jar filled with some fresh solution. Next I reamed out the threaded holes with a pipe cleaner soaked in the solvent, wiped them off again, and dropped all the parts—one set at a time—into fresh acetone as a final degreaser. The clean parts worked like new.

I used the same solution to clean the rust and crud from the bridge base under the saddles. One length-adjusting screw was bent, so I drilled a hole in the workbench top, shoved the screw into the hole up to the edge of the bend, and carefully straightened it with a pair of locking pliers. After running all the parts through the same cleaning process, I put them back where they belonged and used a radius gauge to set the approximate arc. I'll fine-tune the action later.

SQUEEZIN' THE STRINGS

The strings on this '67 Tele were falling off the treble side of the fretboard for two reasons:

1 I needed to loosen the neck and "shift" it back in line with the strings (Step 6, Bolt-on neck quirks);

2 The neck is too skinny! I knew the strings (especially the treble E-string) would barely be over the fretboard after I shifted the neck.

Guitars of this era typically have a narrower fretboard width than earlier models. Measured at the 12th fret, this '67 Tele was more than 1/32" narrower

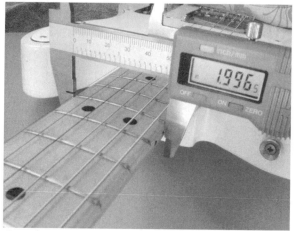

than the '59 Tele (the '67 measured 1.996", the '59 was 2.031"). Combine that with the extreme roundover on the fretboard edge of late '60s and '70s Fender necks (as compared to the less-extreme rounding of earlier models), and the strings get mighty close to the fretboard edge. The first photo is the '67

1967

Tele, the second is the '59. Look how much sharper the edge of the '59 is, and how much more fret width it has! You'll find the problems this Tele neck has on a number of modern guitars, especially bolt-on neck models and the inexpensive imported models that most players start out with.

1959

As a quick test, I pulled the treble E-string back (A) over the frets. I could tell I'd need to squeeze it over at the bridge saddles (toward the center), which would

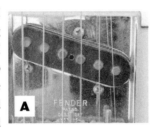

A

entail respacing all the strings on the saddles. I also noticed that when pulled inward, the high E-string no longer ran over the bridge pickup's polepiece. This was because the bridge was mounted slightly crooked, not in line with the neck and pickguard (I take care of that later).

B

I squeezed the threaded saddles (B) a little closer together by carefully studying and marking the portion I would need to remove from the mating ends of the B-, G-, A-, and D- saddles in order for them to move closer together. Then I carefully filed some metal off the ends (C) of the saddles. Once the saddles were a little closer together, I squeezed the string spacing even closer by carefully filing notches for the strings that needed it right on the thread (D). The combination of squeezing the saddles together and notching right on the thread

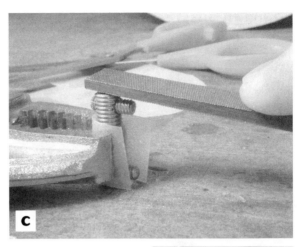

C

D

brought the strings closer together, enough to make my effort worthwhile (and the treble E-string less likely to fall off the edge).

I CAN'T GET NO SATISFACTION

Still not satisfied with the string spacing (though it was improved), I removed the vintage threaded saddles, saved them for posterity, and installed a set of Vintique's Danny Gatton smooth-bodied brass saddles that are angle-drilled for good intonation. Then, because the saddles were smooth, I could notch the strings even more exactly where I wanted them. The B-string slot was right on the edge of the height-adjusting hole, but it worked. However, now the real mismatch between the narrow neck and the string spacing at the bridge was apparent because the treble strings ran at quite an angle to the string

grooves I had made. Even though my string notching had improved the spacing, the E- and B-saddles' length-adjusting screws were in a straight line opposed to the angled strings. This caused the strings to pull the brass saddle away from the others. The B- and E-strings were too far from the G-string, and again too close to the fingerboard edge.

THINKING OUTSIDE THE BOX

Next I did something that I had never done before that I was very pleased with. If you have a Tele that suffers like this one, take it to a good repair shop and see if they'd be willing to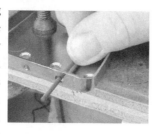

do what I did (or do it yourself—it wasn't hard). I took the parts off of a Stewart-MacDonald #99 Tele-style bridge and filed the sides of the holes for the E- and B-saddles' length-adjusting screws, creating an oblong shape that ran toward the G-saddle. I

hoped this would relieve the tension caused by the pull of the strings, and it did. Next, I drilled six string-mounting holes in the #99 bridge, making it a "top-loader," and in-

stalled the pickup and the Gatton saddles into this new bridge. I drilled the six string holes closer together than usual, and now all six strings ran straight to their saddle spots, and lined up perfectly with the neck. As a top-loader, the guitar sounded different, but good. It had a brighter, more "jangly" sound.

CROOKED BRIDGE AHEAD

I'd satisfied myself with that fix, but knowing that Dave Hussong couldn't sell a vintage guitar altered that way (even though it played better), I reinstalled the original bridge with threaded saddles. Since I had shifted the neck, the strings lined up well with the fingerboard edge, but of course, with the wide string spacing of the original saddles, the treble E-

string was too close to the fretboard edge again. I decided to straighten the bridge—for real—because that would be a major improvement. Many of you could do this job easily, but you may want to ask a pro to do it.

With only the two outside E-strings installed, and not tuned very high, I removed three of the bridge mounting screws—leaving only the one on

the bass side. The strings pulled the bridge into alignment (parallel with the pickguard), and the treble E-string was centered over the polepiece. I couldn't use the other three screw holes any longer, however, because the holes were misaligned. With the bridge removed, I drilled out the three holes, glued in some 1/8" wood dowels, and drilled new holes that lined up with the new bridge location. I used two bits—a 7/64" bit for the screw thread, and a 9/64" for the screw's smooth shoulder. Now the strings lined up

on both the neck and the pickup, and the strings were a little less likely to fall off the fretboard edge. Dave Hussong was happy.

That's enough on dismantling, cleaning, and maintaining Tele bridge parts for sure (and you clean any rusted bridge parts in a similar fashion).

Let's move on to Gibson hardware.

Gibson's Stop-Bar tailpiece and Tune-O-Matic bridge

People often ask me, "Should the stop-bar tailpiece be screwed tightly to the body?" It's commonly thought that fastening the stop-bar tightly to the body produces more sustain, which may or may not be true. Certainly it changes the sound, so decide for yourself if you like it or not. Depending upon the year your Gibson was made (see "neck-to-body angle," below), tightening the stop-bar tailpiece down to the body produces certain results:

1 It puts so much tension on a Tune-O-Matic bridge that it sinks in the center (see "collapsed bridge," below) and bends the support studs.

2 It causes the strings to touch the back edge of the bridge, which kills any free-string sound and natural harmonics and overtones occurring between the saddle contact points and the tailpieces—harmonics which, to me, are an important part of the sound of these guitars.

3 It can cause the two threaded height-adjusting posts of an ABR-1 Tune-O-Matic bridge to bend forward, toward the neck.

4 The string tension stiffens. With the tailpiece high, strings are easier to bend. Screw the bridge to the body, the strings stiffen, and bending becomes more difficult. Try this experiment that Trev Wilkinson showed me:

Screw the tailpiece to the body and bend the B-string, noting how far you have to push it to achieve a semitone. Then raise the tailpiece and repeat the bend. It will be easier to achieve the same semitone. Notice however, that you have to bend the slinkier string farther to achieve the same semitone (the stiffer string produces the semitone with less travel, but it's stiffer).

5 When a string is tight it's easier for the high (treble) frequencies to get through than it is for the bass frequencies. Could this be the the "sustain" that people are hearing?

THE NECK-TO-BODY ANGLE'S RELATION TO THE BRIDGE AND TAILPIECE

On Les Pauls made from 1954 until the late '60s and on other solid-body and semi-hollow ES-style models that followed the Les Paul, the neck-to-body angle was a very precise 4 degrees. I don't know exactly when it happened, but by the time Gibson relocated to Nashville, the neck angle had increased to 5 degrees and, at times, even 6 degrees. Gibson's Kalamazoo builders were highly skilled and had a long history of guitar building behind them. It's reasonable to expect that it would take time for Gibson to set up a new factory in Nashville, train new builders, and bring them to the level of guitarmaking that had existed in Kalamazoo.

When fitting a neck to a body, a builder must be able to hold close tolerances and set a neck at exactly a certain angle, which is a difficult task. Four degrees—plus or minus very little—had proven to be the optimum neck pitch for the ABR-1 Tune-O-Matic bridge. At 4 degrees, the bridge sits low and close to the body, with sometimes as little as a 1/16" inch clearance below the treble height thumbwheel

in a normal setup. With these low-profile (by design) bridges, you can tightly screw the stop-bar to the body. This ensures that the string angle over the bridge body is not so great that it will warp or collapse the bridge body, and that the strings will not hit the back edge of the bridge body. You don't have to tightly screw the stop-bar to the body on these models, but you can if you want to. (I prefer to keep the tailpiece up off the body at least 1/8".)

It may seem absurd that 1 degree can make a big difference, but as soon as the neck angle changed to 5 degrees, it made a huge difference at the bridge end. The bridge may be as much as 1/4" higher than bridges used with a 4-degree neck pitch, depending on whether or not the builder at the factory set up his jigs and fixtures to the high side of 5-degrees or to the low side.

So if the top of your Gibson's highest bridge saddle (where the strings rest) is higher than 11/16" to 3/4", the neck is probably set at a 5-degree angle, and your bridge may, over a period of time, collapse if you screw the stop-bar down. You may also end up with strings contacting the rear edge of the bridge. If the bridge saddle top measures less than 11/16" (a 5/8" range is common, as in the photo on previous page), the neck is most likely set at a 5-degree angle, and you can screw the stop-bar tailpiece down if you like (probably without undesireable results). Try several different setups and give them each a few weeks of tone trial.

REMOVING A RUSTED STOP-BAR TAILPIECE

This black Les Paul provided perfect examples for much of this book, from its hard-to-adjust neck (Step 2) to its rusted stop-bar tailpiece and collapsed Tune-O-Matic bridge.

The mounting studs of the stop-bar rusted firmly in place—no doubt from hard-earned sweat. I unscrewed it with a large 1/2" blade screwdriver that fit the slot as closely as possible, to avoid slipping onto the body. It doesn't hurt to dribble a little cleaning solution down into the anchors beforehand.

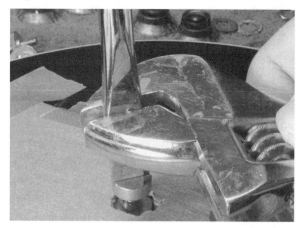

To protect the top, I masked off around the studs with thick cardboard in case I slipped, and used a good-sized wrench to turn the screwdriver blade. Slowly, each stud gave up its grip. I dry-brushed their rusty threads then bathed them in the solution. I cleaned the bridge height-adjusting posts,

too. I also derusted the threaded anchors in the body with a solution-dipped cotton swab.

STRAIGHTENING A COLLAPSED TUNE-O-MATIC BRIDGE

I measured the Les Paul's fretboard radius at a perfect 10", yet the bridge wasn't even close to the normal Gibson 12" T.O.M. radius. Having collapsed, it was concave. With the bridge saddles removed you can really see the warp if you place a ruler along the front edge of the bridge body.

To remedy this, block the bridge on each end and slowly clamp the bridge straight—or even slightly beyond straight (overarching it, actually). If you go too far or too fast, however, the thin metal of the bridge saddle screw holes may split, as in the photo opposite  page. Squeeze the bridge gently, by degree, checking occasionally, until it's back where it should be. Now the strings resting in the saddle slots have a

good radius, although it is the factory 12" radius and doesn't match the 10" fretboard radius perfectly enough—we'll take care of that soon.

Note: *The same forces that cause a bridge to collapse also can cause it to lean forward, bending the threaded support studs. Even though the guitar shown here (a Gibson Trini Lopez) has a 4-degree*

neck set, the studs were tilting forward. Using the technique shown here, you could simply straighten the bent studs while they remain in the body; I don't, however, because the pressure on the stud can chip the vintage finish around it. Instead, I use two pairs of pliers or locking-pliers and tighten two thumbwheels firmly together onto one post. Then I can remove the stud by turning both of the thumbwheels together (counterclockwise)—and sometimes with my fingers, sometimes with one

set of pliers holding both wheels (slowly and carefully). Then I either replace the bent stud or drill a hole that fits the stud into a piece of scrap wood, shove the stud into the drilled hole—up to the bend—and straighten it with any small tube as a lever. You can prevent bridge studs from collapsing (and firm up each stud's coupling to the top) by adding an extra thumbwheel at the bottom of the post and turning

it counterclockwise against the top (if you don't think it looks bad).

DISMANTLING AND CLEANING THE ABR-1 BRIDGE

With the strings and tailpiece set aside, I removed the bridge and removed the adjustment screw retainer clip by gently pry-ing the thin wire out of its hole and up over the screw head. Once you clear that screw the clip comes right off. I removed the saddles and screws and kept them in order. Then I removed the screws from the saddles and gave them a bath in the solution. A solvent-soaked pipe cleaner and a cotton swab were good tools for clearing the threaded holes in the saddles and for cleaning the saddle body. After reassembly, perform the steps in reverse order to reinstall the retainer clip. I push the wire in the bass side hole, lift it over the screw heads, stretch it around that last screw head, and push the clip into its hole with my thumbnail.

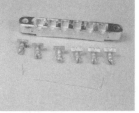

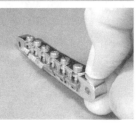

CHANGING THE BRIDGE SADDLE RADIUS ON A TUNE-O-MATIC

In order for the saddles to reach a 10" radius, I had some filing to do—mostly on the outer strings, graduating toward the center, and hopefully leaving the D-and G-strings pretty much alone.

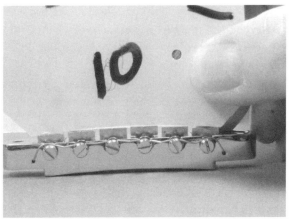

I used two drywall screws to fasten the bridge to a scrap of wood clamped to my benchtop, and screwed all the saddles to the back edge so I could reach them with 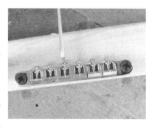 the file. You can take each saddle out to shape it, and sometimes I do—it's nice to have them held tight in the bridge base though.

Note: *Since the string slots were spaced evenly in the saddles, I turned the low E- and A-saddles around so their slanted backside faced forward. I used a small "triangle" file from the hardware store to quickly deepen the slots, then created a rounded shape with my homemade nut files wrapped with various sandpaper grits to finish the job. I did use a real nut file (.038") at one point.*

On the ABR-1 Tune-O-Matic bridge, Gibson always faced the low E- and A-saddles (and sometimes the D-saddle) backward so the sharp edge would be closer to the back wall for intonation. This was necessary for the heavy strings being used at the time, although I've always wondered why Gibson didn't move the bridge back a little so that the saddles could all face forward, with the strings leading up the ramped edge to their take-off points. With the lighter strings being used today, you can usually face the saddles with their flat faces forward, (except on the rare occasion that a string won't intonate properly). Also, if the saddle slots are not well centered, turning them around will change the string-to-string spacing—in that case you should replace the saddles.

I deepened the smaller string slots with a razor saw, and smoothed them with a series of wet-or-dry sandpapers (ranging from 400 to 1000 grit) folded into sharp edges that fit in the slots. Now the outer two E-string slots, and to some degree

the A- and B-string slots, were too deep, so I used a smooth-cut lawnmower blade sharpening file to lower the tops of the saddles. I followed with a smaller spark-plug file 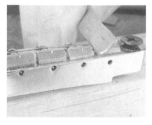 to reshape the saddles until they looked right, removing any sharp edges and corners. Last of all I removed any file marks and gave the saddles a good polish with 500-grit wet-or-dry sandpaper.

The final, lowered saddles looked pretty much as if they hadn't been touched, a little on the rough side compared to the bridge saddle shaping below, but quite Gibson-ish, and the radius was 10".

SUPER-SMOOTH SADDLES

Here's a glimpse of how I prefer to shape Tune-O-Matic bridge saddles— these were on a customer's Les Paul. The string notches hold the  string, yet expose it for a clean sound. All sharp edges are gone, and with them any file or sanding marks. The saddles, sanded to 1200-grit sandpaper, feel completely smooth. If you rest your hand on a bridge like this it is extremely comfortable. The plating is lost during the process, however, but you don't notice it. A little cleaning from time to time with the "solution," followed by a little furniture paste wax on a cotton swab, keeps the saddles from tarnishing.

Note: *Saddles shaped this way work especially well with a vibrato.*

INSTALLING NEW GIBSON TUNE-O-MATIC SADDLES AND NOTCHING THEM FACTORY-STYLE

After all that work, I decided that the original bridge string spacing placed the treble E-string too close to the fingerboard edge (it was much closer to the fingerboard edge than the bass E-string). Also, the treble E-string was not quite over the neck pickup's polepiece. This was really only a minor problem, but since I wanted to show you how to install new bridge saddles anyway, I started over.

WHEN THINGS DON'T FIT, USE A BIGGER HAMMER!

I dismantled the bridge again and installed all new Gibson saddles without notches—that way I could place the strings exactly where I wanted them. Usually this is a simple retro-fit job, but I ran into a small problem. Inspect an ABR-1 bridge, and you will notice subtle recessed ledges, or steps, machined into the bridge top for the two E-strings and the A- and B-strings to rest in. These steps create the 12" bridge saddle radius, since the saddles are all the same height. The new saddles were slightly wider than the vintage ones. The old saddles measured .350", the new ones measured .355" (A). Just .005"

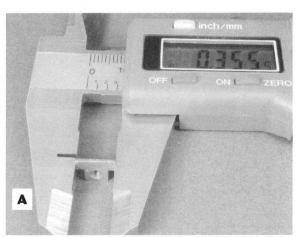

kept them from dropping into their slots (B). After a tiny bit of filing on each end of the offending saddles, they dropped in perfectly.

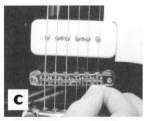

With brand new saddles I was able to place the strings exactly where I wanted them (C) at the bridge before cutting the slots. Once the spacing met my approval, I used the method of notching the saddles that I saw at the Gibson factory. It may seem crude, but in a factory setting it makes good sense. Not so much because it's fast (which it is), but because it's accurate—hit each string with a plastic-faced hammer (D)! This creates a notch (E) because the saddles are relatively soft metal, and the slot location is more accurate than you produce by hand-filing. However, this method does ruin the strings. At the factory they may or may not further hand-file the slots, depending on the model, how well the slots formed, and how the guitar plays.

When I replaced the retainer clip it was a little slack from so much on-and-off handling. Lacking a fresh one, I did something that is sometimes necessary even on new retainers. Using a small, flat-bladed screwdriver, press down in between each string and make a kink in the spring. Start slowly, making slight kinks all the way across and gradually increase the pressure—working across several times—until you create five kinks and the retainer holds the saddle screws tight.

With all that work done, I had a bridge with new saddles and a 12" radius again! So I repeated what I just showed you on the new saddles—lowered them to a 10" radius and reshaped them. The strings did line up perfectly with the fretboard and the P-90 pickups!

SETTING THE STOP-BAR TAILPIECE HEIGHT

The last setup task for this Les Paul was to adjust the stop-bar tailpiece so that it wouldn't collapse the bridge again. This guitar is Nashville-made, but it was between a 4-degree and 5-degree neck pitch.

Photo (A) shows the stop-bar screwed almost tight. The strings are still clearing the bridge body, but we know this bridge collapsed. This is still too much string angle and will probably collapse the bridge again soon. Photo (B) shows a more acceptable height for the stop bar on this guitar.

TOP-WRAPPING A STOP-BAR TAILPIECE

On the 1954 Gold Top Les Paul, the stop bar tailpiece doubled as the bridge. Owners of '54 Les Pauls swear by that model's tone and would not want a Tune-O-Matic bridge near their guitars. The front-loaded strings wrapped over the top of the bar. Set-

screws on the bass and treble sides of the stop-bar screwed against the studs to adjust the string length for limited intonation.

Though it may look a little weird, using the top-wrap on a guitar with a T.O.M. bridge and stop-

bar tailpiece can give you the best of both worlds: a well-coupled tailpiece with strings well clear of the bridge body. The bridge saddles of this Gibson-Epiphone Les Paul have a steep back-angle, and well-spaced, nicely-shaped string grooves cast into them. The D-, A-, and E-saddles were facing backward, so I turned them around. Turned around, they needed almost no final shaping to play cleanly. I was impressed by such saddle detail in a low-priced guitar!

Note: *If your string-winds are right on the edge of the wrap-over (these aren't), the string wrap may kink, unravel, and/or break on the edge. An extra string ball end or two slid over the strings before you install them keeps the ball end wraps in the stop bar. Also, pre-shape the bend into the string before stringing up.*

Eliminate the need for extra ball ends by filing relieved grooves for the strings. After filing the grooves, I smoothed them with a .070" wound electric bass string lubed with coarse valve-grinding compound. Now the bar was similar in shape to Gibson's intonated wrap-around bridge/tailpiece used on models like the Les Paul Junior, Les Paul Special, Melody Maker, and some Firebirds and SGs. These were cast with a string-wrap groove, and like other stop-bar tailpiece/bridge combinations, have Allen screws on each support post for adjusting string length. This version has cast-in intonation points.

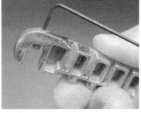

TIDYING UP LOOSE ENDS

Gibson's ABR-1 bridge is a Tune-O-Matic adjustable-saddle model introduced in the mid-1950s, and is still in use today. Variations of it abound. Gibson's simple bridge-tailpiece combination (mentioned above) has plenty of replacements waiting to take its place also—adjustable replacements able to bring those guitars' intonation problems to their knees with hardware that not only has adjustable bridge saddles but extra-long adjustment screws at each end where the bridge anchors on the two bridge studs, making these bridges double-adjustable. The "Badass" bridge of the '70s led the way in this market, and along with Schaller variations, is still in use today. However, in my opinion, these bridges have more artillery than needed to do the job, and they don't couple well.

A relatively new idea is a stop-bar bridge with adjustable sections for setting intonation. They keep the stop-bar look, tone, and solid-coupling, which is nice, and intonate adequately. To my knowledge, this type of bridge was first designed by John Mann

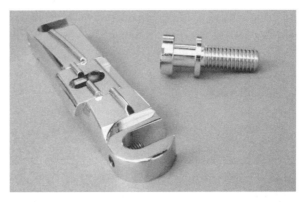

(Mann Made USA), who has taken the concept to even greater heights. The guitar shown here, a Michael Stevens "LJ" model built for Matt Henderson, has a six-saddle-adjustable Mann Made stop-bar built to Stevens' specs. The flanges on the studs, besides being a good machine fit, have wide flanges that keep the bridge from tilting. PRS and others have used stop-bar bridges built by, or fashioned after, John Mann's designs.

Why didn't I think of that?

The locking Tune-O-Matic-style bridge and stop-bar tailpiece from Tone-Pros are real innovations. They're mounted here on a Baker B1H (hollow), built by Gene Baker. Both pieces have set screws that lock them in place. TonePros advertises that "the bridge and tailpiece don't fall off when you change strings," which I agree is a real plus, but more important to me is the improved coupling. The set screw on the stop-bar gives you some extra coupling, which may help to increase sustain, especially if you don't want to fasten the stop bar tightly to the body. The set screw on the bridge, (see photo below) however, is really significant, because it removes the play inherent in all bridges resting on posts and thumbwheels—guaranteeing better intonation and especially good coupling.

"We build mostly adjustable-bridge and stop-tailpiece guitars, and we've switched over completely to the TonePros system and will never go back. Intonation is critically important to our guitars because we build exclusively with the Buzz Feiten Tuning System, which has extremely exacting intonation points [see section on intonation]. Being able to immobilize the bridge is a plus. Why didn't someone think of it a long time ago? The stop bar has been staring us in the face ever since the Les Paul Junior was born. It's not noticeable at all, and it's a total upgrade, making our guitars even better!"—*Gene Baker, Baker Guitars, Santa Maria, California.*

PRS stoptail bridge

PRS has an adjustable "stoptail" bridge (as PRS calls it) similar to Michael Stevens' Mann Made (but the PRS is significantly wider). This comes stock on a number of models including the hollow-bodied McCarty model that's shown here. Like the Stevens bridge, the PRS fits the studs with a very close tolerance, coupling well whether set high or

low to the body. The PRS string ramps in the bridge body, and the bridge saddles, are the most perfect that I have seen. The saddle notches are machine shaped, but as if by hand, before plating. This is one bridge designed to be playable the second it's installed.

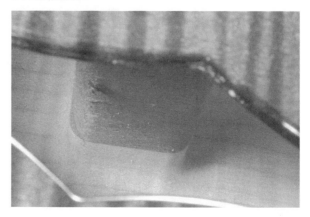

Note: *The PRS McCarty Archtop and the Hollow body model have a top and back carved from solid curly maple. The carving machine leaves pillars of solid maple—connected by a mahogany "sound post," which supports the bridge area and transfers tone. This view (above) through the bass side soundhole shows off this amazing guitar building feat!*

I love the design of the PRS non-adjustable stoptail used on its Santana-model, among others. Instead of moving parts, it has carefully designed intonation points for today's light-gauge strings, and set-screws for increased length adjustment (right). The coupling and tone of this bridge is excellent, and it's super good looking. I wish PRS hardware was available over the counter.

Stop bars, Tune-O-Matics, and tone

My friend Albert Garcia of Whittier, California is one of my best sources for information about a setup's effects on the tone of cool guitars because he's owned and set

up every electric guitar known to man. When he speaks, I listen. Garcia uses the top-wrap and coupled tailpiece on his Les Paul ES-335, and especially on his SG, he says. "I can't believe how close an SG set up that way comes to sounding like a Les Paul."

"With normal string installation (from the rear), and the tailpiece screwed to the body in '60s fashion, the sustain improves because of all the tension on the bridge, but overtones and harmonics are lost. The top-wrap is pretty cool. I don't always tighten the stop-bar down when I top-wrap, though. Sometimes I raise it up to increase harmonics — the more parallel a stop-bar is to the Tune-O-Matic, the more I hear harmonics that I like—the tradeoff is less sustain," Garcia says.

According to Garcia, another reason for that sound may be that when the tailpiece is tight to the body, the threaded studs become immobile. "Since there's slop and air space between the stud threads and the anchor bushings in the body, when they aren't tight, the vibration between them must add yet another color to the tone," he says.

Dismantling Gibson's Nashville bridge

Dismantling a Schaller-made Nashville Tune-O-Matic bridge is easy if you have a couple of small, flat-bladed screwdrivers, as demonstrated on this 1980 Gibson Howard Roberts with a bridge as funky as Howard Roberts playing blues.

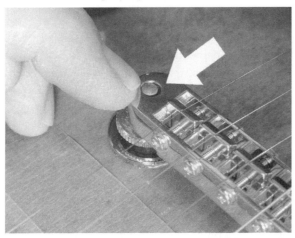

The bridge body was in decent shape, but the saddles were history. I ordered some new saddles for it, and in the meantime used a Stew-Mac 1511-G replacement bridge as a "surrogate bridge" so I could make a nut and refret the guitar. This bridge is styled enough like the Nashville that it fits the stud spacing with only a slight gap (above). I could have used it as a replacement, but it looked too nice to

match the rest of the guitar. Besides, most often imported bridges have pre-cut string grooves. To change the spacing you must file off the saddle

top and start over, which not only ruins the plating but gives you less height to work with. Once the new unslotted saddles arrived, I used all the original screws and springs and replaced the saddles.

■ Most of the saddles had more than one string slot, and someone had worked wax down into the slots—perhaps to keep the saddles from vibrating or moving?

■ You cannot remove and replace the saddles until the retainer clip is removed.

■ To do this, adjust the saddle all the way against the back wall. Then, with one screwdriver, firmly press on the retainer clip from the bottom side while

at the same time using a second screwdriver to back out the screw. The compressed spring clip allows the screw's retaining groove to pass by. Don't try this in your lap! Use a vise or clamp when wrestling with these parts.

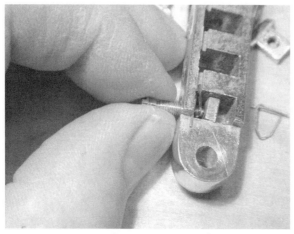

■ Once free from the clip, the screw pulls out and the clip and saddle drop out. Clean off the bridge body and install the new saddles by reversing the order above (press down on the clip to let the screw pass by and into the new saddle).

■ Make sure that the retainer clip has dropped into the screw's clip-groove. If it hasn't, push it in with a small screwdriver.

■ Below is a fresh set of saddles ready to be notched, and shaped to match the fretboard (if necesssary).

OK. If you've gotten this far, here's your guitar mechanic's degree!

5 Whammy bars

Adjustment, maintenance, and setup of tremolos, tremolo bridges, and locking-tremolo bridges

According to the *American Heritage Dictionary*, vibrato is "a tremulous or pulsating effect produced in an instrumental or vocal tone by barely perceptible minute and rapid variations in pitch"; or, "the rapid repitition of a single tone" (most amp tremolos, for example, don't change pitch, but change volume very quickly). I will use the term vibrato in many cases throughout this chapter. There is a huge amount of hardware out there for vibratos, tremolos, and tremolo bridges. Some of the hardware is new, some is vintage. The following advice will help you adjust the parts you have, or, if you're looking for a whammy bar, will help you decide which system is best for you.

Traditional vintage vibrato systems
BIGSBY VIBRATO
Paul Bigsby named his invention the Bigsby Vibrato, a more apt description than "tremolo" for the subtle change in pitch—or slightly more—it lets a guitarist produce. Here are some simple tips for getting the most out of your Bigsby.

On some Bigsby Vibratos, there is a roller bar in front of the retainer bar to which the strings fasten. The roller bar exerts downward pressure on the bridge to increase string angle to the top of the bridge saddle(s) and to help keep the strings in place when plucked or picked. However, the Bigsby Vibrato works its best with only the necessary downward pressure—and no more—on the saddle(s) to keep the strings in place. In my opinion, not every guitar equipped with the roller bar needs one, and the downward pressure can be too great. Whether or not the roller bar is necessary depends on the angle of the neck to the body and the resulting height of the top of the bridge. Try string-

ing up without running the strings under the roller bar and see if you still have a decent string angle to the bridge and some downward pressure. If so, you may prefer the operation and sound of the Vibrato without the bar. Some guitars pick up overtones from the open string length between the bridge and the retainer bar. If that's the case with your guitar, you may choose not to string up this way, but it doesn't hurt to try.

INSTALLING A BIGSBY

You can install a Bigsby only on a guitar with a top strong enough to support it, although they're often mounted on guitars that can't support them—such as the 1969 Gretsch Nashville 6120 described below. The earlier 6120 models like Brian Setzer plays have trestle-supported tops that connect, and strengthen, the top and back and provide support under the bridge area.

After 1963, however, Gretsch removed this support and cut an access hole in the back and covered it with a Comfort Cushion. When you use the Bigsby on these models, the top flexes and the bridge base lifts free. If you own one of these otherwise cool Gretsch guitars (and there are many out there), take it to a repair shop and have two wooden supports custom fit in the bridge area, as shown. These are mahogany, with the grain running top to bottom, 1/2" thick x 2" wide x 2-3/4". I drilled "tone holes" to lighten them and keep the sound airy. Then, with a good bridge setup, the guitar will return to pitch much better.

The tone will improve, too, because the top won't flex. These are not even glued in, although they probably should be.

Before installing a Bigsby on a Les Paul recently, I looked through all my reference books. All but a few of the photos showed Les Pauls equipped with the B5 "horseshoe" Bigsby mounted quite close to the bridge. I clamped one on in that position, but felt the roller bar created too much angle for the Bigsby to work like it should. Also, in my opinion, the arm was too far forward to use when picking in a normal position.

I kept moving the Bigsby back until it rested closer to the top curve, where I could palm the arm

with my pinky and ring fingers, yet with my pick in a desirable playing area. I installed the strings over the roller bar, and they cleared it—but just barely on the bass side. If you string a Bigsby over the roller bar and the strings touch, you can remove the roller from underneath—a single Allen screw holds the

roller in place. It looked a little strange with the roller removed, so I didn't deliver it that way. However, strung over the roller bar, the Vibrato felt smooth and easy like the 1961 Gretsch 6120 I compared it to (which has no roller bar). If you mount a Bigsby on your guitar, give thought to its placement.

A DIFFERENT ARM PLACEMENT

How about this tremolo arm that retro-fits the Bigsby and is adjustable in length? At the time this book went to press, this replacement arm had just become available from guitar shop suppliers. I

find the arm more comfortable and easier to use than the flat Bigsby arm. You also can position it where you like it—both the length and the tilt of the arm are adjustable.

INSTALLING STRINGS ON A BIGSBY

The guitar strings attach to the six pins on the string retaining bar that connects to the spring-loaded hand lever. Bigsby suggests removing the tension spring under the arm so the arm falls down and the string pins are more accessible (I don't bother doing that). Spring or no spring, pre-bend each string around any round object about the size of the retainer bar to produce a round hook shape—it will go on the pin much easier.

Slip each string under the roller bar (if there is one), over the top of the retaining bar, then wrap it down under and onto the anchor pin. Hold the

string onto the pin as you tune until the tension keeps it from popping off the pin. Then use your fingernail to keep the string aligned with the pin as you tune to pitch.

If you have removed the spring, tune the strings taut, but not to pitch, and when all the strings are on lift the tremolo arm and install the arm spring.

KEEP THE COUPLING!

The felt pads on this Vibrato's underside had compressed enough that, even under string pressure, the base of the Vibrato barely touched the top on the

treble side and there was actually a gap on the bass side. I removed the old felts with a knife, then cut several circles of green pool table felt. Lacking thicker felt, I laminated

several circles together with double-stick tape until I achieved the correct thickness. The treble side needed only one layer of new felt, the bass side needed three or four. Then the tailpiece touched the top—which is a must for the Vibrato to work properly!

QUIET AS A MOUSE

I eliminated all the squeaking and spring groans that sometimes afflict a Bigsby by installing round washers cut from several thicknesses of Teflon sheeting. I unbolted the arm from the Vibrato base and replaced the coarse fiber washer between the arm and body with a .030" Teflon washer. Then, I placed one .011" washer under the nut and small spring that fasten the arm onto the retainer bar, and another .011" washer in the spring well. After brushing the two springs clean, I lightly oiled the smaller arm spring and its hex nut, then strung to pitch. Now, under string

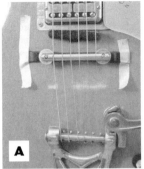

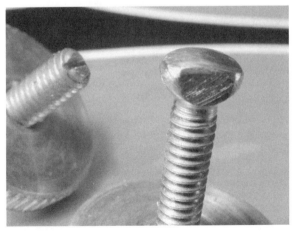

tension, the Vibrato was quiet, cushy, and smoother than any I've played. You don't just find Teflon sheets at the corner store—I buy them from the Mc-Master Carr Company (see page 131 for contact information). The part numbers for 6" x 12" square sheets (the smallest available size) are: 8569K25 (.031" [.79mm] thick) and 8569K21 (.011" [.27mm] thick).

SHIFTING A TAILPIECE

It's common to find a tailpiece that is mounted slightly off center or is worn out at the hinge. Either affliction will pull the bridge to one side or the other—sometimes enough to cause the strings to miss the pickup polepieces and fall off the finger-board. This 1969 Gretsch Nashville was particularly bad; its bridge had been held in place with dabs of glue (I taped the

bridge in place to demonstrate how much the strings were out of line) from bridge to tailpiece (A).

To remedy this, and to avoid plugging and redrilling all the holes for the tailpiece hinge, I loosened the tailpiece screws enough to slide feeler gauges in to find out the thickness I needed to "shift" the tailpiece toward the bass side. I superglued a strip of wood veneer close to that thickness (.028") to the bass edge of the tailpiece hinge, and colored it with an orange marker. Reinstalled, it worked perfectly. (B)

GRETSCH'S SOLID-BAR TREMOLO BRIDGE

When Chet Atkins asked for more sustain in the late '50s, Gretsch introduced a solid-bar saddle on a wood base that was height-adjustable via thumbwheels on threaded posts at each end of the bridge base. Most of these are "rocking" bridges, since the posts have round bottoms that rest in holes in the wooden bridge base. Though intended to move when the Bigsby Vibrato was used, these bridges don't work well because the crudely shaped round of the post bottom and the less-than-round bridge base holes don't provide the intended smooth ball-socket motion. The jagged post bottom, like a shovel digging earth, often catches on the hole when it rocks and sometimes tears chunks of wood from the base. A professional repair tech can tune these bridge bases.

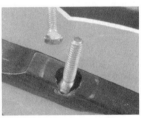

Here's an approach I've used:

■ File off the sharp edges of the V-shaped part of the post bottoms and sand and polish them smooth.

■ Slit a plastic straw and wrap it around the post threads for protection. Then, chuck the protected post into an electric hand drill and run the post bottom backward and forward in the bridge base hole, rocking slightly as you go—burnishing the shape of the post into the base.

■ Also, file a screwdriver slot in the end of the screw so that you can keep the flat sides of the rocker post aligned with the strings—the posts may want to turn sideways when you use the thumbwheels.

■ Put Vaseline in the hole, assemble and adjust the bridge and action, and it will work the way it was intended to.

Many Gretsch guitars equipped with this bridge were built with (improper) low neck angles that made the action impossibly high with the bridge at its lowest adjustment. The common fix for the

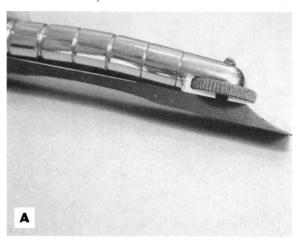

A

bridge was to sand the bottom of the wood base and file some of the metal off the bottom of the metal bar saddle as well. The photos show a superthin bridge base (A) with a filed bar saddle, and then with an un-filed bar saddle (B).

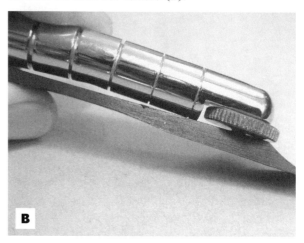

B

The best solution for this problem is to have a pro reset the neck. Then, since replacement bridge bases are not available for this style, have a new (higher) bridge base made to accomodate either a new replacement bar saddle or the original, filed-down saddle (which usually will work). Compare the difference in thickness between the replacement base that I made (on the left) to the sanded-down original.

BIGSBY ALUMINUM BRIDGE AND SADDLE

The bridge that comes with a Bigsby Vibrato has an aluminum base with threaded steel height posts, aluminum thumb-wheels, and an aluminum top saddle. Into-

nation points are staggered along the saddle for the strings and styles of the 1950s. Aside from the fact that it doesn't intonate very well with light strings and an unwound G-string, the machine work on this bridge—at least today's version—is not very good.

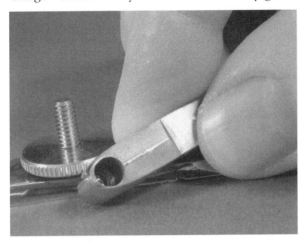

The saddle doesn't return the strings to pitch when you use the tremolo, even though the saddle bottom is slightly V-shaped so it will rock. There is too much slop elsewhere. It looks nice, however, and with metal-working tools and experience, a pro can make it work. Until Bigsby (now owned by Gretsch) redesigns this bridge, I don't recommend it. I do recommend a Bigsby Vibrato, however—I love them! You are better off having a repair tech install a Gibson-style base with a Tune-O-Matic bridge—that's what Brian Setzer uses. (See Setzer's action setup on page 120.)

FENDER'S TREMOLOS:
VINTAGE STRATOCASTER MODEL

Fender's vintage Strat tremolo generally needs some tweaking to reach its peak. Still, the vintage tremolo is here to stay—not only because it looks great and works well if set up correctly, but mostly because a vintage Strat just wouldn't sound the same without it! Compare a vintage Strat to an American Standard. They simply don't sound the same—a big part of the difference in sound is the bridge, and the body rout created for the bridge. Each of these Strats has different advantages and appeal to players.

I picked up a Strat-style "parts" guitar cheap at a guitar show. I knew it wasn't a real Strat, even though some crook had put a bootleg Fender decal on it and attempted a cracked "relic" lacquer finish. I'd planned on refinishing it until Albert Collins autographed the face when I interviewed him for

Guitar Player magazine in 1992. Thanks to this book, I finally took time to set the guitar up.

It was a good subject, too, because along with the normal tweaking and fine-tuning any new or used Strat might need, it had all the problems commonly found on parts guitars put together by hobbyists. Its early '90s Gotoh bridge needed some work, too—here's how I went about it.

FITTING THE BASE PLATE
TO THE SIX MOUNTING SCREWS

Many players set up a Strat tremolo with the baseplate flat against the body. It works that way, and if you break a string the remaining strings won't go out of tune. It takes at least three springs to keep the base flat, however, which stiffens the feel. Leo Fender beveled the front edge of his tremolo bridge so that when at rest it would tilt slightly forward, balanced by the strings and springs, and show about 3/32" of clearance between the bridge plate and guitar top at the rear of the bridge. Tilted like this, the tremolo feels smooth, drops the strings fast, and has an upward pull of about a half step 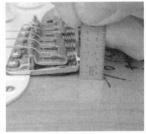 (a semitone). Here's how to adjust a Strat tremolo base plate so it works the way it should.

Remove the back cover plate, the strings, and the tremolo springs. Loosen the the six bridge plate mounting screws (also called pivot screws) until they are not touching the bridge plate. Lightly press the bridge plate flat to the body and forward until the six mounting holes contact the smooth shank of the screws. These mounting screw holes are countersunk on the underside of the bridge plate to produce thin, beveled edges (knife edges). These edges bear against the mounting screw shank and act as a pivot point.

Leaving the four middle screws high and untouched, and still keeping that slight pressure against the screws, tighten one of the two outside screws until the bridge plate moves almost imperceptibly—just starting to tip on the bevel. When it moves, barely loosen the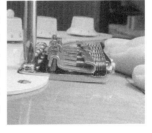

screw until the plate rests flat again. Repeat the process on the other outside screw.

Still keeping pressure on the bridge against the screws, tilt the tremolo forward the approximate amount that you would tilt it and look for a tiny clearance between the plate and the flat underside of the screw. This photo shows too much clearance, but if you tighten the screw down on a piece of thin paper from a string package as a gauge, you'll be close enough to string up and get everything going. Then, adjust the screws under string—and spring—tension.

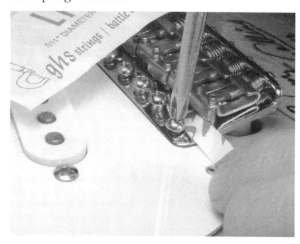

Bring the four other screws down and repeat the process, one at a time, until all six screw heads show a tiny gap when you tilt the bridge plate. In theory, the tremolo plate now is adjusted for proper use, and you can reinstall the tremolo springs and string up. However, if you are looking to make your guitar play GREAT—especially if it is not a real Fender guitar—keep working.

MAKING A STRAT PLAY GREAT
As I said, the 1990 Gotoh bridge needed some improving (the new Gotoh Strat-style bridges don't have the problems mine had—but yours might if it's older).

DISASSEMBLING, FITTING, AND REASSEMBLING STRAT-STYLE BRIDGES
Remove the bridge from the body and look at the back edges of the pivot holes on the underside of

the bridge plate—this edge contacts the screw when the tremolo is tilted. In the photo on the left is a new Gotoh 101. Notice the fine, almost knife-like edges

on the part that contacts the screw. All six holes are identically clean, with back edges that measure a scant 1/32" (.031"/1.2mm). In contrast, on the right is the 1993 Gotoh 101 plate on my Strat. Its holes back edges are pushing 1/8" (.125"/5mm) thick! There is no way two flat surfaces will pivot as smoothly as one flat screw shank with a knife edge bearing against it.

To clean up these pivot holes, I removed the saddles, springs, and adjusting screws, then removed the plate from the sustain block (the heavy block of steel bolted to the under side of the bridge—the part the strings load into from the rear). With a small,

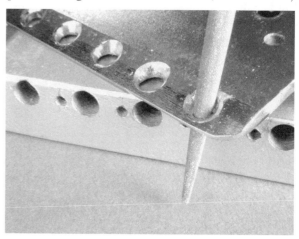

smooth needle file, I back-angled each hole until its edges were thinner and matched in thickness. Some bridge plates may be harder than this one, in which case a file might not touch it. Shop for a bridge with thinner knife edges.

I ran a smooth, flat file over the top of the sustain block where it mounts to the plate (to guarantee good coupling), and used a counter-sink to create a slight bevel on the first sharp edge that

the string hits as it heads toward the saddle. I further smoothed the front string contact point of the bevel, "flossing" it with a .070" wound bass guitar string and some coarse valve-grinding compound.

Note: *If you find a sharp edge on any bridge part that the strings bear against, do your best to deburr it. In the photo, Stevie Ray Vaughan's famous guitar tech, Rene Martinez, is deburring a sharp edge using a Dremel Moto-Tool with a pointed stone grinder. Another trick Martinez used to keep Vaughan from breaking strings*

was to slide a piece of plastic insulation stripped from a piece of small-gauge wire over the string, as shown here on Vaughan's "number one."

I countersunk the six string holes in the plate's top, too (the second sharp edge the string contacts), and burnished them with the .070" string. Next, I countersunk the three larger holes that fasten the plate to the sustain block so the screw heads would rest flush with the plate and not get in the way of the saddle-height screws (which they were—on a real Fender bridge the screws normally would be

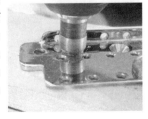

countersunk level with, or slightly below, the plate). I followed by filing and deburring the underside of the plate—removing any raised marks from the manufacturing process and creating a dead-flat coupling surface to the sustain block.

CHOOSE THE CORRECT SADDLE-HEIGHT ADJUSTING SCREWS

The height-adjusting screws were poking uncomfortably above the top of the saddle, so I replaced them with the correct size. Notice the springs of different lengths—the shorter ones go on the saddles that compress closest to the back wall under proper intonation.

Fender makes four different saddle height-adjusting screws: 1/4" (10mm); 5/16" (12.5mm); 3/8" (15mm); and 1/2" (20mm). To accommodate slight differences in neck pocket depth, paint thickness,

body thickness, and neck thickness, which can affect the neck-to-bridge geometry (and therefore the height of the saddles). In general, Fender uses two height-screw lengths—short on the outside two E-strings, and medium for the inside four strings. Fender will normally use either (A): 1/4" and 5/16" (low saddles); or (B) or 5/16" and 3/8" (medium saddles)—leaving the 1/2" saddles for extreme situations. I prefer to use three screw sizes—two short for the outer two E-saddles; two medium for the B- and A-saddles; and two long the G- and D-saddles—because there is less protrusion on the B- and A-saddles.

Often a perfectly set up Strat bridge will fall in between the range of any height screw length, no matter what combination is used. You can shorten a screw by wrapping tape around it to protect it, then clamp it in locking pliers or a vise and file metal off of the bottom.

Note: *I bent and broke off the L-end of this .050" (1.28mm) Allen wrench and superglued it into a small hole in a wood dowel—it makes removing, in-*

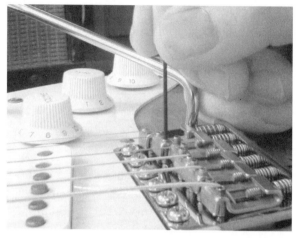

stalling, and adjusting the saddle-height adjust screws much easier. Plastic-handled sets of the straight-shaft Allen keys are available from hardware suppliers.

CLICKETY-CLACK, CLICKETY-CLACK

After all that careful work and reassembly, there was an awkward shifting movement and slight clicking noise when I tilted the tremolo. I removed the four center screws and the noise seemed to go away. Then I noticed that three of the bridge mount holes (the G-, B-, and treble E-holes) were not concentric with the plate. This misalignment between the screws and the plate will cause friction.

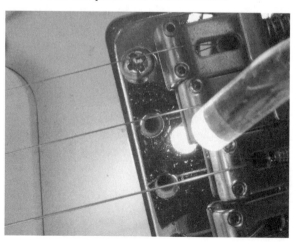

I plugged the three holes and drilled them correctly, but it still clicked. Finally, I traced it down: the bridge was mounted far enough forward and out of line with the neck that the sustain block hit along the treble side of the body rout. A rasp took care of that. The photo shows the three plugged and redrilled holes and how little wood I had to remove. I also concluded that there was friction between the bottom of the bridge plate bevel and the somewhat sticky-feeling lacquer finish. After filing any roughness on the bevel, I lubricated it with a swipe of Vaseline.

SELECTION, PLACEMENT, AND NUMBER OF TREMOLO SPRINGS

No hard rules govern spring placement and the number of springs to use. Fender has two tremolo springs, silver and black, and each has a different diameter and tension. The silver springs, which are larger in diameter, are meant for the Vintage tremolo bridge. The black springs are for the American Standard. They aren't interchangeable (although I often see people do that erroneously).

Fender, however, is no longer the only maker of tremolo springs, and all springs are not equal. Floyd Rose springs are softer than Gotoh springs, and so the story goes. You can match springs by looks, length, and diameter for starters, then you have to use them to feel how they stretch, see how they look when stretched equally, and to hear how they sound when plucked.

As for the number of springs to use, and how to install them, there are a number of options. You'll have to decide what is best for you. Five springs came on the vin-

tage Stratocaster, but few players use that many (Stevie Ray Vaughan did, but he tuned to E-flat). Of course, you must place five springs in a straight row. On vintage Strats, most players who use .009"s use two springs; some players love two springs on .010"s, stretched way out, and others prefer three—usually with the outside two angled in.

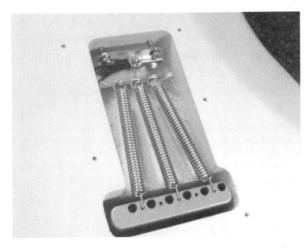

Before beginning my research to write this book, I'd always felt that the springs (whatever number) should run in a straight line so that they stretch equally and have the same tension and sound. That is how I've installed them for years. I figured that players who angled the two outside springs toward the center, rather than in a straight line, had big

fingers and couldn't install the springs along the edge of the tremolo cavity (and it's not easy unless you have the right tool). I use a special hooked tool: It's a Japanese fish hook remover, slightly modified, a gift from my friends Akifumi Koyanagi and Hayahi-San of Tokyo, Japan. Since then, Stewart-MacDonald has made available a variation of this tool.

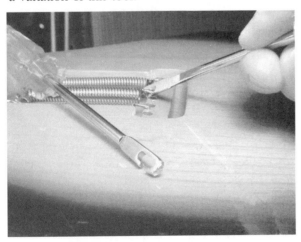

Now, however, after speaking with respected builders and repairmen while researching this book, I am re-evaluating my opinions and trying some new approaches. For example, Tom Anderson's viewpoint is quite different from what I have been thinking.

"I use three springs, and I like them to be opened up some, and never want them closed—open enough that even with the arm pulled back, the springs remain open. I angle the outside springs to center because I like a relatively stiff feel when I push the arm down. The two springs angling to center are already exerting almost enough pressure to balance the strings by themselves. This produces a smooth, cushy feel because the more a spring is open the less resistance it has. As you push down, the angled springs give easily, and the almost-closed middle spring, which is carrying very little of the string tension, offers the resistance that adds a stiffness that I like."—*Tom Anderson, Anderson Guitarworks, Newbury Park, California*

My Strat-loving friend, Albert Garcia, who discusses stop bars, Tune-O-Matics, and tone on pages 54 and 55, uses a different approach.

"For .010"s I use two of the silver springs, not angled toward center, and installed on the second and fourth claw hooks. Then, I tighten the claw down until the rear of the bridge floats 'Fender-style' (approximately 3/32"), and there's a nice, almost drum-like tension. I feel that when I use three springs, the tremolo doesn't return in tune as well because it has more potential to screw up. Actually, I'm of the mind that the fewer the parts the better—fewer things to inhibit movement. For me, two springs balance out evenly, whereas three start to get mushy, because they're backed out more and change the tension of the tremolo arm. Because you have to loosen the claw for three springs, the springs don't stretch as much, and the feel gets a little soggy.

"With my setup, the claw will not always be parallel with the cavity wall. The bass side may be closer to the cavity wall than the treble side, because when I watch the springs open up, I like to see them stretch the same amount—both for the feel of the tremolo, and so that the springs produce the same sound. This is not a proven science, just my opinion, and I am not talking about a tremolo with a tapered sustain block—I am referring only to the vintage Strat tremolo block. If I use .009"s, I also use two silver springs. Springs vary so much in tension, even from the same manufacturer, that you have to test them. It is because of this great variance in spring tension that yours may not be parallel with the wall in the same way that mine are. Variance in spring tension is also a reason that you might choose three springs instead of two."—*Albert Garcia, Whittier, California*

Note: *Albert Garcia is so choosy that when he compares springs, he also looks for the round end of the spring to be flat and bent straight out, not upturned. Any vintage Fender springs that I've checked are always straight. The photo shows two springs, a new one (right) and a vintage one (left).*

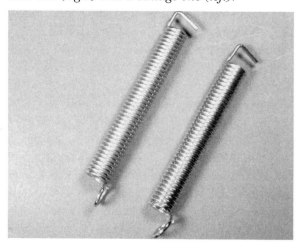

VINTAGE TREMOLO BRIDGE SPRINGS

Use two silver springs for .009"-gauge string sets, and either two or three for .010"s

I have been using two silver springs and .010" -.046" gauge strings on my Strat for some time. For the sake of experiment, however, I set up my guitar with both .009"- and .010"-gauge strings—each time with only two silver springs. After trying each, and following the 10-Step Setup on page 108, I came up with these specs:

With .009"s, the claw was farther from the cavity wall (about 1/2"), and was parallel with the wall. Using .010"s, the same setup resulted in the claw being about 3/8" 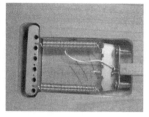 from the wall and slightly farther from the wall on the bass side, in order for the springs to stretch

equally (determined by measuring in between the spring coils with feeler gauges until the same feeler gauge would slip into the coils on both springs equally).

Later, I tried three springs on the .010"s, but, like Garcia, I didn't like the feel as well as I did with two springs. With that setup, the springs measured 11/16" from the wall and the claw was a little more parallel with the wall because of the extra spring. To me, three springs felt mushy, didn't sound as good, and the overall tremolo action was not as smooth and Bigsby-like. Then, I tried Tom Anderson's spring setup and found that it was in between the setups mentioned above.

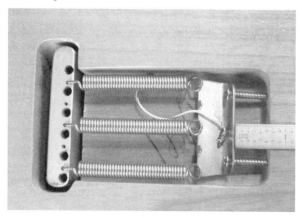

AMERICAN STANDARD SPRINGS

The American Standard springs have a different tension than the vintage ones, and Fender recommends three black springs for both .009"- and .010"-gauge string sets, although they suggest that some players will prefer two springs, depending upon the feel they're after. Following the same tests above (and the 10-Step Setup on page 108), I still preferred two springs on the American Standard tremolo.

KEEPING A STRAT'S TREMOLO ARM TIGHT AND IN POSITION

The vintage Fender and the American Standard tremolo arms, because they are threaded (and because threads wear), loosen over time. You can't just give the arm another turn to tighten it, because the threads won't allow it—the arm would break off! For a number of years now, Fender has dropped a 1/2" x .150" steel spring in the bottom of the tremolo arm hole, putting pressure on the bottom

of the arm and taking up the slack. Be careful when you remove your tremolo arm—the spring falls out easily. If you bend a slight kink into the spring, it will keep it from falling out of the hole. I prefer to leave the arm in the guitar as much as possible to keep the threads from wearing prematurely.

BLOCKING A TREMOLO

Some players who don't want to use the tremolo at all "block" it tight with a piece of wood carefully sized and pressed between the back of the sustain block and the tremolo cavity wall. I've often heard that Eric Clapton prefers a Strat to be set up this way. It doesn't take great woodworking skills to do this, but it takes some. There is no one-size-fits-all wood block, even for the same model of guitar, so you must fit the block until it presses in tight.

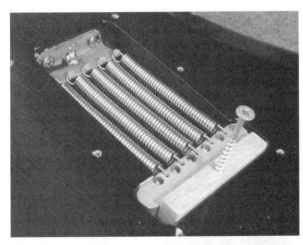

The 1961 Strat shown here is blocked with a flat, rectangular piece of maple measuring approximately 7/16" thick by 1-1/2" high x 2-5/8" wide. I drill a hole in the block to accept a drywall screw to remove the

block if, or when, it's necessary. Of course, I don't leave the drywall screw in the block. Level out any paint bumps along the tremolo cavity wall before pressing the block in for good.

This setup has all five springs, and the claw is tight to the wall—making for a big, springy reverb chamber and great transfer from the sustain block to the body.

TAPERED BLOCKING

Fender's American Standard tremolo has a tapered sustain block, so you must fit it with a tapered block (the vintage block is rectangular). Making a tapered block is more difficult. I found the size needed using two 1/8" thick x 1" high x 2-1/2" long scraps of wood—one taped to the tremolo block, the other taped to the body—and letting them hang down into the cavity (thin edge up). Then, I pressed wood dowels of different diameters, starting with the smallest, between the two pieces to force them against the sustain block and cavity wall. I lightly dribbled superglue on each dowel as I progressed, creating a template.

From the template I took measurements to make a real block, this time from mahogany. I used the same five springs and the claw to the wall as above—and drilled a hole for a drywall screw. If this woodworking is beyond your skills, show this to your repair tech—he or she might not know this trick.

FENDER JAZZMASTER TREMOLO BRIDGE

It's not uncommon to find setup problems with Fender Jazzmasters, Jaguars (which use the Jazzmaster bridge) and Mustangs. The Mustang's bridge is similar to the Jazzmaster's, except it has round, smooth saddles with string grooves instead of saddles made of threaded rod. Also, its saddles rest on the bridge base and are not individually adjustable.

The problem I'm referring to occurs, on occasion but not always, if the neck pocket is routed too deep. The result is a low bridge height—you can't quite get the angle needed from the tremolo to the bridge saddles to keep the strings from popping out when plucked. These tremolos are smooth and have a wide pitch-change range, so it's worth spending the time and money to solve this problem.

Shimming the neck higher in the pocket to raise the bridge and increase the angle isn't a good solution because the pickups don't raise easily, and with enough string angle to solve the problem the guitar feels odd (the strings are too far from the body). Depending on the guitar, and the depth of the neck pocket, sometimes only a slight shim is needed to solve the problem (see page 84).

Another solution, demonstrated here on my '98 Fender Custom Shop Jazzmaster, is to install the Buzz Stop, a device invented by Mark Sampson and

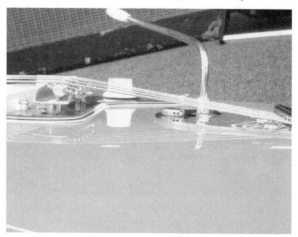

available from the John Sprung's American Guitar Center. The Buzz Stop attaches simply, with the front two mounting screws of the Jazzmaster's tremolo plate.

A unique feature of the Jazzmaster is a sliding lockout lever that immobilizes the tremolo. If you break a string, you depress the lever until the lock-

out slides home—you'll be in tune until you can replace the string. Or, you can keep the tremolo locked if you don't want it to move accidentally.

Both bridge styles have access holes in the hollow bridge posts that allow you to use a .050" Allen wrench to adjust the hardened-steel screws at the bottom. The Allen screws have sharp "rocker points" on their tips. The bridge rocks on these points, which dig into the slightly softer alloy of the metal cups in the body. These Allen screws also adjust the overall bridge height in conjunction with the height-adjustable bridge saddles. However, on many vintage Jazzmasters (and even my Custom-Shop Jazzmaster), because of the depth of the neck pocket rout, the 3/8"-long rocker-point set screws often are too short. Just as you're about to get the string action where you want it, the rocker screws fall out the bottom or barely have enough thread to remain in the post, let alone be considered stable. You need to get as much height from the adjustable bridge saddles as possible because of the short screws—it's a design flaw in an otherwise great axe. Here's how you can correct it.

When Fender reissued the Jazzmaster in the late 1990s, it increased the length of this screw to 1/2" or more (ask your dealer for them if you need additional height adjustment). The new, longer screws took care of my guitar's problem, but even with them, a good deal of the screw remains adjusted out of the post to achieve the right bridge height. There's enough thread left in the post, but not much. Therefore, I put the long screws in, set the action, then

remove the bridge and measure how much screw is exposed. Then, I insert the short, 1/4" (10mm) Strat bridge saddle screws (which will go in only from below) and reinstall the long rocker screw at the premeasured height. From above, I lock down the smaller Allen screw on top of the

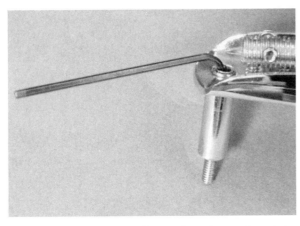

longer, rocker screw. This makes the rocker tight and firm, increases stability, and adds an extra bit of coupling.

I replaced the Jazz-master bridge with a Mustang-style bridge because I thought it would provide better spacing and saddle coupling and allow the strings to move with less friction—it did. The imported, Mustang-style bridge that I bought had adjusting screws of an adequate length (1.5mm Allen screws), and the strings cleared the back of the bridge base. The bridge saddle's vintage 7-1/4" radius was a little rounder than the Custom Shop Jazzmaster's 9-1/2" radius, but the mismatch was hardly noticeable and was not a problem.

ADJUSTING THE ROCKER SCREWS

With either the Jazzmaster or the Mustang bridge, adjust the rocker screws while pressing a finger down on the center of the bridge to keep it centered (not tilted forward or backward). Adjust the two post screws until you feel the screw's points make contact, then adjust the bridge height.

GIBSON'S MAESTRO VIBROLA

Several versions of Gibson's Maestro Vibrola were used on some solid-bodies with flat tops, such as SGs and Fire-birds. The Maestro compares favorably with a Bigsby's smooth feel,

easy semitone pitch bend, and ability to stay in tune. Also like the Bigsby, in use, the strings never leave the saddle contact point as they do with tremolos that tip the bridge saddles forward, allowing the strings to raise off the saddle intonation points when the strings slacken.

The Maestro Vibrola gets its vibrato effect from a simple, tempered "leaf spring," made of steel and bent into the C-shape shown in the photo. The tremolo arm/string holder slides onto the short, flat bend at the front of the "C". The bottom of the leaf spring has a thin piece of felt glued to it, which rests on the face of the guitar.

It's common to find Gibson guitars with a low neck angle, or pitch, on a plane almost in line with the top of the body. As with the Jazzmaster just mentioned, low neck angle means low bridge height, low string angle from the Vibrola to the saddles, and not enough downward pressure to keep the strings from popping out of the bridge saddles—making the guitar unusable without removing the Vibrola and adding a stop-bar tailpiece. Whether or not the bridge is high enough and string angle workable is a fine line and may depend on your picking style.

I bought a used Firebird III reissue that probably was made around 1993. It had the ABR-1 Tune-O-Matic bridge and a stop-bar tailpiece (the original Firebird III never had a stop-bar, always a Vibrola). I bought the guitar because I loved the neck shape (it's just like a real one I had in the '60s), and it was cheap since the headstock had been broken and repaired. Because of the break it's not particulary valuable, so I don't mind hot-rodding it—first with three "Keith-Pegs" (banjo D-tuners) that drop the low E-, A-, and treble E-strings a whole

step into G-tuning instantly, and later with a Graph Tech nut and saddles to decrease friction (see photo—bottom page 69). I gave the saddle slots their final shape with the correct guitar string gauge dipped in Stewart Macdonald's #1201 coarse polishing compound, then burnished them further with wide, waxed, dental floss and the same compound. The end result is perfectly shaped string slots with super-polished, low-friction bottoms.

I further hot-rodded the Firebird by installing a Schaller Fine-Tune Tailpiece. Any lost coupling was worth the tuning stability—especially when drop tuning. If a dropped string is slightly out of tune, I can tweak it in a second (not to mention tweaking the strings in

regular tuning with an eye on the electronic tuner attached to my amp). I wouldn't want a fine-tuning tailpiece on every guitar, but I love it on the Firebird.

All my Firebird lacked was a Maestro Vibrola, and soon I found one (a slightly different version of the one first shown). I decided to use it, even though I'd have to do without the fine-tuning tailpiece (I can always go back). When I clamped it in place, however, I could see that the neck angle and bridge height were too low for the strings to exert any downward pressure on the saddle. The angle was even lower because I wanted to mount the Vibrola farther back than usual. If you have a guitar with this Vibrola, and the downward pressure is inadequate, take your guitar to a repair shop and ask them to read what follows.

I removed the steel spacers that support the rear bend of the Vibrola where it screws to the top and

experimented with filling the hollow U-shape with maple blocks of several heights, all with beveled bottoms. I hoped that with the "C" of the Vibrola resting on the top I could raise the rear screw mount and tilt the Vibrola forward—thereby lowering the string arm and increasing the string angle to the saddles. It worked great.

I carved a final piece to fill more of the hollow area for better coupling and so I could shim the unit high enough that the leaf spring, though still tilted, would not contact the top at all. I liked the smoothness, travel, and sound better like this, perhaps because the leaf spring was floating and the tone wasn't grounded by con-

tact with the top. I think it brought out the full effect of the leaf spring, rather than just bending it in front of the contact point on the body.

Note: *On certain archtop models, an ES-355 comes to mind, and on the Epiphone Sheraton, Gibson used thumbwheels with rounded tops. Gibson also scalloped and rounded the bottoms of Tune-O-Matic bridges where they rest on the thumbwheels so that they would rock better when used with Bigsbys. I found two domed thumbwheels, but no round-bottomed bridge, in my used parts. They did add an extra bit of rock and roll to my unrounded T.O.M. bridge.*

GORDON-SMITH'S LEAF-SPRING "WOBBLE BAR"

Gordon-Smith guitars of Manchester, England, manufactures no-frill, no-nonsense guitars (more than 9,000 to date). Owner John Smith designed the vi-

brato bridge that is shown here, which he calls a "wobble bar." Its pitch change and feel are similar to a Bigsby, although slightly stiffer. "The side effect of the stiffness is that you can put your hand on it when you play it and it

doesn't go all over the place," says Smith, "and you can also do string bends without the vibrato following you and making it hard work. You can get a very fast vibrato with it, too. I think it's a nice compromise."

This simple, leaf-spring vibrato mounts on any solid guitar, flat or arch topped (via a spacer for height), without routing. It attaches with three mounting screws and a spacer bar to give the leaf spring room to operate (see photo page 41). If you tighten the leaf spring screws, the vibrato arm tilts backward about 10 degrees as the flat spring compresses; loosen the screws and the arm tilts forward.

Modern two-point floating vibratos

Nobody provided me with more answers and strong opinions about the function of bridges and vibratos than Trev Wilkinson— inventor of the roller nut used on the Strat Plus from '87 to '93, as well as a number of vibrato bridges in use today. These days, Wilkinson is a guitar manufacturer, building FRET-King and Italia

guitars. As I did, you'll better understand the principles of vibratos and tremolos after hearing what Wilkinson has to say, and be in a better position to decide what kind of vibrato system might appeal to you.

"Anything that moves under a string robs the string of energy. That's why a three-saddle Tele bridge sounds better than a six-saddle bridge—because you have two strings holding down one saddle. Or, look at a good pedal steel, how simply and solidly it's built, and how exceptionally well coupled the strings are. Nothing rings like a steel guitar!

"In vibrato bridge design, the height of the saddle's string contact point—and its relation to the fulcrum point on which the bridge pivots—is critical. If the saddle is too tall, the string gets a leverage advantage over the fulcrum point and you need to increase the spring tension or add more springs. This stiffens the feel and ruins the subtle, easy pitch change, which in my opinion a vibrato should have. But if you want a stiffer feel to the vibrato, increase the saddle height and tighten the springs—but doing this can affect tuning stablility, especially on the G-string.

"To prove the string's influence on the bridge, think of the last time you set up your favorite vintage Strat. When you set the action on a vintage Strat, you can't preset your bridge saddle radius, then raise the string (action) height by simply raising the entire bridge plate using two pivot-point screws the way you can with the American Standard, Floyd Rose, Wilkinson, and some others.

"Your only options are to shim the neck, or the more common option is to raise the saddles for a higher string action. Have you noticed that after you detune enough to raise the saddles that, when you retune, the position of the bridge has changed a lot? That it's tipped forward enough that you must tighten the springs? You gave the strings more leverage, and the entire spring-to-string balance—which is so delicate—needs to be readjusted. The opposite happens if you lower the saddles.

"Another important factor, which also relates to saddle height, is the angle created by the string rising from the bridge at the rear of the saddle to where it couples on the saddle's intonation point. If the saddles are too low, and the rear string angle too shallow, as you depress the vibrato the string tension and coupling to the saddle is lost too quickly, and along with it the sound of the string—they all become slack and mushy. This is not what a vibrato should produce.

"My concept of a vibrato is the subtlety of a note. If you mount a Floyd really well, it still doesn't feel as fluid (nor can it easily imitate the subtle pitch change) as when you set up on old Stratocaster as Leo intended it to be, or a Bigsby—vibratos with some pull-up and push-down, but not too much. The only reason we have the two-point fulcrum tremolos today is because players wanted more pitch change than the old-time vibratos could offer."

I asked Wilkinson why two-point, knife-edge vibratos "flutter."

"All well-balanced, sensitive, two-pivot floating systems have some degree of flutter—that slight shimmering, quaking, almost gurgling-sound (and feel) as the bridge teeter-totters between the forces of the strings on one side and the springs on the other. Take a 12" plastic desk ruler and press half of it flat to a tabletop with the other half hanging free off the edge. Flip the ruler's end, watch it flutter, and listen to the 'boing' sound it makes. Floating vibratos do the same thing, but much more subtley. Flutter is a necessary evil in a well-balanced system.

ELIMINATING FLUTTER

"You can eliminate most flutter by adding a third spring or by raising the saddles. As mentioned above, higher saddles increase the string's leverage over the saddles, requiring tighter spring tension (or a third spring). The result is a stiffer feel, and more tuning instability. Plus, the good qualities of a balanced floating tremolo—smooth vibrato and good return to pitch—are lost.

"You'll eliminate a good deal of flutter if you simply keep the tremolo arm dropped toward the floor—in a neutral position—when you're not using it. The arm's length and weight, when in the playing position and running parallel with the strings (or with the arm at 90 degrees, pointing toward the rear), seems to exacerbate flutter. When dropped to the floor, the arm's weight dampens a good deal of flutter. In my opinion, a heavier arm dampens better than a light one.

"It'd be a hard thing to prove, but I think when

a bridge is parallel to the guitar's face, the knife edge works better because it's pulled straight into the post groove—as opposed to a knife edge on a vibrato with the plate tilted forward. The difference in functionality is probably minimal, but the straight-on knife edge must return more accurately.

"Also, I've always felt that a vibrato system floating off the face of the guitar, whether tiltled or parallel, will come back to pitch better than a vibrato set up to slam against the body. This is because when it floats and you let it return to zero, it goes back past zero slightly, then returns to zero—giving the strings a better chance to recover in the nut slots.

"The Floyd Rose created a whole playing style, and I know that, but are we talking about a playing style or a vibrato? When you start to go down with a Floyd, watch the low E-string, for instance. The string-to-saddle coupling breaks quickly, the string lifts free, and the note goes dead. You don't get the full sound of the strings going down in pitch. The American Standard and Wilkinson VS100 came along to address that problem. Although they have some differences, these bridges are similar in their feel and travel, and they fall somewhere in between a Vintage vibrato and the Floyd Rose.

"If you want the real truth, like you, Dan, I love a Bigsby Vibrato or Gibson's Maestro Vibrola—the saddle remains separate and the vibrato moves the string. I'm from the old school too, as a player—but not as a designer!"—*Trev Wilkinson, FRET-King Guitars, Birmingham, England*

TREMOLO STABILIZERS

Hipshot's Trem-Setter is a spring-loaded device that replaces a tremolo spring and fastens to the tremolo block. The Trem-Setter stabilizes the tremolo and

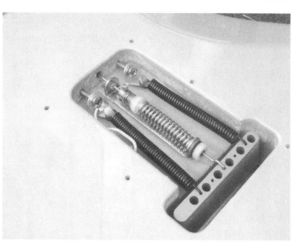

eliminates flutter (some call it "warble")—in fact, that is one of its best attributes. Plus, the Trem-Setter gives the tremolo a positive stop to return to, and helps keep the lower strings from going flat when the treble strings are bent. The drawback to the Trem-Setter is that it alters the smooth feel of a tremolo, and you can feel (and sometimes hear) a slight mechanical movement when you pull it or push it from its resting position. The Trem-Setter is not for eveyone, but you might want to try one. You can read about setting up the Trem-Setter in detail in my book, *The Guitar Player Repair Guide*, or at www.danerlewine.com.

A helpful tip for making the Trem-Setter work more smoothly is to make sure that the hook on the end of the brass pull rod is bent at the same angle as the hole in the sustain block. I stick an Allen key or drill bit in a sustain block hole to judge the angle, then gently bend the hook to match (if it needs it). Also, I file a rounded groove in the hole the hook mounts in to give it more freedom and to eliminate binding and friction.

WD Products offers a Tremolo Stabilizer of a different nature. It's a length-adjustable rigid nylon rod that, after measuring and fitting, installs inside the tremolo spring on the bass side. It makes contact with the spring claw and the sustain block when the tremolo is at rest, and offers a pos-

itive stop for the tremolo to return to after bending. Also, if you break a string, the stop keeps the other strings in tune and it makes replacing strings a cinch. You cannot, however, pull up on the tremolo with this device installed. It installs without drilling or special tools, and is just one more device to help solve tremolo problems that plague some guitarists.

ADJUSTING THE HEIGHT AND BALANCE OF THE AMERICAN STANDARD TWO-POINT FLOATING TREMOLO

In my opinion, the American Standard is Fender's best Strat tremolo. It has no friction troubles, and it's extremely smooth since it "floats" (a floating tremolo has contact with only the pivot posts, and never touches the body). With a well-lubricated nut made of the right material (or the LSR roller nut), it's relatively trouble free, and locking tuners make it even better. I asked the designer of the Standard, Fender Chief Engineer of R&D George Blanda, a 15-year Fender employee and avid guitar nut, to explain the tremolo's setup.

FENDER'S RECOMMENDED SETUP

"The two pivot screws must be adjusted exactly the same distance from the guitar's face, with the plate perfectly parallel to the face from treble to bass side so that the knife edges are on the same plane. The bottom of the bridge plate should be 3/32" above the face and parallel to it from front to back. The neck pitch and string height can be adjusted to match the bridge by using the Micro-Tilt neck adjustment.

"Fender recommends three springs because, even though two springs may feel smoother and the system may be more well balanced, there is a tendency for the tremolo to flutter some with only two springs. Three springs eliminate flutter, so Fender prefers to ship them that way," Blanda says.

Note: *Some players feel that Fender's vintage tremolo has better tone than the American Standard tremolo. Since the vintage tremolo doesn't float, and therefore has no flutter, I think it does sound better.*

ADJUSTING THE AMERICAN STANDARD'S BRIDGE SADDLES

"Set the outside E-saddles as low as you can get them without touching, and adjust the remaining saddles to the American Standard's 9-1/2" fretboard radius. The clearance under the outside saddles can range from 1/32" (.032"/1.2mm) to a maximum of .050".

Note: *The saddles will go lower. You don't want the outside saddles touching because: 1) the*

screws might vibrate loose; 2) if the saddles touch they are more coupled than the others and the sound will be different on those two strings.

"From the two outside strings in, the correct bridge saddle radius will be approximately 3/32" (.093"/2.37mm) on the center G- and D-saddles, and the B- and A-saddles will fall in between. Generally, the screw heads will be hidden within the saddle for comfort and looks."—*George Blanda, Fender Musical Instruments*

Note: *In some cases, when you go lower with the saddles—until they almost touch—you may need to grind off the bottom of one or more height-adjustment screws if their heads protrude from the saddle and cause you discomfort.*

Guitarists seldom agree about setups, and I'm no exception. I prefer to set up the American Standard tremolo with 1/16" of clearance under the plate at the front, and with the tremolo tilted forward showing 1/8" of clearance at the back. This way I get more upward pull and at least as much downward travel. An American Standard with this setup will measure about 9/32" from the guitar's face to the top of the pivot posts.

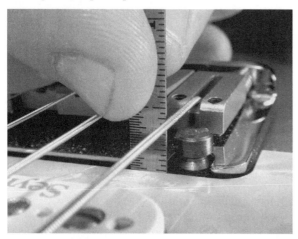

Note: *You can turn the American Standard's pivot posts for height adjustment with the strings tuned to pitch without harming the knife edges.*

WILKINSON VIBRATO BRIDGES

Gotoh now produces its own version of the most recognizable Wilkinson vibrato, the VS100, to Wilkinson's specs. It is called the VS100G, and it retrofits Fender's American Standard guitar. I had to file off a little finish and wood on the treble side of the tremolo body rout to make way for the round vibrato arm mount on the underside of the VS100G's

bridge plate. I used a small rasp, it took five minutes, and it doesn't show.

The saddles are three different heights and they lock to the plate. "I believe this coupling increases tone and sustain," says Wilkinson, "because, during the entire time before the string finally raises from its saddle intonation point (if you drop the bar that far), it is in contact with a saddle that is locked down. The string doesn't need to hold the saddle in place. Also, if saddles can't rise up and move to another position when the tremolo is dropped, tuning stability improves.

"You can adjust the bridge saddles' height screws (for bridge saddle radius) with a 1.5mm Allen key, and the saddles' intonation screws from the rear

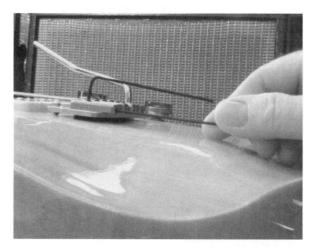

of the bridge as well with a 1.5mm Allen key. You must loosen the 2mm saddle lock-down screws (the top screw with the Allen head in the photo) when raising the saddles to match a fretboard radius or when adjusting the intonation.

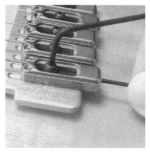

"I designed the saddles low to the bridge plate," says Wilkinson, "with a string angle to the saddle intonation point somewhere in between a Floyd Rose and the American Standard. Since the saddles are three different heights, when they're all tight to the bridge it produces a perfect 15" radius. Many modern guitars have flatter fretboards—within a 14" to 17" range—compared to the 7-1/2", 9-1/2", 10", and 12" radii of most Fender and Gibson models. You'll have superior coupling with the saddles all tight on the plate (if you happen to have a guitar with a fretboard radius close to that). The saddle-height Allen screws are short and never protrude, and since the saddles have plenty of metal and deep threads, even with the center screws adjusted deep to raise the saddles to a vintage radius, they won't fall out the bottom."

Wilkinson sets up the VS100G bridge to float approximately 1/8" above the face of the body and perfectly level, tightens the outside E-string saddles flat to the plate, and adjusts the remaining saddles to the desired fretboard radius. Also, he recommends two springs for .009" or .010" string sets. As with the American Standard bridge, Wilkinson uses stainless-steel saddles that don't require plating and have round string grooves machined into them. Stainless steel is hard, so the strings have difficulty wearing grooves into the intonation point or plating that can cause them to break.

The vibrato arm smoothly presses into a Delrin-lined hole. An Allen set screw puts pressure on the arm and holds it in place (there are no threads to deal with). The arm is smooth and comfortable under your hand, very low profile, and stays where you put it when it's not in use. Also, since it is stainless, you can  bend it to any shape that suits you without heating it.

The VSV is brand new and retrofits a vintage Stratocaster with six mounting screws. "I made this bridge to look and sound like a Strat," Wilkinson says, "yet work like a two-point vibrato. One circular knife-edge mounting hole (on the bass side) locates the bridge, and the other five holes are oval-

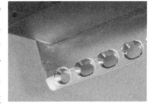

shaped knife edges so they can self-locate on the screw shoulders (similar to what Leo Fender did with the G & L tremolo). It has six mounting screws for good coupling (Fender's vintage Strat tremolo has always coupled well, in my opinion), however, the bent-steel saddles lock down.

"The steel sustain block is unique in that it has staggered holes for the strings to load through. The B-, G-, A- and low E-holes are drilled farther back than the others. These are the strings that have the

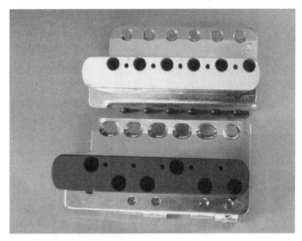

most trouble returning to pitch—especially the B- and G-strings—because their saddles are closer to the back wall (for good intonation). This creates a greater string angle and tighter string tension at the string-to-saddle contact points. After dumping the vibrato, the G-string especially tends to hang up or change position as it tries to even out its tension in relation to the other strings, which have a shallower string angle. As for the low E- and A-saddles, even though they sit lower on the bridge they have a similar problem because, being wound, they drag on the saddle (the low E- especially). Bridge saddles that are not clamped to the plate suffer even more from this problem.

"I use three springs on the VSV because its saddles are taller than the VS100's—it's that string leverage thing again—it takes three springs to balance the leverage of the strings at the saddle.

"We also make the VS200G, originally designed for guitar buider James Tyler of Los Angeles, California, that combines the VS100G plate with the VSV saddles to give a more vintage sound to a two-point vibrato. And finally, the VS100 Convertible (not available in the United States) is a locking version of the VS100G. Locked, it turns the vibrato into a hard-tail bridge via a locking catch on the back cover plate. That's it for now from over the pond. Thanks, Dan!"—*Trev Wilkinson, FRET-King Guitars, Birmingham, England*

HIPSHOT'S BALL-BEARING KNIFE EDGE TREMOLO BRIDGE— A NEW KID ON THE BLOCK

Hipshot's David Borisoff has designed a compact, smoothly-machined tremolo with a solid feel that floats on ball bearings rather than knife edges. It's a new challenger in the tremolo ring (below). The

fact that Sadowsky uses it on all of his nonpickguard floating tremolo guitars speaks well for it (see a Sadowsky guitar setup on page 123). Sadowsky also offers it as an option on pickguard models.

The bridge has two bearings on the treble side, which locate the bridge, and only one on the bass side. The bearings rest in a round groove machined into each post. Having the two bearings on only one

side makes it easy for the single bearing to find a sweet spot to locate on the other post.

Note: *Sadowsky sets up for .010"s using three springs, with the outside two angled toward center. With the intonation set perfectly, the measurement from the nut to the saddle intonation point was 25-5/8" (top right).*

ANDERSON TREMOLO BRIDGE BY FISHMAN

Like Paul Reed Smith, Seymour Duncan, and a few others in the manufacturing end of the guitar biz, Tom Anderson is a great player, and playing guitars is as important to Anderson as building them.

He sets up a floating tremolo bridge differently than all the others—a setup that country players and rockers like Brian May would go for (keeping open strings, or chords, in tune when bending notes). Anderson is using his variation of the Fishman Powerbridge, a fine two-point floating tremolo with piezo elements under each saddle's contact point that gives an acoustic sound at the flip of a switch.

"Our guitars are set up the way I like to play them. If it's a tremolo model, we generally use a Fishman Powerbridge built to our specs, although we do install the original Floyd Rose, too. I like a different two-point tremolo setup than most, and I will put up with a rela-  tively stiff tremolo setup in order to bend strings and use 'double-stops' (holding one string at pitch and pushing anoth- er in pedal-steel fashion) without the other strings going out of tune. I can pound out the big chord like Brian May, then bend the B-string at the 15th fret a whole step and all the strings are in tune. And, of course, flutter is not an issue with my setup.

"I adjust the pivot screws down until the plate is flat on the body, use .010"-gauge strings, and three springs with enough pressure on them to bend one whole step on the B-string before the bridge moves (I use three springs for a setup with .009" strings, too). I can still use the tremolo (without upward pull, of course), because I just want a little old-style vi- brato sound anyhow.

"The arm of our bridge is stainless and thinner than the Gotoh, Floyd, or Wilkinson, which allows for a softer feel than you would think because it flexes before it actually moves the bridge. So real- ly, I set up a two-point like a vintage Strat—when I use the tremolo, the bridge tilts forward onto the front bevel, and returns completely to the guitar's face.

"Even though the bridge is not really floating, I use it because I like its sound. It has a steel block, and even though it adds 4.5 ounces to the weight of my guitars (which  bums me out), it's worth it for the tone it pro- duces. I especially prefer the construction and shape of the witness points (string contact points) on Fishman's sad- dles. Each saddle is hard and polished, and there's an initial contact point before the saddle's witness point. This was intended to create equal pressure on the six individual piezo elements in the power bridge. Though our bridge has no piezos, I think there's a benefit to that initial contact point anyway, because it provides the exact same string angle to each saddle.

"Until the Fishman Powerbridge was avail- able we had been using the Gotoh 1055 two-point bridge from Allparts. It has the Wikinson push- in, unthreaded arm, and better saddles than some others I've tried. I do like this bridge, and will use  it if a customer requests it. However, I have a com- plaint with bridges that use 'powdered metal' stain- less saddles, or any other saddle with a ball-milled groove for the string. In my opinion, the powdered metal process leaves a somewhat gritty feel for the string to catch on, and a ball-end mill cutter leaves a rounded bowl shape where the string heads to- ward the saddle peak. The high E- or B-strings have a tendency to roll up the side of this hollow during a heavy string- bend which, to my ear, can produce a sound  similar to fret buzz. We often found it necessary to polish off the roughness in the saddle slots before even putting the bridge on."—*Tom Anderson, New- bury Park, California*

THE FLOYD ROSE LOCKING TREMOLO SYSTEM

Ibanez is a good guitar for demonstring setting up a locking tremolo system because many of the world's greatest rock guitarists and hard-diving tremolo users play Ibanez models equipped with the EDGE Floyd Rose-liscensed tremolo system. I talked to Jim Donahue, Director of Quality Control and R & D for Ibanez Guitars in the United States, at his office in Bensalem, Pennsylvania. A 16-year Ibanez employee, Don- ahue first worked in the repair and setup shop,  where he set up thou- sands of Floyd Rose Locking Trems. If you can set up and adjust the Ibanez EDGE, built after the original Floyd Rose design, you'll be able to handle any other locking tremolo.

I asked Donahue how the EDGE differs from the lower-profile Ibanez tremolos, such as the LO-TRS and the LO-PRO EDGE.

"On the low-profile models, the fine tuners are lower, more parallel to the top, and less in the way. You can palm the bridge with less chance of the strings going sharp, and your forearm has more freedom. The EDGE, however, because the fine tuners angle upward more, allows for far more up-pull than the other models; because of the up-pull, we install a Block Lock to keep the springs from popping loose during heavy up-pull. The EDGE models have a different feel and sound than the others, too. The LO-PRO EDGE also has the Block-Lock because it too has more up-pull than other Ibanez tremolos (not as much as the EDGE does, though). The LO-PRO has good up-pull because the body cavity is routed deeper on models equipped with it.

TIGHTENING A LOOSE EDGE TREMOLO ARM

Note: *If the tremolo arm of your EDGE or LO-PRO EDGE tremolo feels loose (which only happens after much use), your Ibanez dealer can supply you with nylon pressure clips that will make the arm work like new. Ibanez supplies*

an extra set of clips with each new instrument, and Donahue recommends replacing the entire arm after a couple of years.

CHANGING STRINGS

"Unless the guitar is dirty, the fretboard needs cleaning, or either the bridge or nut needs maintenance, if you change strings one at a time and tune to pitch, you'll keep the tremolo in balance. I prefer to remove the pressure pads at the nut because I don't like fishing strings through them.

■ Shim the rear of the tremolo to raise it forward until the strings slacken, and to keep the tremolo from dropping into the body rout (important on the EDGE because if it drops, you can't access

the string-clamp lock screws). For a shim I use one of two what we call 'fuzzy sticks'—common wooden paint stirrers with felt wrapped around them. One is two paint sticks glued together and measures 1/2" thick; the thinner one measures 1/4". I've seen a product called the Tremolok Gripmaster, a plastic shim with rubber padding, that serves this purpose. I've even used a 9-volt battery in a pinch, jammed into the tremolo cavity.

■ Remove the locking nut's pressure pad for the string you are changing, detune the string, loosen the string-stopper screw at the bridge, and remove the string.

■ I start the string at the peghead by running the free end through the tuning post. Let the ball end fall where it may, you'll clip it off soon.

■ Run the string under the retainer, up and through the nut, and down to the string-stopper screw and firmly tighten it.

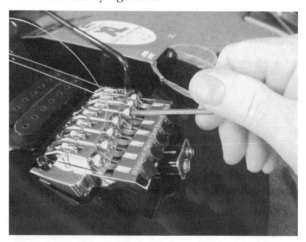

■ Back at the headstock, use enough slack string to lift the string over itself as you make a wrap around the post and start to wind. As the string winds around the post, the second wrap goes under the string and locks it.

■ Remove the fuzzy stick, tune the string to pitch, stretch it a couple of times, and lock the nut. Finally, cut off the excess string (and the ball end). For me, the fewer winds around the post, the better.

■ Put the fuzzy stick back in, change the next string, and so on."

SHIMMING THE LOCKING NUT

Note: *I describe locking nuts, and how to shim them, on page 37. However, Donahue has a couple of inside tips to share:*

"We have two ways of adjusting the height of the locking nut. For both methods, first block with the fuzzy stick, then remove the string retainer bar and the rear nut mount bolts so the nut is loose.

1 Drop the bar farther than the fuzzy stick has it propped, and the nut will be loose enough to raise up as you slide in the shim (you may need to wiggle it into position with a thin tool). Remove the fuzzy stick, the nut will drop back in position, at pitch, and you can check your new action height. If you're happy, retighten the mounting screws and you're done; if not, try again with a different shim or shims.

2 I prefer this second method because I can install the shims easier: Remove the nut's pressure pads to free the strings, and drop the bar enough that you can lift the nut block out from under your strings and set the shim in place easily. Reinstall the rear mounting screws and pressure pads and lock down the strings. Remove the fuzzy stick, you're still in tune, and can check your adjustment."

IS IT OK TO TURN THE HEIGHT-ADJUSTING PIVOT STUDS UNDER STRING TENSION?

"Yes. It won't harm the knife edges at all. However, the EDGE and LO-PRO EDGE have pivot screws with secondary stud lock screws on their bottoms. Always loosen these screws (counterclockwise) and back them into the main pivot screw while making a height adjustment, then retighten the stud lock screws. These stud lock screws are a deluxe feature and provide extra stability and better coupling on these higher-end tremolo models.

SETTING THE FINE TUNERS

"I set all the fine tuners in the middle of their travel, except for the treble B- and E-strings—those I

back out as far as they can go, then screw them back in two turns.

WHAT IS THE PROBLEM IF A FLOYD ROSE WON'T RETURN TO PITCH?

"I know of two main reasons why a Floyd Rose wouldn't return to pitch—one causes the strings to return sharp, the other causes them to go flat. Both problems are easily solved.

WHAT IF THE STRINGS RETURN SHARP?

"If you drop the bridge and the strings return sharp, the locking nut is loose. Wood shrinks when it dries, and the screw threads can lose a little grip on the locking nut. The string tension in front of the locking nut is pulling toward the tuners, and when you drop the bridge, the strings pull the nut toward the tuners and hold it there, causing the strings to return sharp. Pull the tremolo back until the locking nut is back in place, then tighten the two rear mounting screws and the problem is solved.

WHAT IF THE STRINGS RETURN FLAT?

"When strings return flat, it's usually on a new guitar, and it's because the bridge is tilting forward since the brand-new tremolo springs need a little time to stretch in. Usually after one change of strings (a week or so of playing), the problem stops. Today at Ibanez, we prestretch our springs to eliminate this problem. Also, if you've had the guitar for some time, the tremolo springs can stretch to their limit and weaken. In this case, put on a fresh set of tremolo springs.

A PRE-SET BRIDGE SADDLE RADIUS NEEDS NO ADJUSTMENT

"The original Floyd Rose (and other Floyd-licensed versions available today) has a 10" bridge saddle ra-

dius that is reached by having saddles of three different heights resting on a flat plate. Guitars factory equipped with these Floyds (such as the Schaller version, which is a good one) will have the correct radius to match the very common 10" fretboard radius found on many guitars since the Floyd Rose was first introduced. However, if you install a Floyd-style tremolo on a guitar with a different fretboard radius, you must place thin metal shims under the bridge saddles to raise whichever ones need it until the bridge saddle radius matches the fretboard. Then lock the saddles down tight with a 2.5mm Allen wrench.

"In contrast, both our EDGE and LO-PRO EDGE tremolo have the correct 17" (430mm) radius cast into the bridge base. Therefore, we need only one saddle and no shims. The only exception to this is the Joe Satriani Model—it has custom-stamped shims to raise the center saddles to the 12" radius that Joe prefers."

Note: *There is a variation on the Floyd Rose Original Tremolo, called the WDFR, that does not require shims to adjust the saddle radius. It is avail-*

able from WD Music Products. It's the only Floyd Rose-licensed tremolo I've seen with locking saddles that are individually height-adjustable (no shims required). Also, notice the five holes drilled at the front of the sustain block. These give the spring hooks freedom to move at the bottoms of their holes—eliminating any possibility of the hooks hanging up and causing friction. This is a really neat idea!

HOW MANY SPRINGS DOES THE EDGE HAVE, AND SHOULD THE EDGE REST PARALLEL TO THE FACE?

"We make our own springs at Ibanez, and recommend that you use three on all of our Floyd-licensed tremolos, both for .009"- or .010"-gauge strings.

WHY DO PEOPLE SLANT TWO OUTSIDE SPRINGS TOWARD CENTER?

"Some good player (it may have been Jimi Hendrix) probably installed the springs that way, people saw it, and the fad started. There's no good reason, from a spring-tension point of view. However, if you have big hands like guys like Jimi and myself, it's hard to get your fingers in there to install the springs along the tremolo cavity wall. I'll bet that's how it started,"—*Jim Donahue, Ibanez Guitars, Bensalem, Pennsylvania*

In the setup section, we will set up both a Fender vintage tremolo bridge and the Ibanez EDGE floating tremolo bridge. The procedure for both models is the same you would use for all similar tremolo systems, including vintage Fender style and two-point floating systems. See you there!

6 Bolt-on neck quirks

Shifting a bolt-on neck

The 1995 Strat Plus featured here belongs to my friend Luke Berchowitz, who bought it used while away at his first semester in college. During the holidays, Berchowitz brought his Strat home to show me. He had no idea that his parents were going to surprise him with a used, but mint, Fender Deluxe-Reverb amplifier on Christmas morning. Later in the week, Berchowitz brought the outfit to my shop

for a checkup. The amp was perfect, but the Strat needed a setup and the neck needed to be shifted over in the pocket. Many bolt-on-neck guitars suffer from misaligned necks, which cause the strings to fall off the fingerboard to one side. In this case, the strings fell to the bass side of the fingerboard. I had the exact same problem with that '67 Tele that we did so much bridge work on in Step 4—remember that its neck also needed shifting? Berchowitz fixed his neck while watching me fix mine, and he got a lot of satisfaction from doing the job himself. His mother was pleased with him too.

Both necks needed to shift toward the treble side. Sometimes you can see plenty of space between the neck and the body, and there's obviously room to move it over a little. If that's the case,

simply loosen the screws a bit and rest the body on its side. While holding the body with your armpit, gently but firmly force the neck in the direction it needs to go. Then, hold it in position as you tighten the screws.

Berchowitz's Strat, however, showed no gap at all, and my Tele had a gap of .002" between the neck and the wall of the neck cavity in the body—not enough to move very far. We both needed to remove the necks and clean out any dirt or paint in the neck cavities.

Berchowitz took off the strings (leaving them in the body) and removed the neck from the pocket while I did the same. (Notice that he's holding his fingers around the Phillips head screwdriver tip to keep it from slipping off the screw onto

the neck plate or finish.) You may have to gently pry the neck out of the cavity because the painted surfaces of the neck and body cavity stick to each other after time.

Often, a tightly fitted pickguard will shrink around the end of the neck and hold it in place, like on the Strat Plus in the picture (this is not Berchowitz's Strat Plus). Notice how much plastic I scraped away from the pickguard overhang to give the neck a little breathing room?

If you're alone and have no one to hold the body for you while you gently pry the neck from the pocket, lay the guitar on its back on a padded tabletop. Hold the body with your forearms as you use both hands to pry the neck upward and out of the pocket. Or, lay the guitar face down and pry the body from the neck. The latter method makes it difficult to see what's happening with the fit, and you must be careful not to chip paint. If the job daunts you, have a professional remove the neck for you, then take the guitar home and clean up the pocket yourself as we do here.

Berchowitz filed off some thick paint that had rolled over the edge of his guitar and into the corner of the cavity that the neck would bear against when forced toward the treble side. If he hadn't removed the paint, the pressure from shifting could have popped finish off of this delicate wall, or even worse, cracked  the wood. When I file paint around any routed area, I make all the file strokes carefully and deliberately, going in only one direction (the direction in which the file's teeth cut)—not back and forth. Back strokes chip paint off. You should file toward the inside of the cavity, away from the painted edge.

The Tele needs some more work. With a file, I removed a good amount of paint from the bass-side cavity wall, the bottom, and the same thin lip of the cutaway as on Berchowitz's guitar. Several thick bumps of paint in the cavity bottom were acting as a shim in the pocket, creating a gap that guaranteed a poor fit and lousy coupling of the neck to the body—the most important connection on a bolt-on-neck guitar!

NECK MOUNTING SCREWS
NEED CLEARANCE THROUGH THE BODY

While reinstalling the neck into the body, Berchowitz had trouble pushing the neck mounting screws through the body's four clearance holes. In fact, they tightened into the body as well as the neck. I prefer to see clearance holes drilled through the body for the screws to pass through before they thread into the neck with a good strong bite. When a Fender guitar is new, the screws pass through with a snug but clean fit. However, in humid climates, the wood can swell enough to grip the screw threads.

Or, as in the case of a Danelectro DC3 I'd just purchased, it appeared that the manufacturer did not drill any body clearance holes. The factory builders must have used only one drill bit to assemble the neck and body—drilling straight through from the back and into the neck like carpenters fasten drywall to a stud! The screws threaded deep into, rather than passing through, the holes in the body and were hot when I removed them—friction

caused by an undersized hole that can easily cause a screw's head to twist off. Waxing the threads lessens the chance of breaking off a screw head during installation or removal, but choosing the correct drill sizes, and using clearance holes, is best. I fixed my Danelectro while Berchowitz fixed his Strat Plus.

Fender puts wax on the screws when it first installs them so they'll thread in easily. However, the wax often picks up paint, excess buffing compound, and sawdust (especially as

the screws are removed). You don't want to reinstall that dirt into the neck holes, so we both cleaned our threads with a wire brush.

Then, using a #19 (.166") drill bit and drilling

through from the painted backside, we cleared the dirt from each guitar's four mounting holes and passed the screw threads through them several times to dust them out.

The neck on Berchowitz's Strat, a 1985 model, had a date stamped on the end in addition to a dated sticker on the bottom of the neck heel. Therefore, there was no need to leave the adhesive paper on the bottom of the neck. The smooth paper and gummy adhesive let the neck shift even with

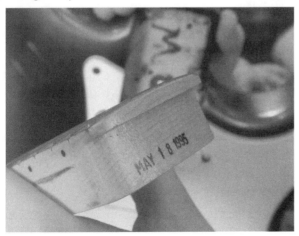

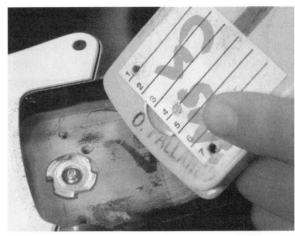

the screws tight. We scraped off the paper and cleaned off the sticky glue residue with lighter fluid. This photo gives you a view of the Micro-Tilt neck adjusting screw in the neck cavity—it bears against a metal plate mostly hidden under the piece of paper.

After we cleaned up the neck cavities and screw

clearance holes, we lightly waxed the screw threads before reinstalling the necks. Here Berchowitz shifts the neck upward toward the treble side as he tightens

the mounting screws. Both necks lined up perfectly and sat much more firmly in their pockets, and we went about setting them up.

SHIMMING A NECK IN THE POCKET: FENDER'S MICRO-TILT NECK ADJUSTMENT

With a bolt-on-neck guitar, you often must slightly shim the neck in the pocket to raise or lower the action as you adjust the bridge. Not every guitar needs this, but some do. In Berchowitz's case, the job was easy thanks to the Micro-Tilt. During a setup, with strings on and tuned to pitch, you can slightly loosen the screws and raise or lower the neck with an 1/8" Allen wrench through the hole in the neck plate, then retighten the screws—an almost instant adjustment.

On a guitar without a Micro-Tilt, you must remove the neck from the cavity and add a shim either at the front end of the cavity (to shim the neck in the direction of the strings and raise the string height, which requires lowering the bridge); or at the rear of the cavity (to tilt the neck away from the strings and lower the string height, which requires raising the bridge). Fender has always used specially made, brick-red fiber shims at the factory. I've seen many a Fender with these shims installed.

My complaint with a single shim like this, or with the Micro-Tilt adjustment, is that it leaves a gap between the neck and body cavity and impairs coupling. In time, because the gap leaves the last 3-1/2" of the neck unsupported, the pull of the screws and the string pull on the neck can cause a kink or warp to develop in the upper fret register (the last eight frets)—causing the strings to note out and the frets to buzz.

TAPER THE SHIM(S)

The best shims are full-pocket neck shims like the one that came from the Fender Custom Shop on my Jazzmaster. It's not easy to make such a thin, delicately tapered wedge of wood (it runs from .040" to zero across 3 inches). Instead, try staggering sever-

al shims along the bottom of the cavity for support, as shown below. Either method is better than using a single shim, which creates a gap.

STAGGER THE TAPER

Choose your thickest shim height and make a shim about 3/8" wide that lies across the end of the cavity. File a tiny taper on its front edge. Then, rest a straightedge on the shim and at the zero point, and fill in the space with several more 3/8" wide shims thin enough to slide under the ruler. These shims could be layers of paper or wood superglued together, or you can whittle, file, or sand shims from any thin scraps of solid wood. Once you make the shims and have them

in place, mark their locations and lightly glue them in place so that when you replace the neck they don't shift. This support is probably as good as the full shim—maybe that slight space even adds a special tone!

You really won't know if you need to shim your guitar's neck until you begin a full setup (full setups begin on page 108). Most guitars don't need a neck shim. If you can set your guitar up with the saddles and pickups adjusted neither too high nor too low, you don't need a shim.

Threaded neck mount inserts

Something to consider, although not for a vintage piece, is to have a repair tech install Vintique's threaded steel inserts in the neck. This is a not a do-it-yourself task, in my opinion. These inserts accept machine screws of the proper length and help the neck fit exceptionally tight in the pocket and couple well. I would certainly think about using these on new work (such as when assembling a replacement neck on a body—

especially one that had never been drilled). If you take your guitar apart to travel, this neck mounting system makes a lot of sense. Bill Kirchen does it all the time with his late '50s Telecaster (see Kirchen's setup on page 113).

Feitenizing a bolt-on neck

By the time you finish this book, you'll know Buzz Feiten (below) almost as well as I do. Feiten tries everything, and anything, in search of better tone (read about the Buzz Feiten Tuning System beginning on page 100). Feiten has impressed me more than any guitarist I've heard—not only for his playing, and he's as good as anyone, but also for his

intelligent approach to studying the guitar and tinkering with it for the past forty years. He is a damn good guitar tech, and does more of his own work than most guitarists I've met. If Feiten likes something, I am bound to try it out.

"Normally," says Feiten, "a shim in the neck pocket is used to increase neck angle (occasionally you will find a shim at the front to decrease neck angle). About ten years ago I had a Telecaster that was really thin sounding, so in desperation (and on a hunch) I stuck a piece of .008" rigid vinyl under the front edge of the neck pocket.

"I'd noticed when messing with the guitar one day that when I loosened all the neck screws slightly and let the neck tilt upward, away from the front of the neck pocket (and then retuned to pitch), that the bottom end and volume of the guitar increased dramatically. Therefore, I decided to stick something in there to hold that new angle. I happened to pick up a scrap of rigid vinyl that was lying on my partner Greg Back's workbench—the vinyl did exactly what I wanted it to do. Now I do this as a matter of routine to all my bolt-on-neck guitars.

"I think that the neck and body each have their own resonant frequencies, and by separating them slightly with the vinyl you allow each to resonate somewhat independently. In addition, a slight change at the front edge of the neck pocket creates a big change in action and bridge height—the geometry changes. I know that Ramirez classical guitars have a 'negative,' or 'reverse,' neck angle—the neck is high, not pitched back, and the bridge is low. It's my opinion that this makes them sound better by increasing the volume and altering the low end in a way pleasing to me, and I believe the principle is the same for an electric guitar."—*Buzz Feiten, Los Angeles, California*

I asked my friend Tom Humphrey about Feiten's remarks regarding Ramirez and negative neck angle. Humphrey is a classical guitar builder and maker of the revolutionary Millennium guitar—which has a radical, negative neck set.

"I think when Buzz describes an increase in volume and a change in the low end," says Humphrey, "that possibly what he's hearing is an overall change in the timbre of the instrument. The trebles will get fatter, however, on an acoustic guitar the timbre of the bass will rise unless the soundboard is simultaneously thinned.

"It doesn't surprise me that his experiment produced results that were pleasing to him. When you raise the timbre, you are rearranging the partial tones. Therefore, the quality of the sound changes. Timbre is what makes a Martin a Martin, and a Gibson a Gibson, [and a Humphrey a Humphrey—*Dan*]. Put simply, timbre is the quality of a sound that distinguishes it from other sounds of the same pitch and volume. It's the distinctive tone of an instrument or a singing voice."—*Tom Humphrey, classical guitar builder, Gardiner, New York*

Feiten's idea will certainly stir up some controversy, but it can't hurt to try it out as long as the threads in the neck's screw holes are healthy. I stabilize neck screw holes by dribbling water-thin superglue into them, followed quickly by a pipe cleaner to suck up any excess. The superglue hardens the threads, which formed when the factory originally installed the neck mounting screws. When the glue is dry (a minute or two), I lightly coat the screw threads with beeswax, which "chases" the threads and makes them crisp.

I can't agree with Feiten on principle because he is saying that a bad neck-to-body connection is better than a good one. This is exactly the opposite of what many of us believe, and it's certainly the opposite of the method of smaller builders I know who fit a bolt-on neck in the pocket to extremely close tolerances and with great tone transfer.

"Let me qualify what I've said," Feiten counters. "I don't want total decoupling, that is not optimal. I want a tight fit on the sides of the neck pocket, and only a slight separation on the bottom. Also, you must install the shim as follows.

"Tuned to pitch, loosen the front screws more than the rear. Loosen the rear screws just a hair, and the front screws just enough to slide in the shim—about 3/8" wide—until it hits the neck screws and

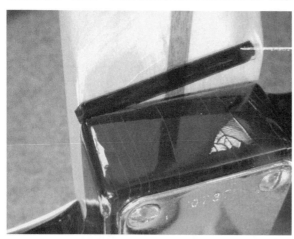

comes almost, but not quite, to the front of the pocket (for good looks). Tighten the rear screws first (be sure you are tuned to pitch), then tighten the front screws until you make firm contact. Don't just insert the shim when you're not tuned to pitch and tighten all four screws the same—that acts as a clamp and creates pressure that can bend the heel of the neck and create a hump in the end of the fretboard

that you don't want. Tightening the screws my way, I don't get any hump.

"Also, I think the gap the shim creates improves the overall acoustic sound of the guitar—unplugged. I'm a firm believer that if a guitar doesn't sound good acoustically, it won't sound good plugged in, either."

I tried Feiten's experiment, and I did hear a difference in tone. However, my questions are these: Is Feiten, in fact, getting the sound improvement from slightly separating the neck from the body? Or is it from the negative neck set? Or is it a combination of both?

For more proof, I would have to run a test wherein I would reroute the cavity at the appropriate backward slant to create a negative neck angle, yet still have firm neck-to-body contact. (This is something that you would want a repair tech to do—don't try it yourself.) For an even better test, I would need to compare two identical guitars (as close as two guitars can ever be) at length: one set up Feiten's way and one with the negative neck rout instead of a shim.

7 Cleaning dirty finishes and hardware

A guitar's finish becomes dirty and hazy because dirt particles land on the finish, which always has a thin film of oil on it no matter how often you clean it. The oil and dirt create a "build" that hardens in time and becomes quite tough to remove. When you remove the dirt, because of its abrasive qualities, you could remove the finish, too (or scratch it), especially on vintage pieces. Vintage guitar finishes are almost always traditional nitrocellulose (furniture) lacquer. The finishes are thin and delicate because much of what makes up nitrocellulose lacquer—including solvent, plasticizers, and cellulose—evaporates over time and the finish loses thickness. Thirty or forty years of wear, cleaning, and polishing also weakens the finish. That's why using the right cleaning technique is important—not only on vintage guitars, but to keep new guitar finishes in good shape and from wearing out prematurely.

However, I believe that dryness and brittleness are part of the reason old guitars have killer tone. So, if you clean and polish a new guitar regularly, it might look good but may not sound as good as guitars that are polished only occasionally. After thirty years, the finish of a regularly polished guitar is less likely to be dry and brittle, because the finish will absorb polish and remain softer. Some automotive polishes are formulated to soften, brighten, and rejuvenate a finish—I do not use that type of polish on guitars. I dry polish my guitars somewhat regularly (or use the moist-breath treatment described below), but liquid polish (with the right polish) only occasionally.

New guitar finishes, as well as finishes on older guitars that have been maintained, are easy to clean. No doubt, there are any number of cleaners on the market that can do the job. However, I'm picky about the cleaners I'm willing to use on a guitar's finish—new or used. Normally only some parts of a guitar are dirty, and the dirt quickly comes off with spot cleaning followed by dry polishing with a soft, clean rag. The following list describes cleaners that I use, in the order that I often use them. There is no one way to clean a finish—it depends on the dirt and what is holding it to the finish. Always start with the least-invasive cleaner.

■ Moist breath: My first strategy when cleaning any finish is to blow my hot, moist breath directly onto a finish (or hardware), then immediately rub the finish with a soft, clean rag or paper towel. Often that is as far as I need to go, especially for spot cleaning or hardware.

■ Saliva: Used only as a spot cleaner and sparingly on the tip of a rag, saliva often removes dirt that all other cleaning agents won't.

■ Deionized water: Available from chemical supply houses and hospital suppliers, deionized water is so pure that it doesn't even conduct electricity! Normal water has either a negative or a positive charge, and would actually repel dirt if the charges were the same. Deionized water has no charge. It's hungry to pick up any ions, positive or negative, that contain the various minerals and other particles that make up dirt. Deionized water does a much better job absorbing and removing water-soluble dirt than tap water. Use it sparingly on a clean rag only dampened—not wet—with the deionized water. I buy mine from VWR Scientific, part number VW 3234-4. Cost: $13.00 per gallon plus shipping.

■ Warm water: In the absence of deionized water, substitute warm water. Again, sparingly on a clean rag.

■ Murphy's Oil Soap: At times I will use a touch of Murphy's Oil Soap to loosen stubborn dirt. I add it in small amounts to warm water and use it sparingly on a clean rag dampened with the soapy water.

■ Liquid cream polish. Cream polishes also are called "polish/cleaners," because they shine as they clean. As a general rule, if the liquid is a light tan cream, it's a cleaner formulated for removing heavy oxidation. It also leaves a good looking, "polished" surface.

If the liquid is a white cream, it's a polish that will clean a not-too-dirty finish and polish it to a finer degree than the tan cleaner. If you clean a dirty finish with tan cleaner, you could go over it with the white polish to get the best shine. Brands of liquid cream polishes have come and gone on the market. You should make sure that you find a brand that does not contain silicone. However, stay away from automotive polishing compounds, which can be harsh. No matter what brand of liquid cream polish/cleaner you try, be sure to test it on a small area first (or on a guitar that you don't care about).

■ Naphtha (lighter fluid): Naphtha is a good oil, grease, and oxidation film remover. Used sparingly—and quickly—it will not harm lacquer. (Don't leave a naphtha-soaked rag sitting on a guitar's finish.) Naphtha is not likely to harm any of the modern polyester and polyurethane finishes, which seem impervious to most solvents. For a greasy finish or oily film, naphtha is my first choice. Follow it with any of the previously mentioned cleaning methods.

No matter what type of cleaning method or product you're using, be sure to use only clean, soft rags. Some of my favorite sources are well-used (and cleaned) baby diapers, T-shirts, and flannel—all 100 percent cotton, of course.

Once I've tried the water and soap-based methods listed above (including saliva), if the dirt still won't budge I try liquid polishes or naphtha. If the finish is intact—without "checking" (the thin cracks old instruments and furniture finishes often have)—I will use either. If a guitar's finish is checked, I use the moist-breath treatment first because it won't hurt anything, and then naphtha since it has no color, and the cream polish as a last resort (both used sparingly).

Note: *Any liquid will "blush" a finish if you leave a pool of it on the guitar. Blush is the whitish-blue haze you might see on the finish of an old tabletop after someone leaves something wet on it. A blush usually will go away once the water, which the finish absorbs, dries, and evaporates.*

Also, avoid polishes or cleaners that contain silicone! Beware of silicone when you're guitar shopping, too. Many music stores use ArmorAll, which contains silicone, to keep guitar cases looking shiny. Lacquer, glue, stain, and other guitar parts just don't get along with the slippery aftermath of silicone. Subsequent repairs to an instrument exposed to silicone will be a hassle, and it requires the skill and chemicals of a professional to remove.

Beware of soft finishes!

Have you ever sat in an old, wooden-armed chair and felt the gummy surface sticking to your skin? That's a soft finish, and it can happen to a guitar, too. There are natural plasticizers (triglycerides) in your body that transfer through the skin—especially your hands. Lacquer breathes, allowing moisture and certain chemicals such as polishes, cleaners, and plasticizers to migrate through. The plasticizers go right through the finish and make the wood their home. Once a finish has softened, there's no cure except to allow it to completely air dry, and even then it may never truly be hard again. The area of a guitar most likely to suffer from this is the part of the body where you rest your arm when playing, although it also happens to the neck or any area that contacts your skin. It's most common on dirty, neglected guitars, because the oxidized dirt acts as a lid, holding the plasticizers down in the finish. If your axe suffers from these symptoms don't try to rub, clean, or polish it away—you'll just make it worse. That's a job for a pro, and often the diagnosis is not good.

Cleaning technique

Take a small section of a clean, dry rag and fold the corners into the center. Bunch the corners and loose parts into your palm, so that your fingers and thumb are pinching the rag into a ball shape.

This ball of cloth is a good tool for cleaning and polishing your guitar's finish. Use it with polish, naphtha, or water, or use it clean and dry.

A TYPICAL CLEANING SCENARIO

Fog up an area with the moist-breath treatment, then quickly polish off the dirt. If the dirt doesn't transfer to your rag or if a haze remains, follow with a rag dipped lightly in naphtha, since it breaks down grease and sticky residue. Try a small area and see if it works. If not, follow with a rag barely dampened with water (it's a toss-up which to start with—naphtha or water). If the dirt transfers

to your rag, give the whole instrument (or the area to be cleaned) a light wiping. Whether you're using naphtha or water, the rag should be damp—not quite dry, even—not wet. Follow all of those steps before switching to a polish or cleaner. The top of the Les Paul in the photo was filthy around the areas most difficult to clean (the toggle switch, pickups, etc.). I used deionized water first and removed much of the

dirt, then switched to naphtha to remove what the water left behind. Naphtha is an especially good cleaner for plastic pickup covers and plated metal hardware. I followed with liquid polish—you can

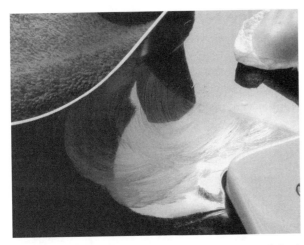

see the dirty haze that the polish and rag lifted away—leaving a shiny surface behind. What naphtha or water won't remove, the polish or cleaner will.

Note: *Naphtha, and most liquid polishes, are petroleum products and you should wear plastic gloves and safety glasses when using them. Work in a well-ventilated area and keep away from sparks, electric heating coils, or open flame.*

USING POLISHES: EXPERIMENT AND WORK IN SMALL AREAS

Always test a small area or an area that doesn't show (under a tailpiece or pickguard). Sometimes I even remove a tuner to test a product on a finish. Once you're satisfied with your test, follow the product's instructions, which usually will advise you not to cover a larger area than you can polish off within a reasonable amount of time. Some polishes are supposed to harden before you remove them, some aren't. I don't like to let a polish harden to a haze that's too dry, because it seems as if I'm waxing a car—I don't want to shine the dirt, I want to soften it and remove it!

With naphtha or cream polish work small areas at a time (no larger than 4 square inches to 6 square inches). As the dirt starts to loosen, pick it up with your rag using a quick, upward twist of the wrist. When one side of the rag is dirty, switch to a clean part; otherwise, you'll put the dirt right back on the finish. Remember, the finish, rag, and dirt all are warm from the friction of rubbing, which allows the dirt to either lift away from or return to the finish. Another cleaning trick is to move the dirt to an edge, where you can pick it up more easily.

Work in particularly small areas on the dirtiest

parts of your guitar—cutaways; where your arm or leg contacts (if you sit and play); the butt-end, where a guitar may rest on a bandstand; and the back of the neck. Cover your fingertip with a rag to work these areas. In these photos, I am using liquid polish to remove heavy dirt and oxidation. This 1952 Telecaster may never have been cleaned, and I only cleaned a small area to show its owner (Jim Weider) what it could look like. The part of the cutaway to the right of the dark smudgy area is an "after" shot. In the second shot, I'm using my fingertip and a rag—with white liquid polish—to clean the rest of the cutaway. I quit after removing this much oxidation from the very front end of the body where the neck rests in the neck cavity—to go further might have removed the finish itself.

The back of the neck was very dirty and didn't feel good—especially right behind the nut. Before cleaning, I could have sworn the neck had been cracked and repaired, and told Weider so. He said it had never been broken. He was right—the dirt had built up in a ridge that looked like a break. After cleaning, the "break" was only a worn lacquer area.

USING NAPHTHA (LIGHTER FLUID) TO REMOVE OIL

People often squirt oil where they shouldn't or onto tuner parts that aren't meant to be oiled. The oil soaks into the wood and softens it—sometimes causing the screws holding the tuners to the peghead to lose their grip in the wood. The same black '78 Les Paul we've been following throughout the book was so dirty that I removed the tuners to clean the front and back of the peghead. In the course of cleaning, I

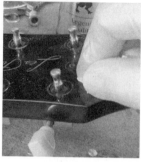

switched from water or polish to lighter fluid to remove excess oil that built up under the tuner bodies and wicked down into the sidewalls of some of the tuner mounting holes drilled in the peghead.

After sponging the oily areas with paper towel dipped in lighter fluid, I dried the areas repeatedly with clean paper towel and left the areas to dry for

an hour. Meanwhile, the film of oil on the tuners had picked up hair and dust, and the tuners themselves were wet with oil. I used cotton swabs dipped in naphtha

to clean the tuners thoroughly, and wiped them completely dry with paper towels.

I then switched back to cleaning and polishing with the white cream polish. The thin layer of

white cream dries almost as soon as it's applied, so I went back over it with a clean rag only seconds after applying it—removing dirt and polishing the lacquer at once.

Cleaning hardware

I illustrated a lot of heavy-duty hardware cleaning beginning on page 43. For more routine hardware and for preventative maintenance, I use most of the same cleaners listed above for finishes. The exceptions are plain water and soap. I also sometimes use cream polishes that are formulated especially for metal. I don't think metal polish is much different from finish polish, but I suspect that metal pol-

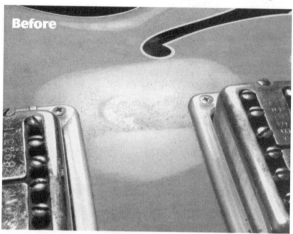

Before

After

ish has something in it that leaves a protective coating on metal. That coating probably isn't good for lacquer. So, I may clean metal with a guitar polish, but I wouldn't clean a finish with metal polish! While using liquid polish to clean dirt from the worst areas of this 1968 Gretsch Nashville (under the pickguard is always a grungy place), I decided to clean the pickup surrounds and the crusty, gold-plated covers that were starting to corrode.

Gently remove the covers, I used a screwdriver tip to pick up most of the steel wool particles that were magnetized and clinging to the polepieces (if you use steel wool on an electric guitar, protect the

pickups from the residue). Next, I used masking tape to pick up whatever wouldn't cling to the screwdriver tip. The covers were only starting to corrode, which was good because you cannot remove cor-

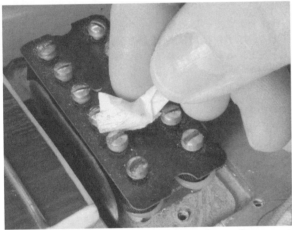

rosion. It actually is metal plating that salty sweat has eaten away. You can clean corrosion though, along with the parts of the plating that have oxidized only with dirt. I used a cleaner, a polish, and naphtha on these covers. Afterward, I coated the plating with some automobile wax to protect it (sometimes I spray them with lacquer).

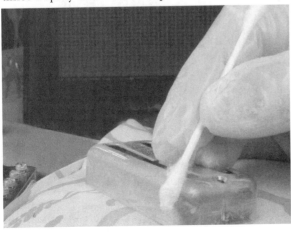

8 Setting the intonation and tuning your guitar

Setting a guitar's intonation is the process of adjusting the bridge saddles under each string to a fixed position so that the guitar plays as closely in tune as possible. It is the last adjustment you make in the setup process. If you do the best setup in the world, yet can't set the intonation accurately, your guitar will play out of tune and all your hard work will be for naught. A guitar's intonation dictates whether or not a guitar can truly be in tune—and drives some guitarists to quit playing the guitar and pick up a horn or keyboard.

The strings on a guitar have two stopping points—the nut and the bridge saddles. The scale-length of a fretboard, and the precise adjustment of the two string-stopping points, determines whether or not a string will have accurate intonation. You achieve standard intonation when any string fretted at the 12th fret is in exact tune with the same string played open. The exact point at which any string's intonation is correct is different for each string and is determined by the following factors.

Fretboard scale length

With a proven formula, guitar manufacturers can calculate any scale length and determine where to place the frets for a guitar to play in tune. Guitar manufacturers select a scale length that they believe will produce the best sound and be comfortable for the player of a particular style of guitar. There are a number of different scale lengths on electric guitars—the most common ones are:

Long-scale guitars have tighter strings, a stiffer action, frets that are farther apart (requiring a longer reach), and more power—particularly in the bass strings—than guitars with shorter scales.

■ 30" (762mm): Fender Baritone guitar ("six-string bass").

■ 28-5/8" (728mm): Tom Anderson Guitarworks.

■ 25-5/8" (651mm): Some Guild models.

■ 25-1/2" (648mm): Fender, Guild, many Gretsch and Gibson archtops, most other builders.

Medium-scale guitars are easier to bend notes on and have a shorter reach for smaller hands. In my opinion, they're more responsive to finger-style playing, yet lack the power in the bass strings of the long-scale guitars. Long- and medium-scale guitars are the favorites of blues players.

- 25" (635mm): Danelectro, PRS, others.
- 24-3/4" (628mm): Gibson and many others.
- 24-1/2" (622mm): Numerous Gretsch models, such as the 6120.

Short-scale guitars have a much shorter reach for small hands. The really short scales, such as a 22-1/2" Musicmaster, are good guitars for kids or beginners.

- 24" (610mm) and 22-1/2" (572mm): Some Gretsch models, Fender Mustang.
- 23-1/2" (597mm): Gibson Byrdland and ES-350.
- 22-1/2" (572mm) Fender Duo-Sonic, Musicmaster, and some Mustangs (rare).

String-length compensation and intonation

Because the strings rise at an angle from the nut to the bridge, they're actually longer than the scale length by the time they reach the bridge. And, because they're raised above the frets, the strings stretch when fretted. Action height, neck relief, string tension and diameter, and fret size play an important role here, too. Also, as the strings head toward the bridge, they fan out to match the fretboard as it widens—another factor that will slightly affect a string's length.

To make up for these factors, you must compensate for the extra string length by adjusting the bridge saddles until the guitar has good intonation. This is why adjustable bridge saddles are so nice—they can accommodate any string gauge, action setting, fret height, and neck setup.

Paul Guy, who builds and repairs guitars in Stockholm, Sweden, has written a book, *The Guitarist's Handbook* (due for publication in Sweden by FUZZ Media AB in the spring of 2001). It is a history of the guitar  and offers players useful tips and information for getting more out of their guitars. It also includes an unprecedented explanation of guitar temperament, compensation, intonation, and tuning, which Guy was generous enough to share here. Here's how Guy describes the need for string length compensation.

"All the strings will end up slightly longer than the theoretical scale length, which is the distance from the nut to the 12th fret multiplied by two. The thicker the string, the more its tension increases when fretted. The lower strings therefore need more 'compensation,' as this small increase in string length is called. A plain string needs more compensation than a wound string of the same diameter, so, in most cases, the high E-string will be shortest, the B-string a little longer, a plain G- a little longer still, the D-string a little shorter than the G-, the A-string a little longer than the D, and the low E- is the longest of all. Heavy gauge strings need less overall compensation than lighter gauges. This is because they are already at a higher tension than lighter gauges, and thus the percentage of tension added by fretting the strings is relatively less than for lighter gauges."—*Paul Guy, Stockholm Sweden*, The Guitarist's Handbook

FINDING THE THEORETICAL STRING LENGTH CENTER AT THE BRIDGE SADDLES

Measuring down the centerline of the neck, between the G- and D-strings, the distance from the front of the nut to the center of the 12th (octave) fret is half the distance of the scale length. Repeat that distance from the center of the 12th fret down to the bridge saddles (still on center), and imagine a line running perpendicular to the center line—this is the spot at which the scale length ends, and where the center of the bridge saddle theoretically should fall. As a general rule, if I center my long ruler on the fretboard (between the D- and G-strings) and measure from the nut to the bridge, the actual scale length (say it's 25-1/2" [648mm]) will need approximately 1/8" to 3/16" of compensation—plus or minus 1/32".

COMPLETE THIS CHECKLIST BEFORE ADJUSTING YOUR GUITAR'S INTONATION

You can set your intonation accurately only if you've correctly made all the adjustments detailed in this book up until this point. Here is a brief checklist of those adjustments, in the order you should make them, before you set the intonation:

- The frets are level and crowned to the center so that the string intonates on the center. (Take your guitar to a repair tech to have the frets dressed.)
- You have adjusted the truss rod for desired fretboard straightness or relief.
- The bridge saddles have the correct radius, and

you have set the string height so that it coordinates with the nut height and the neck adjustment.

■ You have filed the nut slots to the front edge take-off point, and the overall nut height is in harmony with the truss rod adjustment and the string height (i.e., the strings are not too high over the 1st fret, because that would cause them to note sharp).

■ Set your pickup heights. (You don't have to adjust the pickup height to set intonation, but it's part of the setup, and if the pickups are too close to the strings they may pull the strings out of tune.)

■ Install new strings 24 hours before setting the intonation. Stretch them several times, retuning each time, then let them settle in. Then set the intonation, wait another 24 hours, and check it again. The intonation can change overnight (the strings usually go flat), and you may need second and third minor adjustments before the intonation is perfect.

TYPES OF ELECTRONIC TUNERS

The equal tempered scale on a guitar fretboard divides the octave into twelve exactly equal semitones of 100 cents each (1 octave = 1200 cents). "Cent" (some pronounce it "sont") is the unit of measure. Only expensive tuners can tune within one cent. You don't necessarily need one-cent accuracy, but the average person can hear within two cents against a reference pitch.

If you want to explore the fine points of pitch adjustment, as Buzz Feiten does with his Buzz Feiten Tuning System (BFTS, described on page 100), you need a tuner with a one-cent window. Until KORG introduced the DT7, the only tuners capable of such accuracy were the more expensive tuners used primarily by piano tuners and professional repair shops. Professional electronic tuners cost anywhere from $700 to as much as $1,000 or more and can read and display a note instantly in "real time." Most inexpensive tuners need time to sort the note being played from among eighty-eight possible notes, creating a delay between what you play and what you're actually seeing on the tuner.

Buy the best tuner you can afford. If you expect to own many guitars and plan to set them up yourself, consider owning a professional tuner. They are far more accurate than inexpensive tuners. Some tuners that have worked for me are pictured, starting from the least expensive to the most expensive, with both the retail and discount catalog prices.

Sabine Chromatic Tuner ($69/$50): Reading within approximately five cents, this tuner is good enough for playing in a band and setting acceptable intonation. The LED display is dependable, and the tuner senses the note being played (you don't need to press a button to select a note). You can read the LED display on a dark stage.

Boss TU-12H ($109/$80): This tuner has a three-cent window and a needle that moves smoothly and comes to a stop. It also senses the note being played.

Korg DT7 ($120/$85): KORG designed this new tuner for Buzz Feiten. I prefer this to both of the above tuners. If you own a guitar with the Feiten system, you'll want this tuner because in addition to the chromatic setting it has built-in Feiten settings for electric guitar, acoustic guitar, and electric bass. It has a one-cent

window, a very steady LED display, and the tuner senses the note being played. On the Feiten setting, the tuner reads nearly in real time because it is programmed to exclude all but six notes (E, A, D, G, B, E). I recommend this for anyone buying a new, relatively inexpensive tuner.

Campbell PST-2 ($525): The PST-2 is a good professional tuner with much going for it. It has a tenth of a cent window; two programmable channels; real-time sam-

pling; regulated power supply (it's immune from household current variations); a crystal oscillator that gives a stable, constant source frequency; and it's a true strobe. This is a good tuner for the professional shop or serious do-it-yourselfer.

Peterson AutoStrobe Model 490 (approximately $659): I've used the Peterson 490 since it came out and have been pleased with it. It reads within a tenth of a cent, and is used by many professionals. Also, Peterson just introduced a $300 strobe tuner, the VS-1, with capabilities that

match the more expensive tuners. Finally an affordable strobe tuner for the average player!

For playing out, I mount my KORG DT7 tuner on a flat piece of wood screwed to the top of my Tone King Imperial am-

plifier. I strap the tuner to the board with a Velcro strap (although I plan on supergluing Velcro to the bottom of the tuner and to the piece of wood).

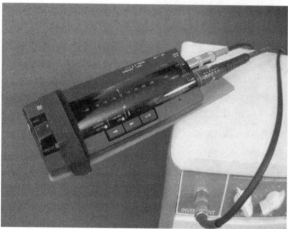

MOST PLAYERS SET INTONATION AND TUNE TO THE "ATTACK"

Before setting intonation or tuning a guitar, you must decide which part of the note you're tuning to. When you pluck a string, it rises instantly to its "transient peak" (it may even go slightly sharp), then drops, or decays, to the "dwell" tone. I call tuning to the transient "tuning to the attack," and tuning to the dwell "tuning to the decay." You must decide if your playing style benefits from tuning to the attack or to the dwell. A light-touch, low-action, light-string player may be better off setting the intonation to the decay. However, I suspect that most players set intonation and tune to the attack.

My tuning mentor, Buzz Feiten, recommends tuning to the attack—using a soft attack on the E-, B-, and G-strings, and a firmer attack on the wound strings. Using his signature KORG DT7 tuner, Feit-

en doesn't mind if the tuner reads a tiny bit flat of the green "in tune" display. "You never want the light to go into the sharp zone," Feiten says, "but I don't mind tuning a little flat because I know I'll be playing slightly sharp when I attack the strings—most of us stretch the strings slightly sharp if we use a medium attack or stronger."

SET INTONATION WITH THE GUITAR IN THE PLAYING POSITION

It's important that you adjust intonation with the guitar on its side in the playing position. I sit in a chair so I'm comfortable, and so that the guitar chord running to the tuner isn't jamming into the benchtop. Within easy reach are my adjusting tools (small screwdrivers or Allen wrenches) and a good A 440 tuning fork. Before I use an electronic tuner, I always tune to pitch using my tuning fork to keep my ear in training. Using your ear, a pitch pipe, tuning fork, or electronic tuner, tune each guitar string to A 440 pitch, then set the intonation one string at a time, as follows.

THE MOST BASIC APPROACH TO SETTING INTONATION

■ Play the open string, then with the note still ringing in your mind or displayed on a tuner, play the fretted note at the 12th fret. The two notes should be the same—a perfect octave. A tuner's display should register the octave or your ear should hear it.

■ If the fretted octave note is flat, move the bridge saddle forward (toward the neck), a little at a time, retune, then check the fretted note again.

■ If the fretted octave note is sharp, move the bridge saddle back (away from the neck), a little at a time, retune, then check the fretted note again.

Note: *A variation on the above method is to chime the open string harmonic at the 12th fret and tune the fretted note to match the chimed harmonic. Most experts agree that this is not an accurate way of checking the 12th fret octave. I suggest using the fretted note method explained above.*

THINGS THAT CAN MAKE SETTING INTONATION DIFFICULT

■ Learning to master the right attack on the open string, how to read the rise and fall of the note, and then master the right attack on the note fretted at the 12th fret takes practice. You must learn to attack the string when you are setting intonation in a way that suits the way you actually play the guitar.

■ You must be incredibly accurate when fretting a note while setting intonation (it's nice to be accurate when you're playing too, of course). If you squeeze hard, especially with modern, high frets, you will sharpen a note too much and all your intonation settings will be wrong. If you fret lightly you may get the actual note, but if you squeeze harder when you play you will be out of tune. So you must learn to fret notes, while setting the intonation or when playing, in a way that suits your playing style. Your fretting hand is just as important to your attack as your picking hand.

■ If you have trouble achieving accurate intonation, try lowering your pickups a little (especially the neck pickup). The magnetic pull of pickups that are set too close to the strings can pull a note out of tune—especially when you're dealing with something as delicate as setting intonation.

DON'T CAUSE THE TUNER TO GIVE YOU A FALSE READING

It's natural to keep your fingers on the tuning key as you tune a note to pitch. However, the weight of your hand and pressure against the peghead can move the neck and pull the note sharp or flat. Don't touch the tuning key, or the neck, when deciding if the open-string note is in tune. Drop your hand away from the neck momentarily as you let the note register. Fretting at the 12th fret doesn't normally cause sharpness or flatness because the neck is stable in that area on most guitars. Some guitars, like Gibson's SG, have a great deal of neck free of the body and require more gentle fingering at the 12th fret.

NASHVILLE CATS

Joe Glaser (left in photo) and his fellow repairmen at Glaser Instruments in Nashville, Tennessee, work for some of Nashville's most demanding guitarists, including a host of Nashville's session players. Glaser offered to explain how they set intonation in his shop (one of the earliest Feiten System authorized retro-fit shops).

"We don't rely on the octave harmonic because it is not necessarily in tune with the open string. Since guitars can be in tune in one place and out in another, we attempt to average out the error while identifying areas of playing priority. A string that seems particularly out of tune may need to be replaced, and sometimes all the D-strings in a box will have the same untuneable defect. We tune to pitch, adjust the relief, set the action quickly, check the nut height carefully, set the intonation quickly, then look at the note played gently at the 1st fret. If it is sharp, we know that either the nut is too high, or the string has worn off the leading edge of the nut slot and its take-off point is too far back. This cannot be stressed too much!

"Then we set the final action and set the intonation so that the 7th, 12th, and 19th frets share the same degree of accuracy and error. Still, it doesn't matter what a guitar does on the bench. What counts is what happens when the red light is on or the song begins—when notes are part of a chord, and chords are part of a song, with or without other instruments. We adjust with that in mind.

"We watch the players, looking at where they play on the neck, and how hard they grip—are we dealing with 'white fingernail' grip? We may deal with that by overcompensating the intonation—moving the bridge back, and in a worst-case scenario, shortening the nut-to-first fret distance on certain strings (usually a plain G- or low E-string will get the most correction). A guitarist playing with a piano will be sharp to its bass range and flat to the trebles, since a piano can easily have twenty-five cents of stretch over its range. We may need to take that into account in setting the intonation.

"Still, there is a certain harmonic interference of real life. Thirds will never sound in tune, particularly on the top of a chord. Strings are imperfect, the harmonicity of music is imperfect, as are instruments and player technique. We don't set perfect intonation, we carefully try to make the best of it. That is what I find remarkable about Buzzy Feiten's discovery. Buzzy started with the music, ears first, tuning, tweaking, measuring, retuning, retweaking, remeasuring until he was happy—backward, but so obvious. Not everybody chooses the same tuning solution, but everybody chases the same thing — friendly notes. And remember: the tuner is not in the band!"—*Joe Glaser, Glaser Instruments, Nashville, Tennessee*

LEARN TO TRAIN YOUR EAR

Before electronic tuners came along, and before I could afford a strobe tuner, I set intonation by ear to an A-440 tuning fork that I have had for thirty-five years. Even now, after using a Peterson strobe tuner, I may readjust the tuning until it pleases my ear on my own instruments. I always give customers a perfectly strobe-tuned guitar as a starting point, and hope they will not be afraid to readjust their guitars by ear. Almost all guitar players tweak their tuning after tuning up to any brand of electronic tuner.

Many of today's players grew up with a guitar tuner and never learned to tune without one. That's a shame because they're not getting ear training or learning to trust their ears. They're helpless without a tuner. You should learn to set intonation by ear, without your tuner, if only for the training. Besides, you must train your ear if you want to play with other people.

There's a big difference between playing or practicing alone in your room and playing with other people. Anyone who's spent much time in a band with two guitar players and an electric bass player knows that even if all three tune to the same electronic tuner, they'll each retune certain strings until the sound is pleasing to their ears. Then they'll further fine-tune their guitars until the whole blend is right as a group. Guitars are not as perfect or exacting as a good tuner, and tuners don't have taste, personality, or ears. We retune for the inadequacies of our guitars and ourselves. I seldom pick up someone else's guitar without tweaking the tuning a little bit. The same goes for anyone picking up one of my guitars. And, when you play with a keyboard and guitars, the tuning issues get more complicated. Develop those ears!

Tuning your guitar

Now that you know how to adjust your guitar's intonation, and since we covered all the adjustments that comprise a setup earlier, all you have to do is tune it up and play. Here's some advice from a number of people who I respect on how to tune a guitar. This section is not a casual, easy read. It's a reference section. You could experiment with all of the tuning methods listed in several hours and find the method you think you like, but you'll have to use each method for a while to see if it truly works for you.

PAUL GUY'S TIPS ON TUNING

Here's more from Guy's upcoming book. Note that several of the tuning methods he advises not to use are exactly the ones that guitarists often do use. Thanks, Paul!

"5/7" HARMONICS METHOD—TERRIBLE!

"This method seems to have a strange attraction for many guitarists. Perhaps it's a relic from the beginner stage, when it was difficult to get the harmonics to ring at all. Somewhere deep in the unconscious the impression is formed that the method must be good because it 'sounds so professional,' and was so difficult to learn. Perhaps because it's such a convenient method, and leaves the fretting hand free to tune with, many guitarists cling stubbornly to harmonics tuning, despite the recurrent tuning difficulties it causes.

"All the mystery effectively hides the simple fact that the method cannot possibly work, as all harmonics are pure intervals and the guitar is constructed for the tempered scale. With the exception of the octave and double octave harmonics (octaves are pure in both the pure and the tempered scales), harmonics should not be used for fine-tuning.

"When players use the 5/7 method, they follow these steps:

■ Tune the high (treble) E-string to a reference, and tune the 5th fret harmonic on the low (bass) E-string to the open high E-string.

■ Next, tune the 7th fret harmonic on the A-string to the 5th fret harmonic on the low E-string.

■ Then tune the 7th fret harmonic on the D-string to the 5th fret harmonic on the A-string.

■ Now tune the 7th fret harmonic on the G-string to the 5th fret harmonic on the D-string.

■ Finally, tune the 5th fret harmonic on the B-string to the 7th fret harmonic on the high E-string.

"Many users of this method also delude themselves that the 4th fret harmonic on the G-string should sound the same frequency as the 5th fret harmonic on the B-string.

"A guitar tuned this way will, quite simply, not play in tune. The reason is simple—the 7th fret harmonic on the A-string sounds the note E, the fifth. But this is a pure fifth interval (to be pedantic, an octave and a fifth). The tempered fifth is lowered two cents from pure. The resulting open A note will therefore be two cents flatter than the tempered A we want. The interval between the low E- and A-strings should be a tempered fourth, which is raised two cents from pure. Since the A-string has been tuned two cents flat, the E-to-A interval will be flat by the same amount.

"Two cents isn't much, but when you tune the D-string to the A-string the same way, the D-string ends up four cents flat. When you get to the G-string you will be six cents flat. Tuning the 5th fret harmonic on the B-string to the 7th fret (pure fifth) harmonic on the high E-string leaves the open B-string sharp by two cents. The resulting major third interval between the open G- and B-strings will be eight cents sharp.

"Trying to tune the B-string to the G-string by harmonics will really get you into trouble. The 4th fret harmonic on the G-string sounds the major third of G, which is a B note. But again, this is a pure interval. The tempered third is raised fully fourteen cents from pure. Tuning the 5th fret harmonic on the B-string to the pure third on the G-string will leave the B-string fourteen cents flat. Try it and then compare the 4th fret B note on the G-string to the open B-string—you'll see what I mean. It should be obvious by now that harmonics—other than octaves—are not to be trusted! They are useful for the initial coarse tuning, however, as the fretting hand is free to tune while both strings are sounding. Just don't try to use them to fine tune.

TUNING TO A CHORD—HOPELESS

"Tuning one chord so that it sounds perfect just causes all other chords to sound terrible. In tempered tuning, all chords are slightly out, but all by the same small amount. Remember that the tempered scale is always a compromise that enables us to play all chords and intervals, in all keys, with the same relative accuracy. It therefore follows that there is not one chord on the guitar that tunes absolutely pure. Thus it is a total waste of time to tune the guitar to one particular pure chord and expect it to sound pleasing anywhere else. If you can't swallow these facts, then for your own peace of mind, you're probably better off if you give up the guitar

and get a flute or a sax or something instead. With experience, though, you can develop an ear for even-tempered tuning.

OCTAVE METHOD—EXCELLENT

"Any tuning method using octaves is correct in principle. There are many variations—one way is to tune the open B-string one octave below the 7th fret B on the high E-string, the open G-string one octave below the 8th fret G on the B-string, the open D-string one octave below the 7th fret D on the G-string, the open A-string one octave below the 7th fret A on the D-string, and—you guessed it—the open low E-string one octave below the 7th fret E on the A-string. But we're back to small errors affecting the following strings again. To avoid this, and because tuning errors become more obvious further up the fingerboard, make your comparisons using only fretted octaves between the 7th and 12th frets, and try tuning in this order:

1 Tune the bass (low) E-string two octaves below the treble (high) E-string: With the treble E-string tuned to a reference note, tune the 5th fret harmonic on the low E-string to match the open treble E-string.

2 Tune the D-string to the (in-tune) treble E-string; compare the octave between the 7th fret B note on the E-string and the 9th fret B note on the D-string.

3 Tune the G-string to the (in tune) treble E-string also; compare the octave between the 10th fret D note on the E-string and the 7th fret D note on the G-string.

4 Tune the B-string by comparing the octave between the (in-tune) 7th fret A note on the D-string to the 10th fret A note on the B-string.

5 Tune the A-string by comparing the octave between the 7th fret E note on the A-string to the (in-tune) 9th fret E note on the G-string.

PAUL GUY'S TUNING METHOD

"If you tune all the strings to the same reference string you can avoid a small error on one string affecting the others. For example—I tune the 5th fret E note on the B-string, the 9th fret E note on the G-string, and the 14th fret E note on the D-string, all to the open high E-string (which has been tuned to a reference pitch). Then I tune the 7th fret E note on the A-string one octave below the open high E-string, and the open low E-string two octaves below the open high E-string.

"I then check that the 5th fret harmonic on the low E-string sounds the same pitch as the open high E-string. (Since octaves are pure intervals, we also can tune using the octave and double-octave harmonics—above the 12th, 5th and 24th frets.) I fine-tune as follows:

■ The A-string: Tune the 12th fret harmonic on the low E-string to the fretted 7th fret E note on the A-string.

■ The D-string: Tune the 12th fret harmonic on the A-string to the fretted 7th fret A note on the D-string.

■ The B-string: Tune the 12th fret harmonic on the B-string to the fretted 7th fret B note on the high E-string.

■ The G-string: Tune the 12th fret harmonic on the G-string to the fretted 8th fret G note on the B-string.

"Finally, I check that the 12th fret harmonic on the D-string sounds the same pitch as the fretted 7th fret D note on the G-string. This method has worked well for me—and for many of my customers—for many years. It also is extremely effective at getting the best available results out of a poorly adjusted instrument.

TIPS FOR ANY TUNING METHOD

■ Learn to attach the strings to the machine heads properly!

■ Never try to tune down to a note—first tune below the target pitch, then stretch the string, then tune up to the note to avoid problems caused by the "play" in 99 percent of tuning machines. Make a couple of deep bends (you don't have to actually play the note, just bend to settle tension), then fine tune.

■ Before tuning a string that you suspect is out, check it against both adjacent strings. Many guitarists make the mistake of tuning the wrong string! Oftentimes you think your G-string is sharp when in fact it's the D-string that's flat, for example. I do sometimes, and when I watch other people tuning, it seems to me that they do, too.

■ When tuning a guitar with a vibrato arm, tune the string, give the arm a good shake, stretch the string, give the arm another shake, and fine tune. On the plain strings I also like to bend the string a whole tone a couple of times (somewhere around the middle) before fine-tuning."—*Paul Guy, Stockholm, Sweden*, The Guitarist's Handbook

TUNING ON THE OPEN RANGE, COWBOY STYLE

Michael Stevens of Stevens Electrical Instruments in Alpine, Texas, is one of the world's great electric guitar builders and an avid horseman and cowpuncher. Here's how Stevens tunes a guitar when he's sitting around the campfire or performing at a south Texas dude ranch. Stevens learned this in the Guild of American Luthier's Data Sheets 31-60, sheets 45 and 45-2, author unknown. (The Data Sheets were a collection of guitar and other stringed-instrument-related articles compiled by the Guild over many years, and are no longer in print.)

Tuning the 1st and 6th strings: First, you must be relatively in tune to some source—an A-440 tuning fork, pitch pipe, electric tuner, or a piano on either the low or high E-string. Let's choose the high (treble) E-string as our source string—tune it to the source. Then, tune the harmonic of the low (bass) E-string until it is in pure unison with the source string. When you have properly tuned these two strings with each other, continue as follows.

Tuning the 4th string: Play a harmonic on the (in tune) 6th string at the 12th fret, and as this harmonic sounds, adjust the 4th string until the note E on the 2nd fret is in pure unison. Now you have the open E (1st string), the E note on the 4th string at the 2nd fret, and the open E (6th string) tuned pure. That is permissible because they are octaves.

Tuning the 2nd string: Play a harmonic on the (in tune) 4th string at the 12th fret. As this sounds, adjust the 2nd string (D-string) until the D note at the 3rd fret is in pure unison. As you have used two fretted notes for reference, and as the frets are positioned for tempered intervals, you now have the open 1st, 2nd, 4th, and 6th strings in "equal tempered tuning."

Tuning the 3rd string: As it is easier to adjust a string while listening to a continuous reference tone, you may first try the following. Play a harmonic on the (in tune) 4th string at the 12th fret and, as this sounds, adjust the 3rd string (G-string) until the D note at the 7th fret is in pure unison.

Double check: Now make this check to see if you were accurate and if the instrument plays true when fretted at the 7th fret on the G-string. Play a harmonic on the (now tuned) G-string at 12th fret, and as this tone sounds, play the G note on the 1st string at the 3rd fret. The two tones should be in pure unison. If they are not, either you are at fault with your tuning, the instrument's scale length is inaccurate (at least at the 7th fret), or the string may be bad. Go back to the beginning and carefully check each step up to this point. If the tones are still faulty, readjust the 3rd string until the harmonic at the 12th fret is in unison with the G note played on the 1st string at the 3rd fret. Do not tamper with the 1st and 4th strings, because it is the 3rd string you are trying to bring in tune. When you have the 1st, 6th, 4th, 2nd, and 3rd strings in tune, in that order, continue with the 5th string.

Tuning the 5th string: Play the note A on the (in tune) 3rd string, at the 2nd fret. Listen to this pitch carefully and now adjust the open 5th string (A-string) until the harmonic at the 12th fret is in pure unison. Strike the harmonic at the 12th fret first, then fret the 3rd string. With the harmonic still ringing (move quickly), tune the open A-string with your left hand.

When you follow these steps, the strings will be tuned perfectly to equal temperament. No further tuning adjustments should be necessary.

A QUICK METHOD FOR TUNING A GUITAR

This simple tuning method works well for me.

■ Get the treble E-string in tune to A-440, then tune the open B-string to the open treble E-string—listening to the interval of a fourth. It's easy to hear the fourth in that register.

■ Play the A note fretted at the 2nd fret of the G-string, and compare it to the open treble E-string—you're listening for a perfect fifth interval.

■ Fret the 2nd fret E note on the D-string and compare it to the treble E-string open. Double-check this by fretting the E note on the 14th fret of the D-string.

■ Now tune the 7th fret harmonic on the A-string (an E note) to the open treble E-string.

■ Finally, tune the 5th fret harmonic on the bass E-string to the open treble E-string.

TUNING UP AFTER REMOVING THE STRINGS ON A LOCKING-TREMOLO SYSTEM

Tuning any tremolo-equipped guitar is tougher than a non-tremolo "hard-tail" guitar because the strings and springs counterbalance each other. Tuning one string changes everything, so you have to tune and retune the guitar a number of times until it finally settles in at pitch. As you will see in the setup section, beginning on page 108, tuning and setting intonation while the tremolo is blocked makes sense during a complete setup (when all the strings are removed and the bridge saddles are not intonated properly). Once the setup is correct, you can change strings one at a time and follow the tuning method described next. However, there often are times when you'll be removing the strings entirely. Perhaps you'll remove the bridge, too, to clean the entire guitar and fretboard and maintain the hardware. Tuning all the strings from scratch can take forever, as the tensions of the strings and springs keep fighting each other. In that case, follow the blocking method shown on page 78.

Here, Jim Donahue, Director of Quality Control and R & D for Ibanez Guitars in the United States, describes his method of tuning a well-balanced, locking, floating tremolo system.

"I use the fuzzy stick (see page 78) when changing all the strings at once. I install all the strings at the same time, and with the tuning keys I put enough tension on the strings to roughly hold the bridge in a floating position. Then I remove the fuzzy stick to tune. Here are the steps I follow:

1 First I tune by ear to an A-440 bell or tuning fork. I hit the 5th-fret harmonic on the A-string, and tune it sharp by a half step. (As you move up the strings while tuning, the bridge rises up and the strings go flat. By tuning sharp initially, I eliminate the excess tuning needed to keep up with the flatting strings.)

2 Tune the E-string harmonic to the sharped A-string harmonic.

3 Tune the D-string harmonic to the A-string harmonic, but sharpen it.

4 Tune the G-, B-, and treble E-strings using the sharped D-string as your reference, but by that time they will all be flat again.

5 Go back to the A 440 bell. This time tune the 5th-fret harmonic on the A-string sharp by a full step

6 Do as before (the low E-string, the D-string off the sharped A-string, and on up), without the extra sharping on the D-string this time. You probably will still be a little flat, but close. At this point you can get serious and start to fine tune.

7 When you reach pitch, stretch the strings in a couple of times, retune, and you're there! Install the nut's pressure pads (you may notice a slight sharping on some strings as the clamp squeezes them, but nothing that a tweak of the fine tuners at the bridge can't fix.)—*Jim Donahue, Ibanez Guitars*

IMPROVING INTONATION ON A THREE-SADDLE TELECASTER

Earlier in the book, I mentioned that Vintique's Danny Gatton-model replacement bridge saddles can help you achieve better intonation on a three-saddle Telecaster (see page 43). When I dropped by the *Guitar Player* magazine booth at the winter National Association of Musical Merchants show in Los Angeles in 1998, my friend and fellow author Dave Burrluck was interviewing Jerry Donahue about his method of setting the intonation on a three-saddle Telecaster. Since Donahue is one of the world's greatest Tele players, I eavesdropped and was intrigued by what I heard. Donahue's approach to setting non-angled, vintage-style Tele bridge saddles doesn't rely on mechanically changing the angle of the saddles as Danny Gatton did. Instead, Donahue uses his ear and a unique approach to tuning.

Burrluck later published Donahue's comments in his excellent book, *The Player's Guide To Guitar Maintenance* (Miller Freeman Books, 1998). Burrluck was generous in sharing that knowledge with readers of this book.

PRO'S PERSPECTIVE: TUNING HELL

"The Hellecaster's Jerry Donahue is very particular when it comes to setting up his guitars. Over the years he has developed a very neat method of not only solving the intonation problems of a three-saddle Telecaster bridge, but also, Jerry believes, making any guitar with a six-saddle bridge play more in tune. Here's how he sets up his three-saddle Telecasters.

"Tune all open strings as normal, but set the center bridge saddle so that the G-string fretted at the 12th fret is marginally sharp of its harmonic, which is in tune. (The D-string fretted at the 12th

will therefore be marginally flat of the harmonic.)

"Now, using the tuner, adjust the G-string so that its fretted note at the 12th fret is in tune, effectively flattening the G-string. A root position E-major chord should sound in tune to your ear, with the G-sharp (first fret G-string) slightly flat, but not so much flat that a root-position E-minor chord sounds out.

"Jerry finds that the top strings are usually fairly in tune, but sets the B-string fretted at the 12th very slightly sharp of the harmonic; the top E-string fretted at the 12th, and its harmonic, should be the same.

"On the low E- and A-string saddle, Jerry sets the A-string in tune—fretted at the 12th and the harmonic. Again, he finds the difference here is almost always minimal; he usually flattens the low E-string very slightly anyway."—*Dave Burrluck*, The Player's Guide To Guitar Maintenance

Donahue actually is "stretch-tuning," or tempering, the intonation of his guitar so that it intonates better throughout the range and is more pleasing to the ear. It's Donahue's instinctive and simpler approach to what Buzz Feiten has taken to another level with his Buzz Feiten Tuning System. Here's my report on the BFTS, one of the most talked about guitar advancements in recent years.

BUZZ FEITEN TUNING SYSTEM

A Feiten Family, from left to right: Washburn Centurion CT5BB ("Blackburst"), Tom Anderson GuitarWorks Cobra, Gene Baker HB2.

No doubt you've noticed that I've mentioned Buzz Feiten and his tuning system throughout this book. That's because I'm impressed. I first played a guitar set up Feiten-style in 1998 at Chandler Guitars in Kew, Richmond, England after meeting Chandler at a London music trade show. Charlie Chandler (right), a top United Kingdom repairman, had set up his own Stratocaster this way after be-coming one of the first authorized installers of the BFTS. I didn't spend more than a half hour with the guitar, but my feeling then was exactly the same as today—I love it.

Tom Anderson recently loaned me his personal guitar for several weeks so I could get a real feel for the Feiten system. Shortly after I got to know Anderson's guitar, Feiten and his partner Greg Back visited my shop for an intense four-day retrofit clinic, attended by several repair techs and builders from around Ohio. We all converted our guitars to the

Feiten system, including two hand-built acoustics, a mandolin, a Fender Precision bass, a Fender Stratocaster, and my Gibson Firebird. Everyone went home happy.

Greg Back

Tom Anderson builds all of his guitars with Feiten's setup and, as of this writing, the only major company to utilize the Feiten system was Washburn International. Washburn began using the BFTS on all of its U.S. model electric guitars (and basses) in 1998, including signature models endorsed by Dimebag Darrell, Paul Stanley, Jennifer Batten, and Nuno Bettencourt. Several other great electric guitar makers, including John Suhr and Gene Baker, build with the Feiten system. Some controversy exists over the Feiten system because it's different, and many play-ers are skeptical about it. Here's my take on what it's all about.

Feiten moves the nut toward the 1st fret by a carefully measured amount that relates to the guitar's exact scale length and type. Feiten and his partner Greg Back spent years calculating exactly how much to shorten the fretboards of acoustic, electric, and electric bass guitars. Each guitar type, and each scale length within a type, requires that you remove an exact amount of wood from the end of the fretboard. That amount relates to a measurement calculated for the particular scale length at hand, with a level of accuracy of plus or minus .003". Just moving the nut forward is not revolutionary. Some other builders do it too, knowing that it helps to eliminate sharpness inherent in the 1st position. There has been much literature regarding nut placement available within the trade.

Feiten's system is unique because, after moving the nut forward, he sets the saddle intonation and the tuning of each string differently than you would a "normal" guitar. Feiten uses intonation parameters that he discovered after trying to quantify what he was hearing as a player. When he played in the Bette Midler band, being in tune with the keyboard was important. Whenever his guitar tech handed him a freshly strobed guitar, Feiten immediately would start tweaking it. Eventually he decided to measure that tweaking in order to teach his tech how to tweak it for him. Soon he was moving the saddle around as he experimented with the intonation at the bridge, and recording his findings, until he was satisfied that what he had come up with worked. For other believers and me, the outcome is a guitar that plays more in tune everywhere on the neck.

Some builders and technicians suggest that simply moving the nut is all that's needed to fix a guitar's intonation problems. I tried that and yes, the guitar played in much better tune in the 1st position and up to about the 5th fret. Still, it did not play nearly as in tune—nor was it as harmonious—as when completely "Feitenized." The melding of the notes was not there, and the sweetness didn't come through.

According to Feiten, when you shorten only the nut, "you're just wounding the problem—you have to kill it! Simply moving the nut doesn't solve the problems between the strings—you haven't balanced them against each other. However, if in addition to moving the nut you adjust the intonation offsets properly, the notes and overtones are working with each other, not fighting each other. When you have soundwaves that are fighting each other, it kills the sustain and tone."

Feiten stresses that you must let new strings settle in for 24 hours (after stretching them several times and retuning to pitch) before the adjusting the final intonation. I advise this for setting intonation on a non-Feiten guitar as well.

I'm not suggesting that owners of rare vintage guitars convert their guitars (although I have converted my Gibson Firebird quite happily). I highly suggest, however, that players intrigued by the system purchase any of the excellent low-priced guitars on the market and have a qualified installer Feitenize it (see *buzzfeiten.com* for an installer near you). Or, if guitars by West Coast builders Tom Anderson, Gene Baker, and John Suhr are beyond your price range, Washburn offers Feiten system guitars for as low as $699. You could get a new guitar—and the system—in one fell swoop.

The Feiten system could be a particularly great help for beginning players, because it helps you learn to be in tune and play with others. I'm not the only guitarist sold on Feiten's system. For example, **Steve Vai** and a number of other great players are Feiten believers. Here are some comments on the BFTS

from some of these players and Feiten himself.

Tom Anderson: "It's the most significant improvement in guitars I've ever seen. What else could you do to a guitar that has as big an effect as this?"— *Tom Anderson, Tom Anderson GuitarWorks, Newbury Park, California*

Gene Baker: "Buzzy made a huge breakthough that was right in front of us all these years. He discovered that it didn't matter what you did to the guitar before you played it, it only matters what happens when you actually play it. It's a brilliant break-

through."—*Gene Baker, Baker Guitars, U.S.A., Santa Maria, California*

Paul Guy: "Once you get used to the BFTS, it becomes very hard to even listen to a guitar intonated to standard specs, let alone play one. It's the best thing that has happened to the guitar in the last 400 years!"—*Paul Guy, Paul Guy Guitars, Stockholm, Sweden*

Gary Brawer: "Stu Hamm was in the studio, having trouble playing a part in tune. When I walked in he was literally playing while staring at the tuner. He had me Feitenize his bass right then and there. He stopped the recording, sent me back to my shop, and I gave it to him the next day. It solved his problem completely. Then Buzz's partner, Greg Back, and I Feitenized the rest of Stu's basses."—*Gary Brawer, Gary Brawer Stringed Instrument Repair, San Francisco, California*

Pete Anderson: "Buzz has created the ultimate plane bomber—a huge step in taking the guitar toward its ultimate position. The sweet pitch struggle is most troublesome with multiple bends, not so much for single note bends. If you're playing double-stops or steel-bends as I do, that is the whole

gag. You get to the sweet spots of the notes so easily."—*Pete Anderson, guitarist and producer, Little Dog Records, Burbank, California*

Dave Burrluck: "The Feiten system makes a lower priced guitar sound more expensive. If it only gave me another 2 percent out of my guitar—and it's far more than that—then I am up for it, because I need all the help I can get.'—*Dave Burrluck, reviews editor,* Guitarist *(UK), author of* The Player's Guide To Guitar Maintenance, *and co-author of* The PRS Guitar Book: A Complete History of Paul Reed

Smith Guitars (both from Miller Freeman Books).

Sid Poole (foreground above) with Dave Burr-luck testing out two of Poole's latest creations. Poole, based in Kent, England, is one of the finest guitar builders in the UK...and probably the world!

Joe Satriani: "I tour with two of my Ibanez JS Chrome Boy models. One is in the normal tuning and the other is set up with Buzzy's system. I play

three songs with one guitar and then switch. Buzzy's tuning makes my guitar a little less aggressive sounding—it makes it more sonorous. As I told Buzzy years ago, I was intrigued with the idea of multi-tracking the two tunings together to create an interesting blend. You hear that sound on my *Crystal Planet* and *Engines of Creation* albums."—*Joe Satriani, San Francisco, California*

Buzz Feiten: "I believe that when Satriani says 'normal tuning,' he is referring to tuning the guitar to equal temperament, the standard method for setting intonation. That's the system we have always used when laying out the fret placement for the guitar, and for tuning the guitar, to make the pitch of

every note equidistant from every other note. It was achieved on the guitar to an extent, but we are married to the fret placement. Equal temperament on a guitar exhibits exactly the same problems that it does on the piano—some chords are in and some chords are out.

"Another type of intonation is the 'mean tone,' or 'just' intonation, whereby you tune the guitar for a specific chord or key, and typically a chord tuned that way will exhibit a 3rd that is nine cents flat. 'Just tuning' is what slide guitar players use when they tune (tune the 3rd of a chord nine cents flat). You are using just tuning when you flatten the G sharp in an E-major chord. A 3rd tuned nine cents flat pleases the ear, however the ear will not tolerate a 3rd that is sharp. A 'just-tuned' 3rd on a guitar throws any other chord out of tune that has that string in it because any other note played on that string will consequently be too flat.

"Play a barred A chord at the 5th fret, and then a barred D chord at the fifth. With equal temperament, the barred A chord will be perfectly in tune and the barred D chord will be really sour because the B-string will not be in tune. So we all flatten the B-string to fix that D chord, but then we ruin the barred A chord. This starts the 'chasing your tail around the equal temperament syndrome.' It is impossible to 'tune' around the problems inherent in equal temperament. In a three chord group—simple triads—you can get two out of three notes in tune on a good day, but one of the three will always be out of tune.

"The reason that temperament works on a piano and a guitar is because the ear is very forgiving of pitch adjustment of the so-called perfect intervals—i.e., 4ths, 5ths, and octaves. However, the ear will not tolerate the slightest bit of sharpness in a 3rd, 6th, or a 10th (the so-called imperfect intervals). This is not new information; piano tuners figured out four hundred years ago that stringed instruments must be tempered in order to play pleasantly in tune regardless of key and regardless of chord shape. Piano tuners 'borrow' pitch from 4ths, 5ths, and octaves to sweeten up 3rds, 6ths, and 10ths, and that is what my system does—it brings the overall intonation of the guitar into a much tighter focus. My tuning system gives you pleasant intonation anywhere on the fingerboard, regardless of chord shape, and you are no longer limited by the problems of normal intonation.

"Open tunings, such as DADGAD, open G tuning (DGDGBD), and the open A tuning (the same as open G, but one step higher in pitch), also sound much more pleasant on a guitar with the Buzz Feiten System. For those open tunings, tune to the normal chromatic side of the tuner and you'll be fine."—*Buzz Feiten, Los Angeles, California*

DECIDE FOR YOURSELF

Though many players love it, the Buzz Feiten Tuning System is not for everyone—and only an authorized retro-fitter is qualified to do the installation. You must have a guitar Feitenized by someone trained by Buzz Feiten and Greg Back, or one of their authorized training centers (there is more to it than I had imagined).

Some players don't hear the difference at all, some hear it as a subtle change, and others (myself included) consider it a Godsend. Along with all the positive comment, I also heard some negative reactions. In the course of my research I spoke with several builders and repair techs who either don't feel the BFTS is significant enough for them to change their direction, or they simply don't hear it. However, I have yet to hear a negative comment from a guitar player.

If you're serious about your music, and want the most from your guitar, consider trying the system the next time you need a professional setup—one that entails fret dressing and a new nut.

If you'd like to test the waters, have an authorized Feiten retro-fitter make you a "shelf nut" (below)—one that fits the normal nut slot and hangs out over, and onto, the fretboard. I did this on my

Stratocaster as a test, before actually cutting back the fretboard on my Firebird. Satisfied with the results, I went ahead and gave the Firebird the full treatment. A shelf nut won't harm anything and will give you a chance to decide if the Feiten system is for you (on a guitar that you know well). Expect a shelf nut to be expensive because it's labor intensive.

Also, it may be more difficult to set the BFTS parameters on a some Gibson guitars than it is on a Fender Strat or Tele. This may be especially true on some Gibson models with the original ABR-1 bridge because it is narrower and has less bridge saddle adjustment than the newer, wider, Nashville bridge, and because not all Tune-O-Matic bridges are placed in exactly the same spot.

Now let's move on and set up some guitars!

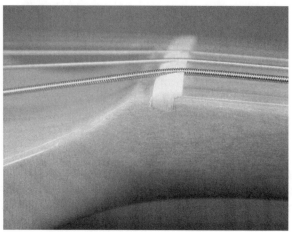

Putting it all Together

Here's where the adjustments detailed in Steps 1 through 8 come together to produce a setup. But before we get started, I'll describe a couple more things that play a role in any guitar's action: fret size and shape and fretboard radius.

Get to know your frets

Every guitar player worries about strings that buzz on the frets. Frankly, some buzz will exist on all guitars because both the strings and the frets are metal. However, technicians try to eliminate as much buzz as possible, and a good setup can be only as good as the guitar's fretwork. You should have a qualified professional perform any necessary fretwork—including accurately leveling and rounding your frets to center—before you start your setup (frets that are not rounded to center can throw off the intonation). This is also a good time to have a repair tech make a new nut if your guitar needs it.

When you take your guitar to a repair tech for fretwork, it's a good idea to know what you want the tech to do—a fret leveling or a refret? Listed below are some common fret heights and widths that you can compare to your guitar as well as to the measurements listed in the setups that follow. These measurements will help you determine if you need to have a pro refret your guitar completely or simply level your frets and "dress" them by rounding (crowning) them to center. Or, even if your frets are in good shape, you may decide to try frets with a different height or width. The measurements below reflect my opinion of fretwire size ranges for both new and worn fretwire (worn fretwire has been leveled and dressed a number of times). To measure fret height, refer to page 5 and use the fret gauge included at the back of this book.

■ High frets measure from .048" high to .055" high and range in width from .080" to .115". My favorite fretwire is .048" high x .093" wide, because it leaves room for plenty of future fret levelings and is great for bending strings.

■ Medium-high frets measure from .046" high to .041" high and range in width from .078" to .108". Vintage Gibsons often had .043"-high frets when they were brand new.

■ Medium-low frets measure from .041" high all the way down to .034" high (a .034"-high fret usually is a result of wear and fret leveling). They may

be as wide as .103" (Gibson), as narrow as .078" to .080" (Fender), or anywhere in between. Any frets leveled or worn below .035" high, although they can be leveled and dressed, will never be easy to bend strings on, and, in my opinion cannot produce satisfactory results for most blues players.

■ Low frets measure from .034" high down to .025" high and can be any number of widths. Normally frets this low have had many fret levelings and should be replaced. I know of only one guitar that came with new wire this low: Gibson's Les Paul Fretless Wonder, circa 1960. Some players, like Leon Rhodes, prefer low frets because they prefer low action, like to play fast riffs and chords, and don't bend strings (check out Rhodes' setup on page 120).

FRETBOARD RADIUS

There are about six common, popular fretboard radii (the arch across the fretboard width). With the exception of compound radius fretboards, most fretboards have a cylinder-shaped radius and fall into these categories:

■ 7-1/4" (184mm): This is the vintage Fender fretboard radius and is great for playing chords. However, even with well-dressed frets, unless the strings are set high the extreme arch will cause the treble E-string (and sometimes the B-string) to "fret out" (buzz or become dead). To illustrate this, set a straightedge on a cylinder, skew it, and see how it rocks.

Note: *Notice in the setups that feature a fretboard with a 7-1/4" radius that many players raise the treble E- and B-strings higher than the G- and D-strings. In essence, they're flattening the bridge saddle radius more than the fretboard radius. The increased string height allows the player to bend strings without fretting out, producing a strong, clear tone. Many players keep the bass E- and A-strings high, too, for a strong open bass-string attack.*

■ 9-1/2" (241mm): Introduced on Fender's American Standard and used since the 1930s on Gibson guitars. It's flatter than the vintage radius, allowing clean string bending with relatively low action.

■ 10" (254mm): A 10" radius became popular with the Floyd Rose locking tremolo system (the Floyd's nut is machined at a 10" radius). A 10" radius allows you to make easy bends with a low-action setup.

■ 12" (305mm): This is the common Gibson electric radius, though you'll find many Gibsons with a 9" radius or 10" radius. A 12" radius is good for blues bends—one reason many blues artists play Gibsons.

■ 14" (356mm) to 16" (406mm): These flatter fingerboards are popular on most "rock" guitars (and used on numerous vintage Gretsch guitars). Allows for low action and easier string bends than others.

COMPOUND RADIUS FRETBOARDS

Guitar fretboards also may be shaped in a compound, or cone-shaped, radius. The radius of a compound fretboard is most pronounced at the nut, flattens progressively along the fretboard according to a mathematical formula, and continues to flatten until the final radius is reached at the bridge saddles. Usually a compound radius flattens enough in the upper register that string bending is easy and buzzing is not an issue. If you don't like playing guitars with radii in the 14" to 16" range, you might not like a compound radius fretboard.

All Warmoth Guitar Products necks have a compound radius, and many private builders and repair techs use the compound radius, too. However, you cannot convert a guitar into a compound radius during a refret if the existing radius already is too steep or if the fretboard isn't thick enough. It can be an expensive job, too, if the tech must remove pearl inlays.

STUDY YOUR FRETBOARD

A fretboard—even one made in a factory—often has more than one radius along its length. It may even flatten progressively, creating somewhat of a compound radius. If your fretboard's radius changes along its length, next time you have a guitar tech replace your frets you may also want to have the tech change the radius so that it is consistent (I usually choose whichever radius predominates). The tech may be able to convert the fretboard into a compound radius. Discuss your options in detail with any repair tech before leaving your guitar for repair.

Setup checklist

When I set up a guitar, I usually go through two sets of strings unless the guitar comes in with brand-new strings. I need one set to use while I work, and a second set just prior to setting the intonation (because strings wear out, kink, or break during the work). These are the steps I follow during a setup:

✔ Remove the old strings and clean the fretboard. Also, clean any dirty hardware or fix it if it's in bad shape.

✔ Install fresh strings (if necessary).

✔ Make an initial truss-rod adjustment and check that the frets are level. If they aren't, take them to a repair tech for a fret dressing or refret before moving on.

✔ Set the action—the string height over the frets. The action determines the guitar's overall feel and playability. You set the action by adjusting the neck, the bridge saddle height, and the nut height. Raise or lower individually adjustable bridge saddles (Strat, Tele, etc.) with the appropriate Allen key or screwdriver, or in the case of Gibson bridges with bridge saddles that are not individually adjustable, raise

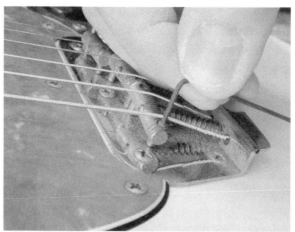

or lower the overall saddle height with the thumb-wheels at each end of the bridge (lower photo opposite page.)

✔ Clean and polish the guitar's finish and check the hardware again.

✔ Adjust the pickup polepiece height.

✔ Install the final strings.

✔ Set the intonation, play the guitar, and stretch the strings (firmly but gently, and without kinking them) to remove any slack. Wait 24 hours to check the intonation again. Make any final intonation adjustments.

Setup measurements

There are no steadfast rules for setting up a guitar, and in the end a good setup is done by eye and feel as much as with measurements. However, measurements are important enough for me to include the specialty tools at the back of this book. punch them out and use them!

With the setups that follow, I provide measurements in fractions and decimals, and include the metric equivalent whenever possible. At times, I provide measurements in decimals and millimeters only. A fraction to metric conversion chart on page 133 provides common guitar setup measurements up to 1/4" (6.4mm).

I often refer to one-half of a sixty-fourth of an inch, or combinations thereof—a much smaller measurement than is printed on most fractional rulers. In those cases, I'll combine a decimal with a fraction. For example, I will denote "three and one-half sixty-fourths" as 3.5/64". Any measurements smaller than one-half of 1/64" are listed in decimals and millimeters. Following are descriptions of the measurements I include with the setups in this book.

■ **Scale:** The guitar's scale length.

■ **Radius:** I provide both the fretboard and bridge saddle radii.

■ **Frets:** I check the distance from the fretboard to the tops of the frets, their width and height, and the shape of the fret crowns (tops) and ends. I list the fret width first, then the height. For example, a Gibson "jumbo" would read .103" x .044" (2.6mm x 1.1mm).

■ **Strings:** I record the string gauge and, when possible, the string brand. Unless otherwise noted, the strings are GHS Boomers or D'Addario EXL (both brands are nickel-plated round wound strings).

■ **Relief:** I check for relief or straightness, usually on the D-string, using the methods shown in Step 2, Truss Rod Adjustment. Measure relief anywhere from the 5th fret to 12th fret, or wherever the gap from the bottom of the string to the top of the fret is greatest. A neck with relief—because it is concave—may appear to have a hump or rise at or beyond the 13th fret. Strings may buzz in this upper register because, since relief is a valley in the center of the fretboard, the upper register frets are on the uphill slope.

■ **Action:** This is the string height over the fretboard. To make this measurement, I capo the strings at the 1st fret to eliminate the nut height as a factor. Then, at the 17th fret, I measure the clearance from the bottom of the string to the top of the fret. At times I measure at the 12th fret—in which case I make a note of it.

■ **Nut:** I measure the gap between the bottoms of the outside E-strings to the top of the 1st fret.

■ **Polepiece height:** While pressing the outside E-strings at the last fret, I measure the clearance from the bottom of the outside (bass and treble) E-strings to the top of each pickup's outside E-string polepieces.

How They Do It: A Guide to the Great Setups

Following are the setup details of some great manufacturers, players, and individual guitars. I'll begin with two role models for setting up most tremolo-equipped, solid-body guitars: a Fender Stratocaster with the vintage tremolo, and an Ibanez RG570 with the EDGE locking tremolo.

Fender's ten-step setup

My favorite setup is Fender's factory approach to setting up guitars. In my opinion, this is the only way to set up a guitar with a tremolo (including locking tremolos). While Fender completes all of the setup steps except for setting the intonation on the production line, I set the intonation during the setup because the tremolo is blocked in a static position.

String the guitar before getting started. Here, I used a set of .010"s. Pre-set the intonation by positioning the saddles farther back than needed so that when you set the intonation later you will need to move the saddles forward, leaving any kink in the string behind the saddle, not in front of it. To do

this, set the treble E-string saddle so that its string take-off point is slightly longer than the exact scale length of 25-1/2" (set it at 25-9/16"). Then, set the remaining saddles farther back in a slanted line toward the bass E-saddle. This should cause your strings to intonate flat and require a forward adjustment when you set the intonation. In the photo is a bridge with the intonation set very accurately (it's one of Eric Johnson's favorite Strats) with a set of .010"s. Use it as a model when you move your saddles back.

1 With no tremolo springs installed, and the claw quite loose (1" from the wall), string up lightly but not to pitch. Use .009"s on the American Standard (factory recommended) .010"s for vintage models.

2 With the strings still somewhat slack, place a wedge of wood between the tremolo sustain block and the rear wall of the tremolo cavity to "block" the tremolo sustain block. The wedge will hold the bridge in a static position once string tension is applied. My wedge for a vintage tremolo measures 2" wide x 1" deep, and tapers from 1/2" to 1/4". (To block an American Standard bridge, use a block measuring 2-1/2" x 1", tapering from 5/8" to 7-1/16", as shown on page 67.) Start tuning to pitch and the string tension will hold the block in place. Shove the block in or pull it out until, when measuring at the back edge of the bridge plate, the clearance between the bridge plate bottom and the face of the guitar is 3/32" for a vintage bridge (page 61), or 1/8" on the American Standard bridge. Tune to pitch, stretch in the strings, and tune to pitch again.

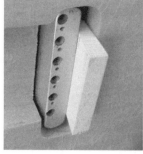

3 Install a capo at the 1st fret to eliminate the nut height as a factor.

4 Make sure the neck adjustment is suitable. Here, my shop-mate Elliot John-Conry uses the "string-as-a-straightedge" technique. If the neck adjustment is not suitable, you'll have to undo (then redo) your string tension and block setup to access the truss rod on necks that adjust at the body end. Or, as

Fender and most pros do, you can pre-adjust the neck to fall within your specs for straightness or relief before beginning this setup. Generally that means some tension on the rod so that the neck is straight or slightly back-bowed. The straight neck will pull into a little relief, and the back-bowed neck will pull straight. For the record, Fender factory specs call for .012" of relief at the 7th fret.

5 With the capo still on, adjust the bridge saddles to set the string height at the 17th fret to match the factory specs (3/32" to 1/8" clearance from the bottom of the string to the top of the fret). Setting each string this way automatically gives you the correct bridge radius.

6 Remove the capo.

7 Check the nut height and lower it to the height you want if it's not there already (factory specs are on the high side, with as much as .022" on the bass E-string and .018" on the treble E-string—still too high for low action).

8 Adjust the pickup height. Pressing the outside E-strings at the last fret, measure the gap from the bottom of the strings to the top of the polepieces. On all three pickups, Fender sets the bass side polepieces at 1/8" and the treble side polepieces at 3/32". I'll detail variations on this later.

9 Play the guitar and check for buzzes, relief, and straightness.

Option: *Although Fender doesn't do this, I suggest that you set the intonation at this stage because it's easier in the blocked position before the tremolo springs and string tension become involved.*

10 Adjust the spring claw equally from side to side until the springs take over the string tension and the block falls out. I clamp the guitar neck in my vise with the face up and work from below so the block

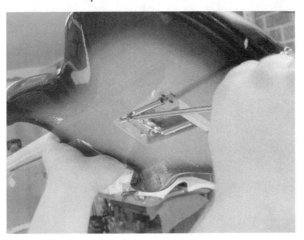

truly falls the instant the springs take over. Without a vise, hold the guitar face up while you tighten the claw. When the block falls, you're done!

Lubricate the friction points!

Rene Martinez, Stevie Ray Vaughan's great guitar tech (see page 63), points out that it's good to make a habit of lubricating all the moving parts of a tremolo system: the mounting screws at the bridge plate, any contact point (witness point) on the bridge, the nut slots and saddle peaks, the point at which the tremolo springs attach to the tremolo sustain block and claw, and under the string trees. This will help the tremolo return to pitch. Good lubricants are petroleum jelly, pencil lead, powdered graphite, spray Teflon (spray the Teflon into a cup, let the solvent evaporate, and dab the remaining lubricant onto the friction points). Rene Martinez uses a mixture of grease and powdered graphite which he calls GraphitAll™ (see list of suppliers).

Note: *I set this Strat up twice—once with .010"s and once with .009"s. See page 60 for photos of the two different spring claw and tremolo spring adjustments.*

Action setup for the Floyd Rose licensed locking tremolo System

I selected two Ibanez models—a six-string RG570 and the seven-string RG7620. Direct from the factory, both of these guitars had identically low, buzz-free, setups, but they have different EDGE tremo-

los: the RG570 has the original EDGE tremolo, and the RG7620 has the LO-PRO EDGE (see page 78 for a description of each).

Before starting this setup, use the old strings (if they are the correct gauges) and measurements listed below to check that the neck adjustment, nut height, and string height are correct. It's hard to raise or lower the bridge once the tremolo is blocked in the Fender style, as we are about to do.

Ibanez factory specs

Most guitar techs measure action at the 17th fret. At the factory, Ibanez measures action at the 12th fret with the strings open, looking for 5/64" (2.0mm) and 1/16" (1.6mm) of clearance for the bass E- and treble E-strings, respectively. Ibanez's relief specification is .010" (.25mm) at the 7th fret, and the pole-pieces are set from 5/64" (2.0mm) to 3/32" (2.4mm). However, the action of these guitars was considerably lower—the necks were adjusted perfectly straight and had low action without buzz.

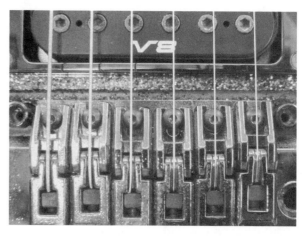

IBANEZ FACTORY SPECS

SCALE	25-1/2" (648mm)	
RADIUS	17" (430mm) at both the fretboard and bridge	
FRETS	.115" x .055" (2.9mm x 1.4mm)	
STRINGS	D'Addario nickel wound, .009"–.042"	
RELIEF	Adjusted perfectly straight and played clean	

	BASS SIDE (LOW E)	TREBLE SIDE (HIGH E)
NUT	.016" (.4mm)	.006" (.15mm)
ACTION		
At 17th fret:	3/64"+.004" (1.2mm)	1/32" (.8mm)
POLEPIECE HEIGHT		
Neck pickup:	1/16" (1.6mm)	5/64" (2.0mm)
Middle pickup:	1/8" (3.17mm)	5/64" (2.0mm)
Bridge pickup:	1/32" (.8mm)	5/64" (2mm)

ADJUSTING THE TREMOLO LEVEL AND SETTING THE INTONATION

With the action set approximately at the above specs, follow these steps. Adjust the action to your individual preferences now if they're different than the above specs.

■ Install your fuzzy stick, Tremolok Gripmaster, or 9-volt battery as described on page 78 and remove the strings.

■ With the strings removed, before restringing, be sure that the bridge saddle lock screws are installed in the front row of holes in the bridge base (there are two holes for each saddle to allow for a wide range of adjustment). The photo shows a perfectly tuned EDGE tremolo on the Ibanez RG570. The measurement from the nut to the front edge of the D-string saddle is 25". Knowing that, and studying the photo (top right), loosen the saddle lock screws and slide each saddle a little farther back than the actual intonation point you expect to hit. This will allow you to creep up on the saddle's exact intonation point with the string pressure pulling the saddle forward, rather than you having to pull the saddle backward against the string pressure.

■ Loosen the spring claw—an inch of clearance will hold the screws into the wood, yet put a small amount of pressure on the bridge. You need enough spring pressure to pull the knife edges into their posts and keep them there with the bridge propped by the fuzzy stick. As with the Fender method above, I don't want the springs to have any major effect on the setup until it's finished. I don't remove the EDGE springs because the Block Lock (described on page 78) holds them into the tremolo. On tremolos without a Block Lock, I would take the springs off just as I did with the Fender Strat.

■ Install new strings. Since I'm starting from scratch, there's no need to change strings one at a time. Install all of the strings at once into their respective pressure pad lock screws at the rear of the saddle. Clip off the ball ends, run the strings under the loosened nut pressure pads, under the retainer bar, and straight into the tuner post holes. I turn the

tuner post holes so that they are in line with the strings, which is the exact opposite of the way Jim Donahue installed strings on page 78. Donahue simply was changing strings on a bridge that was set up and intonated correctly—in that case changing strings one at a time is the way to go because it keeps the tremolo in balance.

■ With the locking nut's pressure pads loose (use a 3mm Allen wrench), tune each string almost taught, but loose enough that finger pressure can push them down easily. When you release the fuzzy stick, the tension of the tremolo springs' pressure will pull the tremolo level or even down into the cavity—this is when you insert the wood wedge and block the tremolo. The bridge must sit parallel to the face, and with all the angles the EDGE has (viewed from the side), it can be hard to tell when it's parallel—especially the LO PRO EDGE, which may sit just below the surface. Use the thin rectangle of steel (the end of the knife edge) that protrudes through the bridge body at each end as a guide.

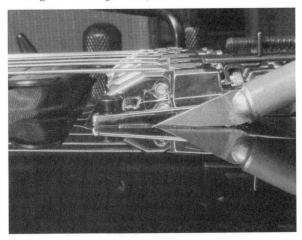

■ For this wedge I followed the wedge-fitting technique on page 67, then fashioned the final one from a hardwood scrap measuring 2" wide x 1-1/4" high, tapering from 9/16" to 7/16".

■ Tune each string to pitch, tighten the nut pressure pads, and stretch the strings. Unclamp the nut and repeat the process to break in the strings. Do this two or three times, then unclamp the nut and tune carefully to pitch. Always tune and set the intonation in the playing position!

■ If you moved the saddles back, all of your strings should be slightly flat when you compare an open string to its fretted note at the 12th fret.

■ Some techs will detune each string as they set its intonation, loosen the saddle lockdown screw, and move the saddle backward by hand. Others will "dump" the entire tremolo forward to slacken the strings entirely, quickly unlock the saddle lockdown screw, and move the saddle by pushing it with a finger or an Allen wrench. Either method will allow

you to move the saddle. However, I prefer to keep the strings at pitch and use the KEY Intonation Tool for Floyd Rose tremolos to adjust each saddle's intonation.

■ The KEY slides in at an angle on the EDGE tremolo, grips the back edge of the bridge, then drops level with the body with a hook that grabs the string stopper screw and keeps the saddle from moving under string pressure.

Note: *Tape a piece of thin, stiff cardboard (a manila folder works perfectly) to the guitar's face so that if the KEY happens to touch the top it won't scratch the finish. On the LO PRO EDGE, which is designed differently and has short string lock screws, techs use a different version of the KEY. It also braces*

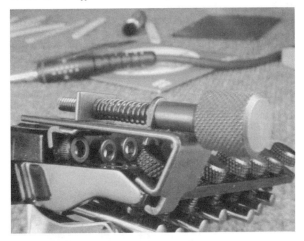

against the back, but reaches forward to grab the string-stopper screw.

■ Tighten the KEY's lead screw until it firmly holds the Allen-head string stopper. Next, slightly loosen the saddle lockdown screw with a 2mm Allen key (detune and push the string aside if you need to so that the Allen key won't mar the string), and slowly loosen the KEY's knurled knob counterclockwise. The saddle will slide forward a bit. Make sure that the string is still at pitch, then check the 12th fret octave, fretting the string accurately. Once the fretted octave note is in tune, retighten the saddle lockdown screw. Retune to pitch and that saddle's intonation point is set.

■ To remove the KEY from the EDGE, I use a 3mm Allen key to push down on the string stop-

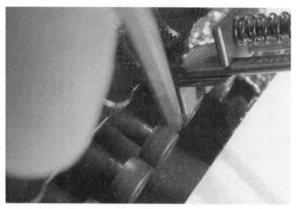

per bolt as I twist the KEY up, out, and free from the string stopper screw. The KEY for the LO PRO removes without this little maneuver.

■ Set the intonation for every string the same way. It is far easier to set the intonation with the tremolo blocked like this. Unblocked, even the weight of the KEY can alter the pitch!

■ Tighten the spring claw, as we did with the Fender Strat, until the block drops free.

Note: *On the six-string Ibanez RG570 pictured, with three springs and .009" to .042" strings, the claw measured 5/16" from the cavity wall on the bass side and 11/32" on the treble side.*

A COUPLE OF WING-NUTS:

John Borchard (left) and Jim Smailes are great guitarists and have played together for years in two of the best bands in Athens, Ohio: the Wingnuts and Real Billy Jive. Borchard and Smailes have lots of guitars and play them all. They're both excellent players, and several of their favorite guitar setups appear throughout this section.

Telecaster masters

Here are tips on Tele setup from several of my favorite guitarists: Jim Weider, Bill Kirchen, and local legend Jim Smailes—long-time veterans of the Tele scene.

Jim Weider replaced Robbie Robertson in The Band around 1985 and played with the group until it disbanded in 1999. Weider's band, The Honkytonk Gurus, recently released the album *Bigfoot* on EKG Recordings, and his instructional videos are available from Homespun Tapes (*Get That Classic Fender Sound* is Homespun's top seller). When Weider visited me,

he also brought: a '52 Fender Telecaster ("Old Yeller"), a '54 Fender Esquire with a vintage Gibson Firebird pickup in the neck position, and a 1960s Silvertone Danelectro slide guitar.

JIM WEIDER'S FAVORITE FENDERS '54 FENDER ESQUIRE, '52 TELECASTER

JIM WEIDER'S 1954 FENDER ESQUIRE		
SCALE	25-1/2" (648mm)	
RADIUS	Untouched, vintage 7-1/4" fretboard radius with a 12" radius at the bridge	
FRETS	.107" x .048" (2.7mm x 1.2mm), with ball-shaped fret ends way out on the fretboard edge so Weider can do E-string pull-offs without falling off the edge	
STRINGS	D'Addario: .010", .013", .016", .026", .036", .048"	
RELIEF	.011" of relief at the 11th fret	
	BASS SIDE (LOW E)	**TREBLE SIDE (HIGH E)**
NUT	.020" (.50mm)	.010" (.24mm)
ACTION		
At 12th fret:	3/32"+.004" (2.5mm)	5/64"+.004" (2mm)
POLEPIECE HEIGHT		
Neck pickup:	6.5/64" (2.6mm)	5.5/64" (2.2mm)
Bridge pickup:	3/32" (2.4mm)	2.5/64" (1.0mm)

JIM WEIDER'S 1952 FENDER TELECASTER		
SCALE	25-1/2" (648mm)	
RADIUS	Resurfaced and refretted many times, with a 10" fretboard radius and a 12" radius at the bridge	
FRETS	.107" x .048" (2.7mm x 1.2mm), with ball-shaped fret ends way out on the fretboard edge so Weider can do E-string pull-offs without falling off the edge	
STRINGS	D'Addario: .010", .013", .016", .026", .036", .048"	
RELIEF	.008" of relief at the 9th fret	
	BASS SIDE (LOW E)	**TREBLE SIDE (HIGH E)**
NUT	.020" (.50mm)	.010" (.24mm)
ACTION		
At 17th fret:	5/64" (2mm)	4/64"+.004" (1.7mm)
POLEPIECE HEIGHT		
Neck pickup:	1.5/64" (.6mm)	1.5/64" (.6mm)
Bridge pickup:	7/64" (2.8mm)	3/64" (1.2mm)

TWANGIN' WITH BILL KIRCHEN

B

Bill Kirchen, one of the kings of twang, played with the original Commander Cody and the Lost Planet Airmen band. Now Kirchen fronts the trio Too Much Fun. With Johnny Castle on bass and Jack O'Dell on drums, they tear the house down. Kirchen's played the same '50s Telecaster since his early twenties.

BILL KIRCHEN'S TELECASTER

	BASS SIDE (LOW E)	TREBLE SIDE (HIGH E)
SCALE	25-1/2" (648mm)	
RADIUS	Years of refrets have resulted in a compound radius, starting at a vintage 7-1/4" (184mm) at the neck and arriving at 12" (305mm) radius at the bridge saddles	
FRETS	Medium width (.093"), high (.047") wire	
STRINGS	Kirchen switches back and forth between D'Addario XL115s (.011" to .049") and XL110s (.010" to .046")	
RELIEF	.020" at the 10th fret—that's major relief!	
NUT	.022" (.58mm)	.011" (.28mm)
ACTION		
At 12th fret:	5/64" (2.0mm)	5/64" (2.0mm)
POLEPIECE HEIGHT		
Kirchen's Tele has Joe Barden blade-style pickups (full-length blade polepieces instead of individual polepieces). I didn't measure the blades, but they were close to the strings and sounded like a Tele ought to.		

This Tele has a Vintique heavy-gauge, stainless-steel bridge plate with three brass bridge saddles angled, Danny Gatton-style, for good intonation. Kirchen has flipped his Vintique control plate and harness 180 degrees, putting the toggle switch (minus a knob) at the bottom end. The volume and tone pots are reversed so that they operate in the normal Telecaster fashion. Vintique makes a Danny Gatton

A

model (A) control plate with the toggle switch knob bent downward—out of the way of the player's picking hand, and a Kirchen model (B) with the switch knob bent upward for easy switching in Kirchen's reverse-plate.

Kirchen had the first Electrosocket Tele jack mount that I'd seen. The jack pushes in the hole and fastens tight with two screws, and is a permanent solution for the no-

toriously loose Telecaster input jack cup. Kirchen also uses Vintique's machine-thread neck mount inserts that screw into the neck and accept machine screws (see Step 6, Bolt-on neck quirks, page 81). These inserts make for great coupling, keep the screw holes from wearing out, and enable Kirchen to take his Tele apart for overseas gigs.

JIMMY SMAILS' 1975 TELE CUSTOM (THREE-BOLT NECK STYLE)

Smailes uses a relatively stiff, high action on his Tele—his setup plays very clean with great tone.

JIMMY SMAILS' 1975 TELE CUSTOM (3-BOLT NECK)

	BASS SIDE (LOW E)	TREBLE SIDE (HIGH E)
SCALE	25-1/2" (648mm)	
RADIUS	7-1/4" (184mm) fretboard, 10" (254mm) bridges	
FRETS	Replaced with .110" X .048" (2.8mm x 1.2mm)	
STRINGS	.010" through .046"	
RELIEF	.009" (.23mm) at the 9th fret	
NUT	.025" (.63mm)	.012" (.3mm)
ACTION		
At 17th fret:	5/64" (2.0mm)	1/16"+.004" (1.7mm)
POLEPIECE HEIGHT		
Neck pickup:	1/32" (.8mm)	1/32" (.8mm)
Middle pickup:	3/64" (1.2mm)	3/64" (1.2mm)
Bridge pickup:	1/16" (1.6mm)	3.5/64" (1.4mm)

Settin' up to slide

Here is Jim Weider's slide setup on a 1960s Silvertone Danelectro with "lipstick-tube" pickups. Weider's repair technician, Dominic Ramos, enlarged the cutaway of this Silvertone for better access. He also installed string ferrules so the strings load from the rear, as on a Tele. The tone improved immensely. The Silvertone's Tele bridge looks like a sawed-off shotgun, with the vintage brass bridge saddles and Weider playing it in open D-tuning.

Jim Weider's Slide Setup (1960s Silvertone)

SCALE	24" (610mm)	
RADIUS	16" (406mm) fretboard, 20" bridge (508mm)	
FRETS	Original, narrow frets, about .030" (.78mm) high. When playing slide, Weider doesn't fret enough to need higher frets.	
STRINGS	.012", .015", .019", .032", .042", .054"	
RELIEF	.020" (.5mm) at the 9th fret	
NUT	The strings become higher across the fretboard going from the bass side to the treble side	

	BASS SIDE (LOW E)	TREBLE SIDE (HIGH E)
ACTION		
At 12th fret:	7/64" (2.8mm)	7/64" (2.8mm)
POLEPIECE HEIGHT		
Neck pickup:	1/32" (.8mm)	1/32" (.8mm)
Bridge pickup:	3/64"+.004" (1.3mm)	1/32" (.8mm)

A 1972 GIBSON ES-345 SET UP FOR SLIDE PLAYING

Alligator Record star Dave Hole, one of the world's greatest electric slide blues guitarists and singers, wrote and performed "Take Me To Chicago—In 1958" years before he even visited the United States.

The Australian's electric slide guitar style is the most unique I've heard or seen. With the slide on his index finger, he plays "upside down," noting the strings from above. Hole's arm, wrist, and hand flow like a dancer's body— with incredibly fluid motions, great vibrato, and HUGE tone. Hole's two greatest influences—Elmore James and Muddy Waters—would be proud to hear him play. Hole's slide setup is high and heavy, though he's able to drop below the neck in order to play rhythm, chords, melody, and turnarounds.

NOTE: *Hole has retro-fitted his ES-345 with Hipshot's Trilogy Multiple-Tuning Bridge, which he presets for G-, D-, and low C-tunings*

Dave Hole's ES-345

SCALE	24-3/4" (628mm)	
RADIUS	10" (254mm) fretboard, 20" (508mm) at the bridge (with the treble E-string raised .007" higher than the actual string radius)	
FRETS	103" x .034" (2.61mm x .85mm")	
STRINGS	"Any kind," says Hole, who makes up a custom set from single strings measuring .015", .017", .024" (wound), .032", .042", .054"	
RELIEF	.042" (1.07mm) at the 9th fret	

	BASS SIDE (LOW E)	TREBLE SIDE (HIGH E)
NUT	.024" (.6mm)	.030" (.8mm)
ACTION		
At 17th fret:	3/32"+.005" (2.5mm)	9/64" (3.6mm)
POLEPIECE HEIGHT		
Neck pickup:	5/64" (2.0mm)	Touching
Bridge pickup:	3/32" (2.4mm)	1/32"+.005" (.91mm)

Hole's polepieces are neither flush with the cover nor radiused—they're staggered in height. Going from treble to bass side, I measured the height of each polepiece as follows. Set your polepieces to these heights, then set the pickup height according to the outside polepieces (above).

Neck pickup: E: raised 1/64"; B: flush; G: raised 1/32"; D: flush; A: flush; E: 1/64"

Bridge pickup: E: raised 1/32"; B: flush; G: raised 1/32"; D: raised 1/16"; A: raised 1/32"; Bass E: raised 1/64"

Les Pauls—the epitome of Gibson solidbody guitars

SETTING UP A 1959 GIBSON LES PAUL WITH HUMBUCKING PICKUPS

I evaluated a 1959 Gibson Les Paul for my friend Rich Hutchinson of the band Xperiment. He bought  the guitar thirty years ago from the original owner. Hutchinson thought the previous owner hardly had touched the guitar, and according to him, "the owner wasn't a good player and not the type to touch any adjustment on his Gibson guitar. He kept it under the bed."

Hutchinson hasn't tinkered with it either, although you'll see that the original owner did remove the bridge at some point—but I suspect this remains an original factory setup.

1959 GIBSON LES PAUL WITH HUMBUCKERS

SCALE	24-3/4" (628mm)	
RADIUS	The fretboard radius was 9-1/2" (241mm) exactly and the bridge saddle radius was 12" (305mm). Gibsons, especially older ones, often have fretboards with a 9-1/2" (241mm) radius.	
FRETS	.103" x .035" (2.6mm x .9mm). The frets were original—I could tell because the lacquer rolling over the plastic binding "nibs" at the end of each fret was unbroken.	
STRINGS	Flat-wound, many years old (Hutchinson hadn't played this guitar for years). The string gauges ranged from .012"-.052" (.3mm to 1.3mm).	
RELIEF	Dead-straight neck—maybe .002" (.05mm) of relief at the 7th fret. A typical great 1950s Gibson mahogany neck that's stout, straight as an arrow, and full of tone.	

	BASS SIDE (LOW E)	TREBLE SIDE (HIGH E)
NUT	.012" (.3mm)	.006" (1.5mm)
ACTION		
At 12th fret:	1/8" (3.2mm)	3/32" (2.4mm)
POLEPIECE HEIGHT		
Neck pickup:	1/16" (1.6mm)	1/16" (1.6mm)
Bridge pickup:	3/32" (2.4mm)	3/32" (2.4mm)

Whether or not it was kept under the previous owner's bed, Hutchinson's old Gibson had some interesting ailments:

■ The plastic tuner knobs had rotted and crumbled—a problem that affects some plastic tuners and binding (not just on Gibsons) used

from the 1920s through the 1950s and sometimes even the 1960s. If your tuner knobs are brownish-yellow, are covered with white dust, exude a strong chemical odor, and feel sticky, remove them from the original tuners and replace them. The chemical that the plastic releases can corrode plated metal parts and infect the finish and other plastic parts around it.

■ The bridge saddle adjusting screws and the saddles faced backward, so that all the strings but the

low E- and A- touched the heads of the screws—not a factory job. With the strings removed, the low E-string was sitting on what originally had been the treble E-string slot—so the original owner changed strings at least once, and put the bridge backwards in the process. Hutchinson left it as he found it.

■ The stop-bar tailpiece was tightened fast to the body. I would have raised the tailpiece slightly, be-

cause the Tune-O-Matic bridge was caving in a bit. However, Hutchinson wanted it left as-is.

■ The pickup polepieces were set up to match the 12" (305mm) string radius created by the bridge sad-

dles. I asked some repair techs and Gibson electric expert Phil Jones about this polepiece adjustment. Jones was the Gibson Custom Shop's first builder, and worked there for fifteen years before joining the world-class, six-man repair team at Gruhn Guitars in Nashville, Tennessee.

"Gibson set the outside polepieces flush to the pickup cover," Jones says. "When flush with the cover, the screwdriver slots of a typical humbucker are at a 45-degree angle. When you raise the middle polepieces to a 12" (305mm) radius, you end up with an almost perfect zig-zag pattern from side to side. In later years, Gibson started putting anything with a slot—stop-bar studs and polepiece slots—in neat, straight lines going at right angles to the strings, to look good."

My friend Albert Garcia of Whittier, California, an expert setup man, uses a set of .010" to .046" strings (.3mm to 1.2mm) on his Les Paul and adjusts the pickups as follows:

"I use the same zig-zag radius setup that Phil Jones described. Gibson used to recommend lowering the B-string, but I don't. I set the polepiece radius, then adjust the neck pickup to exactly 1/16"

(1.6mm) on both sides, and the bridge pickup the same. Since the screwdriver slot in a polepiece means that metal was removed, zig-zagged polepieces place more metal under each string than a polepiece adjusted with the slot going in line with the strings.

"Then I go back and drop the bass side of the neck pickup another 1/32" (.8mm) or so—until it knocks off some of that 'whoofiness' that the neck pickup on a Les Paul always has. I use the exact same setup on P-90s. Also, when I'm done adjusting the polepieces, I remove the pickups and cut the bottoms of the polepieces off—there's less capacitance if you remove the metal, and it tends to brighten up the sound. I wouldn't do this on a vintage, however."—*Albert Garcia, Wittier California*

SETTING UP A 1978 GIBSON LES PAUL WITH P-90 PICKUPS

Here's the final setup for the black '78 Les Paul I've been working on through-out the book. In the end, it played great. I radiused and zig-zagged the P-90 polepieces just like the humbucking pickups mentioned above.

The heads of the two oval-head Phillips screws that hold the P-90s into the body were catching the B-, G-, A-, and D-polepieces when I tried to raise or lower them

(not an uncommon occurrence). I removed the screws, chucked them into my electric drill, and ground their heads against a smooth file to down-size them. It worked perfectly.

1978 GIBSON LES PAUL WITH P90 PICKUPS

SCALE 24-3/4" (628mm)
RADIUS 10" (254mm) fretboard and bridge
FRETS Gibson "jumbo" wire: .103" (2.6mm) x .036" (.9mm) —much-leveled and dressed (but still playable)
STRINGS GHS Boomers—.010" through .046"
RELIEF .002" (.05mm) at the 9th fret (a straight neck)

	BASS SIDE (LOW E)	TREBLE SIDE (HIGH E)
NUT	.015" (.4mm)	.008" (.2mm)
ACTION		
At 12th fret:	1/16"-.003" (1.5mm)	3/64"+.004" (1.26mm)
POLEPIECE HEIGHT		
Neck pickup:	1/16" (1.6mm)	1/16" (1.6mm)
Bridge pickup:	3/32" (2.4mm)	3/32" (2.4mm)

JOHN BORCHARD'S 1954 GIBSON GOLD TOP LES PAUL

This '54 Les Paul Gold Top is pictured with "a couple of Wingnuts" a few pages back. With the wrap-around tailpiece/bridge combination, the '54 Les Paul has a sound all its own.

1954 GIBSON LES PAUL GOLD TOP

SCALE 24-3/4" (628mm)
RADIUS 10" (254mm) fretboard, 12" (305mm) bridge
FRETS Not original—.103" x .040" (2.6mm x 1.0mm)
STRINGS .010" through .046"
RELIEF .010" (.24mm) at the 9th fret

	BASS SIDE (LOW E)	TREBLE SIDE (HIGH E)
NUT	.012" (.3mm)	.008" (.2mm)
ACTION		
At 17th fret:	3/32" (2.4mm)	5/64" (2.0mm)
POLEPIECE HEIGHT	Borchard sets the polepieces to a radius that matches the strings.	
Neck pickup:	1/64" (.4mm)	3/64" (1.2mm)
Bridge pickup:	1/32" (.8mm)	1/64 (.4mm)

Masters of the Stratocasters

ROBERT CRAY'S STRATOCASTER SETUP

I caught Robert Cray's "Some Rainy Morning Tour" at the Mountain Stage live radio show in Charleston, West Virginia. Greg "Zach" Zaccaria, Cray's tech for more than ten years, let me go over four of Cray's Fender Custom Shop "Robert Cray" signature model hard-tail (no tremolo) Strats. Cray has replaced all of the bridge saddles with Graph Tech saddles. Like Stevie Ray Vaughan, Cray uses plastic insulation stripped from 14-gauge AWG stranded copper wire on the treble E- and B-strings.

ROBERT CRAY'S STRATOCASTERS

SCALE 25-1/2" (648mm)
RADIUS Except for one Strat with a 10" (254mm) fretboard radius and a 10" (254mm) bridge saddle radius, all of Cray's bridge saddles had a flatter radius than the fretboards. One had a 10" (254mm) fretboard and a 20" (508mm) bridge saddle radius, and two had a 9-1/2" (241mm) fretboard radius with a 15" (381mm) bridge saddle radius.
FRETS .103" x .041" (2.6mm x 1.1mm)
STRINGS D'Addario nickel wound acoustic or electric, with the following gauges: .011", .013", .018", .028", .036", .046"
RELIEF .017" (.4mm) at the 11th fret

	BASS SIDE (LOW E)	TREBLE SIDE (HIGH E)
NUT	.020" (.5mm)	.014" (.4mm)
ACTION		
At 12th fret:	3/32"+.004" (2.5mm)	1/16" (1.6mm)
POLEPIECE HEIGHT		
Neck pickup:	1/8" (3.2mm)	7/64" (2.8mm)
Middle pickup:	9/64" (3.6mm)	7.5/64" (3.0mm)
Bridge pickup:	1/8" (3.2mm)	5/64" (2.0mm)

TEXAS BLUES SETUP: STEVIE RAY VAUGHAN'S "NUMBER ONE"

Although Stevie Ray Vaughan has been gone ten years, he's more popular today than ever. People are still playing his music—and guitarists mimic his style—the world over. I was lucky to meet Vaughan, along with his friend and guitar tech Rene Martinez, in 1989. Vaughan did as much for the popularity of the blues, and surely the Fender Stratocaster, as any player in history.

STEVIE RAY VAUGHAN'S "NUMBER ONE"

	SCALE	25-1/2" (648mm)	
	RADIUS	Subtly compounded from 7-1/4" (184mm) to 12" (305mm) at the fingerboard end. (Not so much a purposeful attempt at a compound radius, but the result of many refrets.)	
	FRETS	110" x .055" (2.70mm x 1.40mm) They were worn down to .046" (1.20mm)	
	STRINGS	GHS Nickel Rockers: .013", .015", .019" (plain), .028", .038", .058" Note: Vaughan tuned one-half step low to E♭	
	RELIEF	.012" (.30mm) at the 9th fret	

		BASS SIDE (LOW E)	TREBLE SIDE (HIGH E)
NUT		.018" (.45mm)	.012" (.29mm)
ACTION			
At 12th fret:		7/64" (2.8mm)	5/64" (2.0mm)
POLEPIECE HEIGHT		(*Martinez had removed the strings from Vaughan's guitar, so I laid a straightedge along the frets as a reference point and measured the clearance between the straightedge and the polepieces.)	
Neck pickup:		1/32" (.8mm)	1/16" (1.6mm)
Middle pickup:		1/16" (1.6mm)	.004" (.1mm)
Bridge pickup:		1/32" (.8mm)	touching (*see above)

CARRYING ON THE AUSTIN BLUES LEGACY WITH CHRIS DUARTE

Chris Duarte of the Chris Duarte Group was *Guitar Player* magazine's "Best New Player Of The Year" in 1995. A veteran Austin bluesman, Duarte saw Stevie Ray Vaughan play often in the early 1980s. "You wouldn't believe the raw intensity and emotion Stevie had," says Duarte, "I was stunned by him. Watching the different sounds he could get out of a Stratocaster by changing the pickups at certain times in the song taught me the secret of tone. So now, when I play a song, it's not uncommon for me to switch the pickups four or five times on my '63 Strat in a brief period during the song."—*Chris Duarte, Austin Texas*

Duarte's main axe is a '63 Strat with a considerably high action. Duarte plays it in a style equally powerful and raw as Vaughan's.

CHRIS DUARTE'S STRATOCASTER

	SCALE	25-1/2" (648mm)	
	RADIUS	Many refrets have compounded the fretboard from 9-1/2" (241mm) at the nut to 12" (305mm) at the fretboard's end, ending at 20" (508mm) at the bridge saddles.	
	FRETS	.115" x .055" (worn to .045")	
	STRINGS	GHS Dynamite Alloys gauged .011", .015", .018", .030", .040", .050"	
	RELIEF	.017" at the 9th fret	

		BASS SIDE (LOW E)	TREBLE SIDE (HIGH E)
NUT		.020" (.51mm)	.012" (.30mm)
ACTION			
At 17th fret:		3.5/32" (1.4mm)	5/64" (2.0mm)
POLEPIECE HEIGHT			
Neck pickup:		3/32" (2.4mm)	3.5/64" (1.4mm)
Middle pickup:		4.5/64" (1.8mm)	2.5/64" (1.0mm)
Bridge pickup:		5/64" (2.0mm)	1/32" (.8mm)

Note: *Duarte broke the 1st and 4th strings constantly until his guitar tech, Rob Hacker of the Custom Shop in Austin, Texas, replaced the 1st and 4th bridge saddles with Graph Tech saddles. Also, Duarte sweats profusely when he plays—rusting his volume and tone controls solid in a matter of months. Hacker solved the problem by "hermetically-sealing" the wiring harness in a Ziplock bag with holes punched in it for the shafts to pass through!*

BECK BOOGIES

Jeff Beck needs no intro- duction—several genera- tions of guitarists grew up loving his playing and dreaming of playing as well. He is simply one of the greatest guitarists ever. Beck was on tour with Stevie Ray Vaughan in 1989 and provided half of one of the great- est guitar shows I've  seen. At that time Beck was playing a Fender Strat Plus, and he still does today. Recently I spoke with Fender Custom Shop Master Builder Todd Krause for an update on Beck's Strat setup after ten years. Krause's measurements are combined with mine be- low. As Krause says, "Jeff's a tinkerer, so there's no telling how the setup ends up once he's on the road."

JEFF BECK'S STRATOCASTER		
SCALE	25-1/2" (648mm)	
RADIUS	9-1/2" (241mm) compounded by hand to 12" (305mm) or more by fretboard end. Bridge saddle radius: between 12" (305mm) and 14" (356mm)	
FRETS	.098" x .050" (2.47mm x 1.26mm)	
STRINGS	In 1989, Beck used Ernie Ball strings gauged .009", .011", .016", .026", .036", .046". Today he uses a set measuring .010", .013", .017", .026", .038", .048" to start a tour and often raises them to .011" as the tour goes on. I don't know the brand he now uses.	
RELIEF	Beck liked a straight neck in 1989 (the necks I measured may have had .006" relief but no more). Krause has been setting up Beck's guitars with a factory relief of .012"—but I have a feeling Beck straightens it some later on.	
NUT	As he did in '89, Beck uses the Wilkinson Roller Nut. Since they're no longer available, he has his own stash. Todd sets the nut height on Beck's Strats so that, with the strings pressed at the 2nd fret, there is just enough clearance over the 1st fret to show daylight. This is quite low—I set up a Strat Plus this way and needed to raise the low (bass) E-string higher than the treble E-string. I ended up with the following meaurements.	

	BASS SIDE (LOW E)	TREBLE SIDE (HIGH E)
NUT	.011" (.27mm)	.006" (.15mm)
ACTION		
At 12th (1989)	1/16" (1.6mm)	3/64" (1.2mm)
At 15th (2000)	1/16" (1.6mm)	1/16" (1.6mm)
POLEPIECE HEIGHT		
Neck pickup:	touching	3/64" (1.2mm)
Middle pickup:	touching	3/64" (1.2mm)
Bridge pickup:	touching	3/64" (1.2mm)

Since the strings were off the guitar, I laid a straightedge on the frets as a reference point & measured the clearance between the straightedge and the polepieces.

ERIC JOHNSON'S '57 STRATOCASTER

Eric Johnson has many guitars, and this was one of his favorites when I met him in 1998. He usu- ally uses five springs on his vintage Strat tremolo bridge, but sometimes he uses four. "The tremolo springs really affect the tone of the guitar," says Johnson. 'Many times I've replaced the springs, said  'What happened?,' and raced to the old springs and threw them back into the guitar to get back my sound. If they were loose I adjusted accordingly, be- cause the low E-string mustn't go down in pitch when I bend steel licks."

Note: *To soften the brightness of the treble E- string, Johnson had Steve Crisp (Crisp was Johnson's tech some years ago in Austin, and is now with Rick Turner Guitars in Santa Cruz, California) inlay a piece of a 1960s nylon Gibson Tune-O-Matic bridge saddle into the treble E-saddle—a task for your fa- vorite repair tech. Crisp used a modern saddle be- cause it had more metal to inlay into.*

ERIC JOHNSON'S 1957 STRATOCASTER		
SCALE	25-1/2" (648mm)	
RADIUS	Vintage 7-1/4" (184mm) with a flatter bridge saddle radius—between 10" (254mm) and 12" (305mm)— leaving the treble strings higher than the middle strings for good string bends.	
FRETS	.042" x .103" (1.07mm x 2.6mm), fretted out to the very edge with a ball-end shape. "I get several dressings out of a fret job," Johnson says, "and replace them in about a year and a half. I don't like it when they get too low on a Strat because it creates a tension that I don't like. Also, I like them fretted right out to the edge so I don't fall off. Because of that, I move the nut over to squeeze the treble E-string in a little. Rather than alter the vintage fretboard radius, I simply have the frets leveled more in the center so that I don't fret out when bending."	
STRINGS		
RELIEF	None. Johnson likes the neck straight.	

	BASS SIDE (LOW E)	TREBLE SIDE (HIGH E)
NUT		
ACTION		
At 17th fret:	5/64" (2.0mm)	5/64" (2.0mm)
POLEPIECE HEIGHT		
Neck pickup:	5/64" (2.0mm)	3/64" (1.2mm)
Middle pickup:	9/64" (3.6mm)	7/64" (2.8mm)
Bridge pickup:	5/64" (2.0mm)	3.5/64" (1.4mm)

119

Archtops and semi-hollow electrics

A NASHVILLE COUNTRY-JAZZ SETUP ON AN EPIPHONE SHERATON

Leon Rhodes and steel guitarist Buddy Charleton played and recorded with Ernest Tubb's famed Texas Troubadours band of the early 1960s. They created a style of twin guitar playing unlike any heard before or since. In 1967, Rhodes become the staff guitar player for the Grand Ole' Opry, and he's still there today. Over the years, Rhodes has record- ed with everyone from Conway Twitty to Loretta Lynn. "Leon hits the big note," his good friend Son- ny Thomas says. "And there's very few who can do that. I know only one player who can execute like Leon, and that's Pat Martino—and I've been around Nashville a long time!"

For the Opry, Rhodes usually plays a Telecaster or a "tic-tac bass" (a six- string Danelectro baritone guitar tuned low). When Rhodes plays outside the Opry (on the road with Porter Wagoner), he per- forms his signature "jazz with a country flavor," as he calls it, on one of his early-'60s Epiphone Sher- atons. One is cherry red, the other natural.

SETTING UP A GRETSCH WITH BRIAN SETZER

Tom Jones of TV Jones Guitars in Whittier, Cali- fornia, describes the Delrin nut material that he and Brian Setzer favor for tremolo guitars on page 35. Along with Rich Modica, Setzer's guitar tech of six- teen years, Jones sets up and repairs Setzer's gui- tars—including "Smoke," Setzer's famous 1959 Gretsch 6120. Together, the three have worked out a setup that Setzer is happy with and keeps him in tune all night.

Setzer prefers a Gibson Tune-O-Matic ABR-1 archtop bridge with a rosewood base and metal sad-

LEON RHODES' '62 EPIPHONE SHERITON

SCALE	24-3/4" (628mm)		
RADIUS	12" (305mm) fretboard, 16" (406mm) bridge		
FRETS	103" x .028" (2.6mm x .7mm). Rhodes files his frets to that height and crowns them to shape.		
STRINGS	GHS Boomers: .010", .013", .016", .026", .036", .046" Sometimes Rhodes will switch to a lighter GHS Progressive set with the following gauges: .0915", .011", .015", .024", .032", and .042"		
RELIEF	.003" (.1mm) or less (a straight neck)		
NUT	Too low to measure with the tools I had on hand (hardly any clearance with the "third fret press test")		

	BASS SIDE (LOW E)	TREBLE SIDE (HIGH E)
ACTION		
At 12th fret:	1/32"+.002" (.9mm)	3/64" (1.2mm)
POLEPIECE HEIGHT		
Neck pickup:	1/32" (.8mm)	1/32" (.8mm)
Bridge pickup:	1/16" (1.6mm)	3/64" (1.2mm)

BRIAN SETZER'S '59 GRETSCH

SCALE	24-1/2" (622mm)	
RADIUS	A slight compound, from 9-1/2" (241mm) to 11" (279mm) at the fingerboard end. Jones puts the same slight conical radius into Setzer's guitars when refretting them—removing and replacing pearl inlays.	
FRETS	.093" x .048" (2.4mm x 1.2mm)	
STRINGS	D'Addario EXL110 (.010"-.046")	
RELIEF	.015" (.35mm) at the 9th fret. "Brian prefers a loose, high, almost country-style action," says Jones. "He uses a matchbook cover (.012" or .3mm) plus a little more, to keep his relief at .015"."	

	BASS SIDE (LOW E)	TREBLE SIDE (HIGH E)
NUT	.018" (.4mm)	.011" (.22mm)
ACTION		
At 12th fret:	5/64" (2.0mm)	5.5/64" (2.2mm)
POLEPIECE HEIGHT		
Neck pickup:	1/32" (.8mm)	1/32"+.010" (1.04mm)
Bridge pickup:	3/64" (1.2mm)	1/16"+.010" (1.83mm)

The neck pickup measurement is for the polepiece nearest the fingerboard; the bridge pickup measurement is for the polepiece nearest the bridge.

dles because the inherent play in the bridge and saddles lets the strings move just enough with the Bigsby Vibrato that they return to pitch. "The reason this works," says Jones, "is that I removed the zero fret from Brian's Gretsch 6120, cut the fingerboard square, and installed a lubricated Delrin nut. Delrin's the secret to Brian staying in tune. Since the peghead face of his 6120 had been badly damaged, I replaced the entire veneer, ending at the new nut, covering the void left from the original nut spacer and fingerboard end."

TV JONES SPECTRA-SONIC AND GRETSCH'S "HOT ROD"

Here's how Tom Jones sets up his own Spectra-Sonic models (on right in photo). "Follow my set-up exactly—with the almost-straight neck that I prefer—then give the neck .015" of relief, and you will have Brian's setup."—*Tom Jones, TV Jones Guitars, Whittier, California*

I copied Jones' setup on a brand new Gretsch Brian Setzer signature hot rod model (on left in photo)—added in .015" of relief—and went off to relearn some of my favorite Setzer licks. The new Gretsch hot rod is a guitar that cuts to the chase with only one volume control and a toggle switch. It's also lightweight and toneful like an old Gretsch, thanks to a body laminated in the original, thinply, vintage style.

BRIAN SETZER'S "HOT-ROD"

SCALE	24-3/4" (628mm)(longer than the vintage Gretsch)	
RADIUS	A slight compound, from 9-1/2" (241mm) to 11" (279mm) at the fingerboard end	
FRETS	.093" x .048" (2.4mm x 1.2mm)	
STRINGS	D'Addario EXL110 (.010"-.046")	
RELIEF	.003" at the 9th fret	

	BASS SIDE (LOW E)	TREBLE SIDE (HIGH E)
NUT	.016" (.4mm)	.009" (.22mm)
ACTION		
At 12th fret:	3.5/64" (1.4mm)	1/16" (1.6mm)
POLEPIECE HEIGHT		
Neck pickup:	1/32" (.8mm)	1/32"+.010" (1.04mm)
Bridge pickup:	3/64" (1.2mm)	1/16"+.010" (1.83mm)

—The neck pickup measurement is for the polepiece nearest the fingerboard; the bridge pickup measurement is for the polepiece nearest the bridge. Setzer uses TV Jones Filtertron pickups, which have two different polepiece spacings—wider at the bridge, narrower at the neck—so that they locate directly under the strings. Original Gretsch Filtertrons have only one such spacing.

Note: *The Gretsch hot rod model, like Setzer's 6120, also has a traditional nut rather than Gretsch's signature zero fret. However, the nut is not Delrin. If you want your hot rod to be just like Setzer's, have a guitar tech replace the nut with Delrin.*

JOHN BORCHARD'S 1959 GRETSCH ANNIVERSARY

One of the great ones—the straight neck is set at a perfect angle to the body. The original frets are worn, but it plays smooth, I wouldn't change it.

JOHN BORCHARD'S 1959 GRETSCH ANNIVERSARY

SCALE	24-1/2" (622mm)	
RADIUS	16" (406mm) fretboard, 20" (508") bridge	
FRETS	Original—.075" x .030" (1.9mm x .8mm)	
STRINGS	.011" through .050"	
RELIEF	.003" (.075mm) of relief at the 9th fret	

	BASS SIDE (LOW E)	TREBLE SIDE (HIGH E)
NUT	.012" (.3mm)	.009" (.21mm)
ACTION		
At 17th fret:	5/64" (2.0mm)	3/32" (2.4mm)
POLEPIECE HEIGHT		
Neck pickup:	3/32" (2.4mm)	5/64" (2.0mm)
Bridge pickup:	3/64" (1.2mm)	5/64" (2.0mm)

GIBSON ES-350 T (SHORT-SCALE ARCHTOP JAZZ SETUP)

Athens, Ohio guitar guru Ron Scott bought this Gibson ES-350 T brand new in 1958. A close friend of the late Tal Farlow, Scott has played with the U.S. Coast Guard Band, Dick Stabile's Orchestra, Andy Griffith, Bob Hope, Shelley Mann, Gloria De-Haven, and the list goes  on. At 76, Scott still gigs locally all the time. His ES-350's low action responds to a light touch. Scott likes the nut high for strong open strings, and because it helps create an action almost parallel to the frets the length of the fretboard. This Gibson almost plays itself.

GIBSON ES-350 T (SHORT SCALE JAZZ ARCHTOP)		
SCALE	23-1/2" (597mm)	
RADIUS	12" (305mm) at both the fretboard and bridge	
FRETS	A refret worn low, .103" x .030" (2.6mm x .8mm). Scott plays everywhere on the neck and wears the frets down equally.	
STRINGS	Fender .009"-.042"	
RELIEF	Very little—.004" (.1mm) at the 7th fret	
	BASS SIDE (LOW E)	TREBLE SIDE (HIGH E)
NUT	.028" (.7mm)	.016" (.4mm)
ACTION		
At 17th fret:	1/16" (1.6mm)	3/64" (1.2mm)
POLEPIECE HEIGHT		
Neck pickup:	7.5/64" (3.0mm)	7.5/64" (3.0mm)
Bridge pickup:	5/64" (2.0mm)	1/8"+.004" (3.28mm)

JOHN BORCHARD'S 1967 GIBSON ES-355

This is one of the only non-stereo (monaural) ES-355s I've seen, and it's all original—even the frets.

JOHN BORCHARD'S 1967 GIBSON ES-355		
SCALE	24-3/4" (628mm)	
RADIUS	10" (254mm) fretboard, 12" (305mm) bridge	
FRETS	.037" x .085" (.94mm x 2.2mm)	
STRINGS	.010"-.046"	
RELIEF	.003" (.1mm)	
	BASS SIDE (LOW E)	TREBLE SIDE (HIGH E)
NUT	.011" (.3mm)	.008" (.2mm)
ACTION		
At 17th fret:	5/64" (2.0mm)	5/64" (2.0mm)
POLEPIECE HEIGHT		
Neck pickup:	1/32" (.8mm)	3.5/64" (1.4mm)
Bridge pickup:	5/64" (2.0mm)	5/64" (2.0mm)

PAUL REED SMITH (PRS) MCCARTY

This book, like my *Guitar Player Repair Guide*, sports a PRS guitar on the cover—the thicker version of the McCarty model shown here. This PRS came straight from the factory. Smith was nice to send it, since he knew I'd never send it back (just kidding). For a factory setup, it was one of the  best I've seen, although I lowered it even more.

PAUL REED SMITH (PRS) MCCARTY		
SCALE	25" (635mm)	
RADIUS	10" (254mm) fretboard and bridge saddles	
FRETS	.103" x .046" (2.6mm x 1.02mm)	
STRINGS	.012" to .052" nickel wound PRS strings	
RELIEF	.004"—.006" at the 7th fret	
	BASS SIDE (LOW E)	TREBLE SIDE (HIGH E)
NUT	.018" (.45mm)	.006" (.16mm)
ACTION		
At 17th fret:	3.5/64" (1.4mm)	3/64"+.004" (1.28mm)
POLEPIECE HEIGHT		
Neck pickup:	5/64" (2.0mm)	1/16" (1.6mm)
Bridge pickup:	5/64" (2.0mm)	1/16" (1.6mm)

JORMA KAUKONEN'S SIGNATURE EPIPHONE JA RIVIERA

The man who named the Jefferson Airplane, Jorma Kaukonen, lives near me in Southeastern Ohio, where he owns and operates the Fur Peace Ranch Guitar Camp. When he's not teaching, Kaukonen is on the road  with his band Hot Tuna, playing his Epiphone JA Riviera signature model.

JORMA KAUKONEN'S SIGNATURE EPIPHONE		
SCALE	24-3/4" (628mm)	
RADIUS	12" (305mm) fretboard, 14" (356mm) bridge	
FRETS	.093" x .048" (2.36mm x 1.22mm)	
STRINGS	Gibson Brite-Wire nickel wound .011" to .048"	
RELIEF	None—maybe .003" if that (I fretted this guitar)	
	BASS SIDE (LOW E)	TREBLE SIDE (HIGH E)
NUT	.024" (.6mm)	.018" (.44mm)
ACTION		
At 17th fret:	1/16" (1.6mm)	5/64" (2.0mm)
POLEPIECE HEIGHT		
Neck pickup:	4.5/64" (1.8mm)	1/16"+.004" (1.68mm)
Bridge pickup:	1/16" (1.6mm)	1/16: (1.6mm)

GENE BAKER BH1

Once a master builder at the Fender Custom Shop, today Gene Baker's Baker Guitars USA builds great, stylish, guitars that exclusively use the Buzz Feiten Tuning System.

GENE BAKER BH1

SCALE	24-3/4" (628mm)	
RADIUS	12" (305mm) at both the fretboard and bridge	
FRETS	.108" x .046" (2.75mm x 1.2mm)	
STRINGS	.010" to .046"	
RELIEF	Straight neck—maybe .002" (.04mm) of relief	
	BASS SIDE (LOW E)	TREBLE SIDE (HIGH E)
NUT	.015" (.38mm)	.011" (.28mm)
ACTION		
At 17th fret:	1/16" (1.6mm)	1/16" (1.6mm)
POLEPIECE HEIGHT		
Neck pickup:	5/64" (2.0mm)	3/64"+ (1.25mm)
Bridge pickup:	5/64" (2.0mm)	1/16"+ (1.7mm)

DUKE ROBILLARD: SETTING UP A "TRUE" ARCHTOP ELECTRIC GUITAR

When Duke Robillard hits the stage, there's no shortage of guitars. Ro- billard is likely to wield a Strat, a Tele, his new Epi- phone Explorer, or any number of Epiphone's new archtop models— from the ES-295 to the

Broadway to the T-Bone Walker-style Zephyr Blues Deluxe to the Emperor Regent. Robillard calls the Emperor a "true" archtop because its floating pick- up mounts on the fingerboard extension (not into the top), and it has a wooden, non-adjustable bridge.

"The treble E- and B-polepieces don't have much travel, but they're raised as high as they will

go," Robillard says. "The G-polepiece is lowered as far down as it will go because a plain G-string is always a problem on a true archtop. If the top is resonant, it's nearly impossible to use a plain G-string without severely lowering the polepiece to compensate for the vibration of the top. If the pole- piece is up near the string, the guitar goes into feed- back. The A-polepiece is flush to the cover, and the low E-polepiece is lowered into the cover, but not as far as the G-polepiece is."

DUKE ROBILLARD'S ARCHTOP ELECTRIC

SCALE	25-1/2" (648mm)	
RADIUS	12" (305mm) at both the fretboard and bridge	
FRETS	.103" x .043" (1.1mm x 2.6mm)	
STRINGS	D'Addario nickel round-wound: .013"-.056", with a .019" or .020" for the G-string. He sometimes uses a D'Addario flat-wound set with a wound G-string. On archtop electrics with built-in pickups, Robillard uses a D'Addario nickel round wound set measuring .011", .014", .017", .028", .040", and .052". "It's the perfect balanced medium set for an archtop if you're gonna' play both blues and jazz and you need to bend," he says.	
RELIEF	Robillard likes 'em straight—no relief	
	BASS SIDE (LOW E)	TREBLE SIDE (HIGH E)
NUT	.025" (.63mm)	.012" (.3mm)
ACTION		
At 17th fret:	3/32"+.008" (2.6mm)	1/16"+.008" (1.8mm)
POLEPIECE HEIGHT		
Neck pickup:	3/32" (2.4mm)	5/32" (4.0mm)

Guitars that broke the mold

A BIG APPLE SETUP WITH ROGER SADOWSKY

I'd always wanted to play a Sadowsky guitar away from a loud trade show, and this quilted maple solid-body was worth the wait. Built by Norio Imai in the Sadowsky work- shop, it's among the most well-set-up guitars I've played (new or old), and

was the source of my example of a perfect nut on page 28.

"I am amazed, and disappointed, when I see fine, handmade guitars that are poorly set up. Nine- ty-five percent of the guitar is there—beautiful woods, workmanship, and perhaps even tone. Ex- ceptional tone however, can't be produced until that missing 5 percent—a well-cut nut, dressed frets, and a proper setup—is added in. A good setup may comprise 5 percent of the work of building a guitar, but if done properly, it will enhance the playability and pleasure of playing that instrument at least ten times over!"—*Roger Sadowsky, Sadowsky Guitars, New York City*

ROGER SADOWSKY'S SETUP

SCALE	25-1/2" (648mm)
RADIUS	12" (305mm) fretboard, 14" (356mm) bridge
FRETS	.108" x .055" (2.75mm x 1.4mm)
STRINGS	Sadowsky nickel round wound strings gauged .010", .013", .017", .026", .036", .046" Sadowsky uses three tremolo springs for a set of .010"s, but would probably use only two springs for .009"s. "But springs vary too," says Sadowsky, "so it depends." On this setup, the claw is 1/2" (12.67mm) from the cavity wall.
RELIEF	.004" or less (straight neck with buzz-free low action)

	BASS SIDE (LOW E)	TREBLE SIDE (HIGH E)
NUT	.010" (.3mm)	.007" (.2mm)
ACTION		
At 17th fret:	1/16" (1.5mm)	3/64"+.004" (1.2mm)
POLEPIECE HEIGHT		
Neck pickup:	1/8" (3.2mm)	7/64" (2.8mm)
Middle pickup:	5/64" (2.0mm)	1/16" (1.6mm)
Bridge pickup:	3/32" (2.4mm)	5/64" (2.0mm)

This model had two humbuckers and a single-coil pickup in the middle—made by DiMarzio to Sadowsky's specs.

TOM ANDERSON GUITARWORKS

Here's how Tom Anderson set up his personal Cobra model that he loaned me so that I could try out the Feiten Tuning System—another  guitar I want to keep! Anderson's fretwork and his detailing of the fretboard edge are impeccable.

Notice in the photo (above) that Anderson installs a spring-loaded string tree that gives when the string tension changes during tremolo use. On this guitar, Anderson also installed a double set of strap buttons on the butt end—a Dan Armstrong origi-

nal that came to Anderson via David Schecter. Two buttons keep the guitar from swiveling and falling when leaning against an amp (Armstrong's intention). Anderson put two holes in his guitar strap—spaced for the buttons—to hold the guitar against his body better and keep it from falling away. Plus, they allow him to change the way the guitar hangs.

TOM ANDERSON GUITARWORKS

SCALE	24-3/4" (628mm) Most of Anderson's guitars are the longer, 25-1/2" (648mm) scale.
RADIUS	12" (305mm) at both the fretboard and bridge
FRETS	.090" x .054" (2.3mm x 1.4mm)
STRINGS	Elixir from Gore, polymer wrapped, .010" to .046"
RELIEF	.004" (.1mm) at the 9th fret

	BASS SIDE (LOW E)	TREBLE SIDE (HIGH E)
NUT	.015" (.39mm)	.013" (.32mm)
ACTION		
At 17th fret:	3.5/64" (1.4mm)	3.5/64" (1.4mm)
POLEPIECE HEIGHT		
Neck pickup:	3/32" (2.4mm)	5/64" (2.0mm)
Bridge pickup:	5/64" (2.0mm)	3/64"+.002" (1.25mm)

MICHAEL STEVENS LJ

Michael Stevens is one of the world's finest builders of electric guitars and basses (see pages 53 and 98).

The LJ model shown here, which belongs to Matt Henderson of Florence, Massuachusetts, is the perfect weight for a guitar of this style, thanks to hollow chambers in the mahogany body. Stevens' fine arts background is evident in his art-deco styling.

The polepieces of the Tom Holmes custom-wound humbuckers face toward center, and the pickups are slanted. The slant adds treble to the bass

side of the neck humbucker, and a little bass to the treble side of the bridge pickup. The slant works (it's greater under the neck pickup since the strings are closer together) because the strings are running between the adjustable polepieces on one coil and the nonadjustable polepieces, or "slugs," on the other coil. The pickup cover hides the slugs—sort of like a P-bass pickup.

In the middle switch position, a push-push pot

cuts to a very Strat-like, single-coil sound since the polepieces are located in about the same place you'd find the neck and middle pickups on a Strat.

On the neck pickup, the slug side is really close to the strings, and I lower the G-string polepiece flush to the cover while the others are radiused. On the bridge pickup, the B-string polepiece is less than flush by 1/64" (.4mm), the rest, are radiused.

MICHAEL STEVENS LJ		
SCALE 24-3/4" (628mm)		
RADIUS 12" (305mm) at both the fretboard and bridge		
FRETS .090" x .055" (2.3mm x 1.4mm)		
STRINGS .010"-.046"		
RELIEF .004" (.1mm) at the 9th fret		
	BASS SIDE (LOW E)	TREBLE SIDE (HIGH E)
NUT (Very low!)	.009" (.22mm)	.005" (.13mm)
ACTION		
At 17th fret:	1/16"+.005" (1.7mm)	1/16"-.003" (1.5mm)
POLEPIECE HEIGHT		
Neck pickup:	3/64" (1.2mm)	Touching
Bridge pickup:	2.5/64" (1.0mm)	1/32" .8mm)

JOHN CARRUTHERS CUSTOM

This guitar has been Buzz Feiten's main axe for 15 years. "John's been doing guitar work for me for 20 years," says Feiten, "he's the most

brilliant guitar engineer and builder that I know. I'd never let anyone else touch my frets (except, of course, for Dan Erlewine!)."

JOHN CARRUTHERS CUSTOM		
SCALE 25-1/2" (648mm)		
RADIUS 14" (356mm) at both the fretboard and bridge		
FRETS .110" x .055" (2.8mm x 1.4mm)		
STRINGS D'Addario EXL 120+ .0095" to .044"		
RELIEF .005" at the 9th fret		
	BASS SIDE (LOW E)	TREBLE SIDE (HIGH E)
NUT	.018" (.45mm)	.018" (.45mm)
ACTION		
At 17th fret:	3/32" (2.4mm)	1/16" (1.6mm)
POLEPIECE HEIGHT		
Neck pickup:	3/16" (4.8mm)	11/64" (4.4mm)
Bridge pickup:	3/32" (4.8mm)	3/32" (4.8mm)

WASHBURN NUNO BETTENCOURT SIGNATURE MODEL

When Buzz Feiten—an exacting setup tech in his own right—hits the road to present guitar clinics for Washburn, International, he chooses Washburn's Nuno Bettencourt model.

WASHBURN NUNO BETTENCOURT SIGNATURE MODEL		
SCALE 25-1/2" (648mm)		
RADIUS 14" (356mm) at both the fretboard and bridge		
FRETS .110" x .055" (2.8mm x 1.4mm)		
STRINGS D'Addario EXL 120+ .0095" to .044"		
RELIEF .005" at the 9th fret		
	BASS SIDE (LOW E)	TREBLE SIDE (HIGH E)
NUT	.018" (.45mm)	.018" (.45mm)
ACTION		
At 17th fret:	3/32" (2.4mm)	1/16" (1.6mm)
POLEPIECE HEIGHT		
Neck pickup:	3/16" (4.8mm)	11/64" (4.4mm)
Bridge pickup:	3/32" (2.4mm)	3/32" (2.4mm)

Dan's Faves

The next few guitars are my own, and they're some of my favorites. I rotate them in the two bands I play with: the Couch Slugs and The Lorenes.

1956 DANELECTRO U2

This guitar had been re-fretted with a good amount of relief left in the neck when I bought it. Since the neck is not adjustable, the only way to straighten it would be to fret it again. However, I love the guitar and love the way it plays—so in some cases I do like relief! (Just not very often.) This guitar, according to everyone who hears it, is the best sounding guitar I have. I don't plan on changing anything about it—not even the somewhat too low frets.

1956 DANELECTRO U2

		BASS SIDE (LOW E)	TREBLE SIDE (HIGH E)
SCALE	25" (635mm)		
RADIUS	20" (508") at both the fretboard and bridge		
FRETS	.084" x .037" (2.1mm x .93mm)		
STRINGS	GHS Boomers, .010" to .046"		
RELIEF	.018" (.5mm) at the 9th fret		
NUT		.016" (.4mm)	.018" (.44mm)
ACTION			
At 17th fret:		3/64"+ (1.25mm)	3.5/64" (1.4mm)
POLEPIECE HEIGHT			
Neck pickup:		1/64" (.4mm)	1.5/64" (.6mm)
Bridge pickup:		1/32" (.8mm)	1/32"+.002" (.82mm)

FRET-KING ELAN

When I visited Trev Wilkinson's FRET-King guitar company in Birmingham, England, I fell for this combination of Korina (of the mahogany family) and P-90s. The guitar is similar in shape to and hangs like a Strat, however the neck angle is like a Gibson. There's a subtle, dished area in the top for my forearm to rest in that's very comfy. I'm glad I hadn't spent my souvenir money before I came upon this!

FRET-KING ELAN

		BASS SIDE (LOW E)	TREBLE SIDE (HIGH E)
SCALE	25" (635mm)		
RADIUS	Compound from 9-1/2" (241mm) to 12" (305mm), ending at 15" (381mm) at the bridge saddles		
FRETS	.100" x .052" (2.5mm x 1.3mm)		
STRINGS	.010" to .046"		
RELIEF	.009" (.22mm) at the 9th fret		
NUT		.018" (.45mm)	.007" (.17mm)
ACTION			
At 17th fret:		1/32" (.8mm)	1.5/64" (.6mm)
POLEPIECE HEIGHT			
Neck pickup:		1/16" (1.6mm)	3.5/64" (1.4mm)
Bridge pickup:		.050" (1.27mm)	1/32" (.8mm)

GORDON-SMITH

Still in England, I visited Gordon-Smith Guitars in Partington, just outside of Manchester. England's longest-running electric guitar manufacturer, John Smith, his wife Linda, and his friend Chris Smith (no relation) have built over 9,000 guitars in 25 years!

GORDON-SMITH

		BASS SIDE (LOW E)	TREBLE SIDE (HIGH E)
SCALE	25-1/2" (648mm)		
RADIUS	12" (305mm)		
FRETS	.103" x .047" (2.6mm x 1.2mm)		
STRINGS	.008" to .040" from the factory		
RELIEF	None		
NUT		.012" (.3mm)	.006" (.15mm)
		The brass nut screws into the end of the fingerboard—open ended mounting holes allow you to raise the nut up or down, then tighten it firmly in place	
ACTION			
At 17th fret:		1/32" (.8mm)	1/32"+.003" (.85mm)
POLEPIECE HEIGHT			
Neck pickup: (single coil)		1/32" (.8mm)	1/32" (.8mm)
Bridge pickup: (humbucking)		1/32" (.8mm)	1/32" (.8mm)

From left to right: Gordon-Smith owner John Smith, Jenny McCawley, Linda Smith, Chris Smith, and Dave McCawley. The McCawleys are John's sales representatives in England.

The visit meant another souvenir, however, because Gordon-Smith builds original, no-frills, handsome guitars that are very affordable. This guitar has a vintage-style maple neck (no fretboard) and an adjustable rod installed without a skunkstripe! The body is pine and is extremely resonant.

WASHBURN USA CUSTOM SHOP CENTURION CT5BB "BLACKBURST"

This is the only guitar I own that's factory equipped with the Buzz Feiten Tuning System. It's also the only one I have with true humbuckers (both Seymour Duncan— a '59 in the neck, and a Custom/Custom in the bridge). It's a lot like a Les Paul, a style of guitar I hadn't played in years. I'm glad to have it when I need that type of sound.

WASHBURN USA CUSTOM SHOP CENTURION CT5BB		
SCALE	24-3/4" (628mm)	
RADIUS	Compound radius from 10" (254mm) at the nut to 16" (406mm) at the fretboard end. The bridge radius is also 16" (406mm)	
FRETS	.115" (2.91mm) x .055" (1.39mm)	
STRINGS	.009" to .042" (factory set; I switched to .010's)	
RELIEF	.002" or less	
	BASS SIDE (LOW E)	TREBLE SIDE (HIGH E)
NUT	.014" (.34mm)	.008" (.2mm)
ACTION		
At 17th fret:	4.5/64" (1.8mm)	3.5/64" (1.4mm)
POLEPIECE HEIGHT		
Neck pickup:	13.5/64" (5.4mm)	3/16" (4.8mm)
Bridge pickup:	7.5/64" (3.0mm)	3/32" (2/4mm)

FENDER CUSTOM SHOP BAJO SEXTO

This is a favorite of mine. The frets are low and partially covered by lacquer. I don't mind it, however, because with heavy strings and low pitch I'm not bending the strings too much. The bridge pickup is Fender's late-'60s style with staggered polepieces (take that into account when measuring the bridge pickup height). I manage to keep

this neck straight and the strings pretty low with no buzz audible through an amp. It sounds like an electric piano—I love it!

FENDER CUSTOM SHOP BAJO SEXTO		
SCALE	30-1/4" (781mm)	
RADIUS	9-1/2" (241mm) at the 10th fret	
FRETS	.084" x .035" (2.13mm x .88mm)	
STRINGS	.016", .026" plain, .036", .046", .056", .066"	
RELIEF	None	
	BASS SIDE (LOW E)	TREBLE SIDE (HIGH E)
NUT	.022" (.55mm)	.016" (.4mm)
ACTION		
At 17th fret:	4.5/64" (1.8mm)	3.5/64" (1.4mm)
POLEPIECE HEIGHT		
Neck pickup:	1/64" (.4mm)	1.5/64" (.6mm)
Bridge pickup:	1/32" (.8mm)	1/32" (.8mm)

JUNIOR BROWN, TONE PLAYER

Junior Brown and his double-neck "Guit-Steel" —the combination six-string guitar and eight-string steel built by Michael Stevens of Alpine, Texas—play to packed houses around the world. Brown's unique guitar and singing styles are recognized in-

stantly by his fans of all ages. Brown refers to himself as "more of a tone player than anything else," and if you catch him live you'll know why. Here's how he sets up the guitar half of his famous Guit-Steels, "Old Yeller" and "Big Red". Old Yeller resides in the Country Music Hall of Fame and Museum as of now, but Big Red and Brown are inseparable.

JUNIOR BROWN, TONE PLAYER		
SCALE	25-1/2" (648mm)	
RADIUS	12" (305mm) at both the fretboard and bridge	
FRETS	.110" x .052" (2.8mm x 1.3mm)	
STRINGS	.010"-.046" (with an .011" substituted for the .010"). Brown plays a set of strings until the intonation is dead, and he has gone as long as a year on a set of strings. Usually he changes strings about five times a year, however.	
RELIEF	.010" (.25mm) at the 7th fret	
	BASS SIDE (LOW E)	TREBLE SIDE (HIGH E)
NUT	.016" (.37mm)	.010" (.26mm)
ACTION		
At 17th fret:	5/64" (2.0mm)	3.5/64" (1.4mm)
POLEPIECE HEIGHT		
I didn't measure this, but the neck pickup is dropped quite low on the bass side to keep the pickup from pulling the strings out of tune. Brown experiments with pickups often, but you'll usually find him with at least two Fender Bullet, Mustang, or 6-string steel guitar pickups mounted on his guitar—the kind with smooth plastic covers and no visible polepieces. You can find these at vintage guitar shows, but Brown says, "DO NOT tear up an old Mustang or any other fine guitar to get the pickups—I would never do that!" (And Brown's the man.)		

LUCY, ALBERT KING'S FLYING V

I built and delivered Albert King's black-walnut Flying V-style guitar "Lucy," with King's name inlayed in the fingerboard, in the spring of 1972. I'm proud to say that he played Lucy more than any other guitar in his lifetime—she sings on most of King's albums produced after 1972.

The last time I touched Lucy was in 1989, when I gave her a complete physical. I made her a new nut, replaced the last eight frets, dressed all of her frets, replaced and reshaped her bridge saddles, and tuned her up to intonate in King's famous drop tuning of C,F,C,F,A,D. The three bass strings are the same intervals as the G-, B-, and D- bass strings of an open G-tuning, but a whole step lower. Try King's tuning—and his string gauges—and you'll be able to play his licks a lot easier!

LUCY, ALBERT KING'S FLYING V		
SCALE	24-3/4" (628mm)	
RADIUS	12" (305mm) at both the fretboard and bridge	
FRETS	.103" x .043" (2.6mm x 1.1mm)	
STRINGS	.009", .012", .024" (wound), .028", .038", .050"	
RELIEF	.008" (.2mm) at the 9th fret	
	BASS SIDE (LOW E)	TREBLE SIDE (HIGH E)
NUT	.016" (.4mm)	.009" (.23mm)
ACTION		
At 17th fret:	5/64" (2.0mm)	3.5/64" (1.4mm)
POLEPIECE HEIGHT		
Neck pickup:	3/32" (2.4mm)	3/32" (2.4mm)
Bridge pickup:	1/32" (.8mm)	1/32" (.8mm)

Installing strap locks: an extra (special) setup step

As I wrote this book I often surfed the Internet looking for guitar-related questions. One recurring topic was how to install strap locks—nobody wants a new guitar to fall to the floor. Around the same time, Jorma Kaukonen asked me to install a Jim Dunlop Strap-Lock on his brand-new Epiphone Riviera JA

signature model guitar because he didn't want it falling off onstage or anywhere else. There's nothing wrong with the strap button that came on Kaukonen's guitar, it just doesn't guarantee the guitar's safety when his Hot Tuna band gets the joint rockin'.

Generally, a guitar's original strap button, and its mounting screw, are smaller than the replacement parts, so you must redrill the mounting hole

to accept the new, larger screw. Match a drill bit to the screw so that the bit hides the central, "shank" portion and only the thread shows. If the drill bit is smaller than the shank, the hole could be too small and the screw may bind. If that happens, the screw head could twist off, leaving the screw imbedded in the guitar and you on the way to a repair shop. I suggest practicing on a piece of relatively hard scrap wood if you are doing this for the first time. Your local hardware store likely can offer advice about exactly which drill bit to buy for the screw. A good hardware store will have drill bits in all sizes, including "number" drill bit sizes (as opposed to fractional or metric), which is the type of bit I chose for this job.

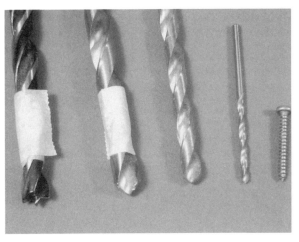

In this case, the correct drill bit was a #34 bit thats measurements were .112" (2.84mm) in diameter. After you drill the hole, rub beeswax or paraffin on the screw threads, then test the fit by screwing it in as far as it will need to go—the wax helps the screw cut and thread into the wood, and the excess wax will remain on the surface (you can clean it up with a paper towel). Unscrew the mounting screw and install the new Strap-Lock button. I placed Stewart-MaddDon-

ald's #4018-B black felt strap-button washer between the strap button and guitar to protect the finish.

Take into account the height of the strap lock's hardware—it may make your guitar ride too high in the case. The strap button with the felt washer measures 9/16" (14.28mm) high, without the felt it measures 1/2" (12.71mm) high. If space is a problem, install the recessed version of the Strap-Lock, which sits flush with the finish. That's my preference for a non-vintage guitar.

To install the recessed version, I used four drill bits, going by degree from small to large. The smallest drill bit (#34) is for the size and depth of the screw and serves as a pilot hole for the others—drill it first. Next, I used a 1/4" bit to enlarge the hole and give the final 3/8" bit (the size of the strap-button insert) a larger hole to bite into. A large drill bit can chip a guitar's finish. Then, I drilled the 3/8" hole to the required depth of 7/16" (11.11mm).

Finally, I used a brad-point bit (far left in the photo), which flattens the V-shaped hole left by the other bits (this is an option, and is not absolutely necessary). Once the recessed fastener is flush to the surface, fasten it with the wood screw. The push-button Strap-Lock fits into the recessed fastener.

Note: *During the entire drilling process, I applied masking tape over the finish to prevent chip-*

ping, and I ran each drill bit in reverse to smoothly center the bit. In reverse, the twist-tip of a drill bit makes a nice countersink since the sharp edges are running backwards.

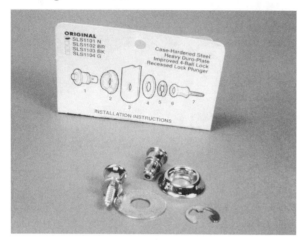

To install the guitar strap portion of the Strap-Lock, follow the instructions. The bottom washer goes on the underside of the strap (A), and is held by a spring clip squeezed in place with pliers or Vise-Grips. Installed, the strap lays close to the surface (B).

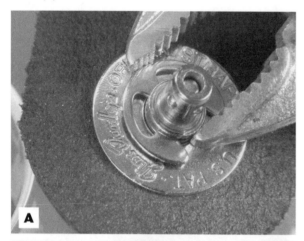

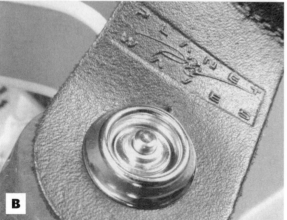

Another popular strap locking system is the Security Lock made by Schaller. It has a grooved, horseshoe-shaped fastener with a plunger that you pull up on to install (the Dunlop Strap-Lock is a push-button retainer).

One of the greatest strap button ideas I've seen came from my friend Dave Senteney—he installed a strap button directly onto the neck-bolt plate using the original neck-mounting screw. The screw still has enough length to fasten into the neck—not a lot, but enough!

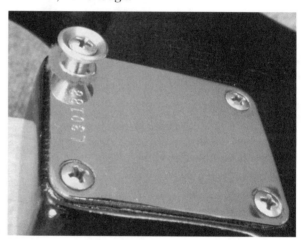

Resources

Builders and manufacturers

Dominick Ramos Guitars
Catskill, N.Y.
(518) 943-1942.

Fender Musical Instruments Corp.
Scottsdale, Ariz.
(480) 596-9690
www.fender.com.

Fred Gretsch Enterprises, Ltd.
Savannah, Ga.
www.sales@gretsch.com.

FRET-King Guitars
www.fret-king.com.

Gibson Musical Instruments
Nashville, Tenn.
www.gibson.com.

Gordon Smith Guitars
Manchester, England
011 44 161 777 9438.

Ibanez
Bensalem, Pa.
(800) 669-8262
www.ibanez.com.

Paul Reed Smith Guitars
Stevensville, Md.
(410) 643-9970
www.prsguitars.com.

Sadowsky Guitars Ltd.
New York, N.Y.
(212) 586-3960
www.sadowsky.com.

Stevens Electrical Instruments
Alpine, Tex.
(915) 364-2487
www.stevensguitars.com.

The Epiphone Guitar Company
A Division of Gibson Musical Instruments
Nashville, Tenn.
www.epiphone.com.

TVJones Guitars
Whittier, Calif.
(562) 693 0068
www.tvjones.com.

Washburn International
Mundelein, Ill.
(800) 877-6863
www.washburn.com.

Builders using the Buzz Feiten Tuning System

Baker USA, Custom Guitars
Santa Maria, Calif.
(805) 739-8990
www.bakerguitars.com.

Buzz Feiten Design
www.buzzfeiten.com

Carruthers Guitars
Venice, Calif.
(310) 392-3919
www.carruthersguitars.com.

Suhr Guitars
Lake Elsinore, Calif.
(909) 471-2334
www.suhrguitars.com

Tom Anderson Guitarworks
Newbury Park, Calif.
(805) 498-1747
www.andersonguitars.com.

Washburn International
Mundelein, Ill.
(800) 877-6863
www.washburn.com.

Tool and specialty suppliers

McMaster Carr Company
(630) 833-0300
www.mcmaster.com.

VWR Scientific
(800) 932-5000
www.vwrsp.com.

Hardware, parts, tools, information

Allparts Music Corp.
Katy, Tex.
(281) 391-0637
www.allparts.com.

DiMarzio, Inc.
(800) 221-6468
www.dimarzio.com.

Dunlop Mfg. Inc.
Benicia, Calif.
www.jimdunlop.com.

Euphonon Company
Orford N.H.
(888) 517-4678, (603) 353 4882.

FRET-King Parts and Accessories by Wilkinson
www.fret-king.com.

GHS Corp.
Battle Creek, Mich.
(800) 388-4447
www.ghsstrings.com.

GraphitAll
www.renemartinez.com.

Guitarmaker's Connection
Nazareth Pa.
(800) 345-3103
www.martinguitar.com.

J. D'Addario & Co.
Farmingdale, N.Y.
(800) 323-2746
www.daddario.com.

JM Rolph Pickups
Highland Ky.
(859) 781-9334
rewinder@cinternet.net.

Joe Barden Pickups
Vienna, Va.
(703) 938-8638
www.joebarden.com

Lindy Fralin Pickups
Richmond, Va.
(804) 358 2699
www.lindyfralin.com.

Luthier's Mercantile International
Healdsburg, CA
(800) 477-4437
lmi@lmii.com.

Parts Is Parts (American Guitar Center)
Wilmington, Vt.
(800) 590 0014
www.guitar-parts.com.

Seymour Duncan Pickups
Santa Barbara, Calif.
(800) S DUNCAN
www.seymourduncan.com.

Stewart-MacDonald's Guitar Shop Supply
Athens, Ohio.
(800) 848-2273
www.stewmac.com.

Tom Holmes Company
Joelton, Tenn.
(615) 876-3453

TonePros
Oakdale, Calif.
www.tonepros.com.

Touchstone Tonewoods
44 Albert Road North Reigate,
Surrey, RH2 9EZ, England.

Vintique
College Park, Md.

(301) 982-9413
www.vintique.com.

Warmoth Guitar Products
Puyallup, Wash.
(253) 845-0403
www.warmoth.com

WD Music Products, Inc.
Fort Myers, Fla.
(941) 337-7575
www.wdmusicproducts.com

Organizations, associations, schools

Association of Stringed Instrument Artisans (A.S.I.A),
(802) 434-5657
www.guitarmaker.org.

Bryan Galloup's Guitar Hospital, Big Rapids,
Mich. (800) 278-0089; www.galloupguitars.com.
*Galloup's school is the site of Stewart-MacDonald's
Annual Great Northwoods Guitar Building & Repair
Seminar. Galloup worked for me in the early 1980s,
and took my fledgling school to great heights after I
left Michigan in 1986.*

Charles Fox,
Healdsburg, Calif.
(707) 431-7836
www.cfoxguitars.com.

Jorma Kaukonen's
Furpeace Ranch Guitar Camp,
Pomeroy, Ohio.
(740) 992-6228;
www.furpeaceranch.com.

Minnesota State College Southeast Technical
(Red Wing Campus), Red Wing, Minn.
(800) 657-4849
www.southeasttech.mnscu.edu.

Newark and Sherwood College, Newark, Notts,
UK. 44-1636-680-680
enquiries@newark.ac.uk.

Roberto Venn School of Luthiery,
Phoenix, Ariz.
(602) 243-1179
www.roberto-venn.com.

The Guild of American Luthiers
(253) 472-7853
www.luth.org.

For an extensive listing of guitar repair and
guitar building schools, visit www.luth.org

Conversion Charts

CONVERSION: MILLIMETERS TO INCHES		
MILLIMETERS	INCHES (FRACTION)	INCHES (DECIMAL)
.1 mm		.004"
.2 mm	.5/64"	.008"
.4 mm	1/64"	.016"
.6 mm	1.5/64"	.024"
.8 mm	1/32"	.031"
1.0 mm	2.5/64"	.039"
1.2 mm	3/64"	.046"
1.4 mm	3.5/64"	.055"
1.6 mm	1/16"	.062"
1.8 mm	4.5/64"	.070"
2.0 mm	5/64"	.078"
2.2 mm	5.5/64"	.086"
2.4 mm	3/32"	.093"
2.6 mm	6.5/64"	.101"
2.8 mm	7/64"	.109"
3.0 mm	7.5/64"	.117"
3.2 mm	1/8"	.125"
3.4 mm	8.5/64"	.133"
3.6 mm	9/64"	.140"
3.8 mm	9.5/64"	.148"
4.0 mm	5/32"	.156"
4.2 mm	10.5/64"	.164"
4.4 mm	11/64"	.172"
4.6 mm	11.5/64"	.180"
4.8 mm	3/16"	.187"
5.0 mm	12.5/64"	.195"
5.2 mm	13/64"	.203"
5.4 mm	13.5/64"	.211"
5.6 mm	7/32"	.219"
5.8 mm	14.5/64"	.227"
6.0 mm	15/64"	.234"
6.4 mm	1/4"	.250"

FRACTIONS OF AN INCH BY "HALF-64THS"			
64THS		INCHES (DECIMAL)	METRIC
		.004	.1
.5		.008	.2
1		.016	.4
1.5		.024	.6
2	(1/32")	.031	.8
2.5		.039	1.0
3		.046	1.2
3.5		.055	1.4
4	(1/16")	.062	1.6
4.5		.070	1.8
5		.078	2.0
5.5		.086	2.2
6	(3/32")	.093	2.4
6.5		.101	2.6
7		.109	2.8
7.5		.117	3.0
8	(1/8")	.125	3.2
8.5		.133	3.4
9		.140	3.6
9.5		.148	3.8
10	(5/32")	.156	4.0
10.5		.164	4.2
11		.172	4.4
11.5		.180	4.6
12	(3/16")	.187	4.8
12.5		.195	5.0
13		.203	5.2
13.5		.211	5.4
14	(7/32")	.219	5.6
14.5		.227	5.8
15		.234	6.0
16	(1/4")	.250	6.4

COMMON SCALE LENGTHS

GUITAR
22-1/2" (572mm)
23-1/2" (597mm)
24" (610mm)
24-1/2" (622mm)
24-3/4" (628mm)
25" (635mm)
25-1/2" (648mm)
25-5/8" (651mm)

BARITONE GUITAR
28-5/8" (728mm)
30-1/4" 30" (762mm)

COMMON FRETBOARD AND BRIDGE RADII

GUITAR
7-1/4" (184mm)
9-1/2" (241mm)
10" (254mm)
11" (279mm)
12" (305mm)
14" (356mm)
15" (381mm)
16" (406mm)
20" (508")

Serious Guitar.

Guitar Player has all the information you need to be a serious player. Because, as the industry-leading magazine, we take the art of playing guitar just as seriously. • All of our editors and writers are experienced players with the special knowledge that only comes from years of hands-on experience. Guitar Player gives you in-depth stories about leading players and new artists on the scene. Our instructional columns, lessons, tips and techniques take your playing to the next level. And our hands-on tests and extensive product information help you find the gear you need. • If you want to get serious about guitar, check us out at a Sam Ash near you or visit www.guitarplayer.com.

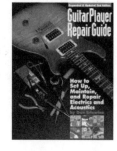

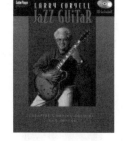
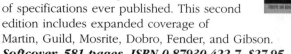